Social Categories in Everyday Experience

Social Categories in Everyday Experience

Edited by

Shaun Wiley, Gina Philogène,
and Tracey A. Revenson

DECADE
of BEHAVIOR

2000-2010

American Psychological Association • Washington, DC

Published by
American Psychological Association
750 First Street, NE
Washington, DC 20002
www.apa.org

To order
APA Order Department
P.O. Box 92984
Washington, DC 20090-2984
Tel: (800) 374-2721; Direct: (202) 336-5510
Fax: (202) 336-5502; TDD/TTY: (202) 336-6123
Online: www.apa.org/pubs/books
E-mail: order@apa.org

In the U.K., Europe, Africa, and the Middle East, copies may be ordered from
American Psychological Association
3 Henrietta Street
Covent Garden, London
WC2E 8LU England

Typeset in New Century Schoolbook by Circle Graphics, Inc., Columbia, MD

Printer: Edwards Brothers, Inc., Ann Arbor, MI
Cover Designer: Mercury Publishing Services, Rockville, MD

The opinions and statements published are the responsibility of the authors, and such opinions and statements do not necessarily represent the policies of the American Psychological Association.

Library of Congress Cataloging-in-Publication Data
Social categories in everyday experience / edited by Shaun Wiley, Gina Philogène, and Tracey A. Revenson.
  p. cm.
 Includes index.
 ISBN-13: 978-1-4338-1093-0
 ISBN-10: 1-4338-1093-X
 1. Social stratification. 2. Group identity. 3. Sex discrimination. 4. Race discrimination. 5. Women. 6. Immigrants. I. Wiley, Shaun. II. Philogène, Gina, 1961– III. Revenson, Tracey A.
 HM821.S622 2012
 305—dc23
                            2011040996

British Library Cataloguing-in-Publication Data
A CIP record is available from the British Library.

Printed in the United States of America
First Edition

DOI: 10.1037/13488-000

APA Science Volumes

APA Decade of Behavior Volumes

Categorization Inside and Outside the Laboratory: Essays in Honor of Douglas L. Medin

Chaos and Its Influence on Children's Development: An Ecological Perspective

Child Development and Social Policy: Knowledge for Action

Children's Peer Relations: From Development to Intervention

Cognitive Fatigue: Multidisciplinary Perspectives on Current Research and Future Applications

Commemorating Brown: The Social Psychology of Racism and Discrimination

Computational Modeling of Behavior in Organizations: The Third Scientific Discipline

Couples Coping With Stress: Emerging Perspectives on Dyadic Coping

Developing Individuality in the Human Brain: A Tribute to Michael I. Posner

Emerging Adults in America: Coming of Age in the 21st Century

Experimental Cognitive Psychology and Its Applications

Family Psychology: Science-Based Interventions

Gender Differences in Prenatal Substance Exposure

Individual Pathways of Change: Statistical Models for Analyzing Learning and Development

Inhibition in Cognition

Measuring Psychological Constructs: Advances in Model-Based Approaches

Medical Illness and Positive Life Change: Can Crisis Lead to Personal Transformation?

Memory Consolidation: Essays in Honor of James L. McGaugh

Models of Intelligence: International Perspectives

The Nature of Remembering: Essays in Honor of Robert G. Crowder

New Methods for the Analysis of Change

On the Consequences of Meaning Selection: Perspectives on Resolving Lexical Ambiguity

Participatory Community Research: Theories and Methods in Action

Personality Psychology in the Workplace

Perspectivism in Social Psychology: The Yin and Yang of Scientific Progress

Primate Perspectives on Behavior and Cognition

Contents

Contributors

Nida Bikmen, PhD, Department of Psychology, Denison University, Granville, OH

Frances Cherry, PhD, Department of Psychology, Carleton University, Ottawa, Ontario, Canada

Nicola Curtin, PhD, Department of Psychology, Clark University, Worcester, MA

Kay Deaux, PhD, The Graduate Center, City University of New York, and Department of Psychology, New York University

Alice H. Eagly, PhD, Department of Psychology, Northwestern University, Evanston, IL

Victoria M. Esses, PhD, Department of Psychology, University of Western Ontario, London, Canada

Susan T. Fiske, PhD, Department of Psychology, Princeton University, Princeton, NJ

Ronni Michelle Greenwood, PhD, Department of Psychology, University of Limerick, Republic of Ireland

Ying-yi Hong, PhD, Division of Strategy, Management, and Organization, Nanyang Technological University, Singapore

Tiane L. Lee, PhD, Department of Psychology, University of Maryland, College Park

Brenda Major, PhD, Department of Psychological and Brain Sciences, University of California, Santa Barbara

Stelian Medianu, MSc, Department of Psychology, University of Western Ontario, London, Canada

Gina Philogène, PhD, Department of Psychology, Sarah Lawrence College, Bronxville, NY

Tracey A. Revenson, PhD, Doctoral Program in Psychology, The Graduate Center, City University of New York

Abigail J. Stewart, PhD, Departments of Psychology and Women's Studies, University of Michigan, Ann Arbor

Scott Veenvliet, PhD, School of Language and Liberal Studies, Fanshawe College, London, Ontario, Canada

Shaun Wiley, PhD, Department of Psychology, The College of New Jersey, Ewing

Foreword

In early 1988, the American Psychological Association (APA) Science Directorate began its sponsorship of what would become an exceptionally successful activity in support of psychological science—the APA Scientific Conferences program. This program has showcased some of the most important topics in psychological science and has provided a forum for collaboration among many leading figures in the field.

The program has inspired a series of books that have presented cutting-edge work in all areas of psychology. At the turn of the millennium, the series was renamed the Decade of Behavior Series to help advance the goals of this important initiative. The Decade of Behavior is a major interdisciplinary campaign designed to promote the contributions of the behavioral and social sciences to our most important societal challenges in the decade leading up to 2010. Although a key goal has been to inform the public about these scientific contributions, other activities have been designed to encourage and further collaboration among scientists. Hence, the series that was the "APA Science Series" has continued as the "Decade of Behavior Series." This represents one element in APA's efforts to promote the Decade of Behavior initiative as one of its endorsing organizations. For additional information about the Decade of Behavior, please visit http://www.decadeofbehavior.org.

Over the course of the past years, the Science Conference and Decade of Behavior Series has allowed psychological scientists to share and explore cutting-edge findings in psychology. The APA Science Directorate looks forward to continuing this successful program and to sponsoring other conferences and books in the years ahead. This series has been so successful that we have chosen to extend it to include books that, although they do not arise from conferences, report with the same high quality of scholarship on the latest research.

We are pleased that this important contribution to the literature was supported in part by the Decade of Behavior program. Congratulations to the editors and contributors of this volume on their sterling effort.

Steven J. Breckler, PhD
Executive Director for Science

Virginia E. Holt
Assistant Executive Director for Science

Preface

A social-psychological approach will not lead us to conclude that men always act one way and women always act another. Instead, this perspective will require us to look at both the person (specifically, the sex of the person) and the situation. Our conclusions will be phrased in terms of interactions between these two factors. (Deaux, 1976, p. 3)

The theoretical framework that I use . . . is one of persons in contexts. Such a framework gives priority neither to the individual as the sole agent nor to the environment as the sole determinant. Rather, the intersection of the two becomes the place of analytic exploration. Almost as a corollary of this assumption, I arrive at no single description of the immigration experience. Different individuals, as members of different groups, arrive in different cultural and historical contexts, and the ways in which their experience plays out depends on the mixture of elements. (Deaux, 2006, p. 3)

The above quotes introduce Kay Deaux's books, *The Behavior of Women and Men* (1976) and *To Be an Immigrant* (2006). Published 3 decades apart, each book introduced social psychology to a new field of study. Differences between women and men, in Deaux's words, had "frequently been considered a nuisance variable" (Deaux, 1976, p. 3). Immigration had been studied much less from a psychological perspective than in other social sciences.

The core of Deaux's perspective at each time—that person and context are inextricably linked and that social psychology should address "hot" social issues—was similar, despite the different social categories and the intervening 30 years. Still, much had changed. Along with other social scientists, Deaux had transformed the understanding of social categories: first, by emphasizing their importance for shaping everyday experience, then by outlining the subjective meaning we attach to them, and more recently by highlighting the ways in which they change and overlap.

The main objective of this volume is to show how a mature social psychological study of social categories can help us understand the similarities and differences between different categorical systems, the way multiple social categories intersect and overlap, and the way they can inform our everyday interactions and public policy. What makes this book unique is its emphasis on the similarities and differences between two category systems: gender and immigration. Consistent with Deaux's research, the chapters in this volume demonstrate that a social psychological perspective can be applied to both. At the same time, people attach different meanings to each. This volume also takes seriously the variations between them.

The second unique contribution of the book is its emphasis on multiplicity. Much of the research on social psychology has considered categories one at a time (Bodenhausen, 2010), despite the fact that we all belong to many and their independent effects cannot be easily partialed out. The experience of race is different for women and men, just as the immigrant experience cannot be captured by studying attachment to the home and the host culture independently.

The third and final contribution of the book is the clear link between the science in each chapter and public policy and everyday life. The chapters address "hot" social issues such as women in leadership, attitudes toward immigrants, and social movements. For budding psychologists the book can serve as an introduction to the way that social psychologists understand social categories in an increasingly complex world. For more established researchers the book highlights the cutting edge of psychological theorizing and research on how social categories overlap and intersect in the real world and how they influence outcomes as diverse as leadership, stereotyping, attributions, and intergroup relations. The book can be used in classes across multiple disciplines, including psychology, sociology, political science, and public policy.

This volume also stands as a tribute to the work of Kay Deaux. The editors and contributors have been inspired by Deaux's work over the past 4 decades as, we suspect, have many of the readers of this book. She has applied theoretical insights to categories that at the time were ignored by much of psychology: gender and immigration. Deaux's name is not synonymous with a single theory or empirical contribution. Instead, she has painted a broad canvas with her work that crosses many topics. Her work bridges psychology and sociology, social psychology and personality psychology, European and American social psychology, and laboratory and field methods. It traces the paths of individuals evolving in a rapidly changing world in which multiple categories and fluid demographic realities have multiplied the interactions between different social groups.

Shaped by her own experience of discrimination based on gender, Deaux set out in the early 1970s to explore the misconceptions about gender difference and their reification in the social world. As with future scholars who would examine the intersectionality of race and gender, Deaux was motivated by a political pursuit. To bring sexism and discrimination toward women into the open and into rigorous social science scholarship was part of a political drive aimed at changing the discriminatory practices of our culture. That political foundation can be found in her research on women in the steel industry, *Women of Steel* (Deaux & Ullman, 1983) and early work on gender stereotypes (Deaux, 1984; Deaux & Lewis, 1984). Another example is the amicus brief on sex discrimination coauthored with Susan Fiske, Donald Bersoff, Eugene Borgida, and Madeline Heilman for the 1989 Supreme Court decision in *Price Waterhouse v. Hopkins* (Fiske, Bersoff, Borgida, Deaux, & Heilman, 1991). A telling example of the broadening of Deaux's research agenda is her more recent work on immigration (Deaux, 2004, 2006; Deaux, Bikmen, Gilkes, Ventuneac, Joseph, Payne, & Steele, 2007; Tormala & Deaux, 2006; Wiley, Perkins, & Deaux, 2008). This scholarship brings to bear her unique social psychological focus on individuals in their social surroundings. Interdisciplinarity, individual agency within socially constructed constraints, a commitment to social action—Deaux is a social psychologist in the classic mold of Kurt Lewin.

The original idea for a volume compiling the research inspired from Deaux's 4 decades of work emerged from a 2008 conference held in Chicago on "Gender Identity and Immigration: A Cultural Dimension to Social Psychology," funded by the American Psychological Association (APA) Science Directorate, with additional support from the Society for the Psychological Study of Social Issues and The Graduate Center of The City University of New York. This volume would not have been possible without the support of the APA Science Directorate. In particular, we thank Steven Breckler and Virginia Holt for their encouragement and support. We also thank APA Books editors Maureen Adams and Jessica Kamish for shepherding this book through the publication process, and Beth Hatch and Peter Pavilionis for guiding us through review. We also offer our gracious thanks to two anonymous reviewers who evaluated the entire volume and made it an even better book. Finally, delivering the final manuscript to APA would not have been possible without the meticulous copyediting and formatting of five promising psychology students from the Social Change and Collective Identity Lab at The College of New Jersey: Cassidy Bartolini, Margaret Diakos, Brittany Gilbert, Priscilla Gutierrez, and Racelle Spokony.

References

Bodenhausen, G. V. (2010). Diversity in the person, diversity in the group: Challenges of identity complexity for social perception and social interaction. *European Journal of Social Psychology*, *40*(1), 1–16.

Deaux, K. (1976). *The behavior of women and men*. Monterey, CA: Brooks/Cole.

Deaux, K. (1984). From individual differences to social categories: Analysis of a decade's research on gender. *American Psychologist*, *39*, 105–116. doi:10.1037/0003-066X.39.2.105

Deaux, K. (2004). Immigration and the color line. In G. Philogène (Ed.), *Racial identity in context: The legacy of Kenneth B. Clark* (pp. 197–209). Washington, DC: American Psychological Association. doi:10.1037/10812-011

Deaux, K. (2006). *To be an immigrant*. New York, NY: Russell Sage Foundation.

Deaux, K., Bikmen, N., Gilkes, A., Ventuneac, A., Joseph, Y., Payne, R., & Steele, C. (2007). Becoming American: Stereotype threat effects in Black immigrant groups. *Social Psychology Quarterly*, *70*, 384–404. doi:10.1177/019027250707000408

Deaux, K., & Lewis, L. L. (1984). The structure of gender stereotypes: Interrelationships among components and gender label. *Journal of Personality and Social Psychology*, *46*, 991–1004. doi:10.1037/0022-3514.46.5.991

Deaux, K., & Ullman, J. C. (1983). *Women of steel: Female blue-collar workers in the basic steel industry*. New York, NY: Praeger.

Fiske, S. T., Bersoff, D. N., Borgida, E., Deaux, K., & Heilman, M. E. (1991). Social science research on trial. The use of sex stereotyping research in Price Waterhouse V. Hopkins. *American Psychologist*, *46*, 1049–1060. doi:10.1037/0003-066X.46.10.1049

Tormala, T. T., & Deaux, K. (2006). Black immigrants to the United States: Confronting and constructing ethnicity and race. In R. Mahalingam (Ed.), *Cultural psychology of immigration* (pp. 131–150). Mahwah, NJ: Erlbaum.

Wiley, S., Perkins, K., & Deaux, K. (2008). Through the looking glass: Ethnic and generational patterns of immigrant identity. *International Journal of Intercultural Relations*, *32*, 385–398. doi:10.1016/j.ijintrel.2008.04.002

Social
Categories
in Everyday
Experience

Introduction:
Social Categories Matter

Shaun Wiley, Gina Philogène, and Tracey A. Revenson

Social categories matter. They shape the way we see ourselves and each other. At the same time, social categories are constructed. They are not "natural" entities that have meaning above and beyond the meaning we ascribe to them in our social institutions, our everyday interactions, and our cultural products (Omi & Winant, 1994). Each of us belongs to myriad social categories—woman, psychologist, African American, immigrant. These categories and the meanings and evaluations that are attached to them influence how we see ourselves, how others see us, and how we interact with the world around us. The ways in which social categories impact people's lives and well-being, as well as the relations among groups, are bound to engage psychologists in an increasingly diverse world. In this book, we address three questions inspired by a social constructionist view of social categories: How do social categories affect people's everyday lives? How do people attach subjective meaning to them? And how can psychological theory come to terms with the idea that people belong to multiple and intersecting categories?

These questions have import for theory development and applications to policy. First, they represent a missing piece in the social psychology literature: Are there differences and similarities across category types? Are social categories stable over time? What happens when multiple social categories clash? Social psychology is uniquely situated to achieve the goal of viewing social categories as both socially constructed and socially consequential. At its best, the discipline focuses on the "meso" level of analysis, examining the social processes that mediate between culture and social structure on the one hand, and individual lives on the other. Thus, social psychology has the potential to move beyond viewing social categories as independent variables (Helms, Jernigan, & Mascher, 2005) to consider the psychological and social processes that reproduce them across time and place. Second, understanding social categorization processes will help us understand how members of marginalized groups cope with discrimination in everyday settings such as school and the workplace, and how we can reduce stereotyping and discrimination among members of society's many cross-cutting categories.

In addressing these topics, we use the social categories of women and immigrants as exemplars for two reasons. First, these are two social groups historically pushed to the margins of society, but in different ways. Second, these categories can demonstrate the notion of *intersectionality,* which is critical to "new look" approaches to social categorization (e.g., Cole, 2009; Purdie-Vaughns & Eibach, 2008). Despite cataclysmic changes in gender roles over the last century, gender operates as perhaps the most naturalized social category. Some assume that it reflects biological essence and remains stable over time; others link it to social roles but consider those roles as unchanging in any time period. Immigrant status is the opposite. For immigrants, who encounter new social categories and new evaluations of old ones, identities and meanings are up for grabs. Members of the host country often expect immigrants to lose their ethnic identities and assimilate to the cultural mainstream, but at the same time exclude them on the basis of language, race, or immigrant status. What's more, old identities take on new meanings in a different context. Women and immigrants' experiences provide a contrast in the everyday experience of social categories. For the former, categories are assumed to be stable; for the latter, they undergo rapid and sometimes dramatic change.

Across cultures, gender is one of the key social categories that structures everyday life. Although a large body of research aims to identify and explain differences between women and men, much of the social psychological research on gender has taken an interactionist perspective, following the work of Deaux and Major (1987). Several decades of accumulated evidence has supported the proposition that gender-related behavior results from the interaction between men and women's own beliefs about their gender and the expectations and assumptions others have. These beliefs and expectations are communicated in social roles, stereotypes, and power structures. Underneath what appears to be a stable category is a plethora of context-dependent negotiations that occur within interpersonal relationships, organizations, and policies.

In contrast, immigration exemplifies a newer social category and is a rapidly emerging area within social psychology (Deaux, 2006). Current research on immigration describes how people adapt when expectations and identifications change. By studying immigration we can begin to uncover how intergroup relations operate in different cultural settings and when the meaning and evaluations of one's category memberships changes. Consider a quote from Mary Waters's (1999) classic study of West Indian immigration: A Jamaican immigrant to England and the United States said, "I never knew I was Black until I left Jamaica" (p. 55). This simple quote illustrates a point that is a primary theme of this book: Categorical differences gain meaning from their cultural context. Although Waters's participant's skin color was the same in Jamaica and the United States, the ideology of race gave it an entirely different significance after her migration.

Social categorization processes, as they are expressed in everyday life, have been a concern for social psychologists in Europe and the United States for several decades and are becoming increasingly relevant for a world that is becoming more and more diverse. As globalization and immigration increase, traditional meanings of gender and nationality are called into question. Thus, understanding how social categories are created and how they affect policy becomes all the more important.

Structure and Content of the Volume

This volume begins with a section on the theoretical foundations of social categories in social psychology. These chapters lay the theoretical groundwork for the remainder of the book, as all the volume's authors use these theories in some fashion.

Chapter 1 is authored by Brenda Major, one of the most prominent researchers on social categories and everyday life. Major synthesizes 2 decades of research on the implications of belonging to a stigmatized social category, inspired in part by her interactionist model of gender (Deaux & Major, 1987). This is followed by a chapter by Gina Philogène that reviews psychological theories of social categories, including social identity theory and self-categorization theory and argues that categories acquire their meaning from their cultural context and that individuals have agency in how they position themselves relative to these cultural meanings. In the final chapter of Part I, Frances Cherry provides a review of how social psychologists became interested in the impact of social categories in everyday life early in the 20th century and how our view of the topic has unfolded throughout our history and into the 21st century. Part II, Gender, and Part III, Immigration, offer contemporary research on the ways two important social categories influence how we interact, how we see each other, and how we see ourselves. We present these chapters in two different sections in part because social psychologists have often studied them separately (for notable exceptions, see Dion & Dion, 2001; Mahalingam & Leu, 2005). As the chapters in this volume convey, however, these categories intersect in important ways, and the social and psychological processes that support them share much in common. We think that presenting them separately makes their overlap all the more apparent. Together, the chapters show how the individual is linked to social structures in the process of everyday interaction.

The three chapters on gender as a social category are written by leading scholars in the area who offer contrasting perspectives on the topic. In Chapter 4, Alice H. Eagly addresses the impact of gendered expectations on leadership and how women and men become leaders. Nicola Curtin and Abigail J. Stewart examine the structure and function of gender identities among activist women. Ronni Michelle Greenwood introduces the notion of intersectionality, or the mutually constitutive relations between multiple social identities in the context of gender. Whereas social psychologists have tended to study identities one at a time, each of us belongs to multiple categories that split apart and overlap depending on the social context. Greenwood highlights how failing to account for intersectionality obscures power differences within social groups and challenges researchers on social identity and gender to study it. The chapters on gender highlight several themes in research on social categories more generally—that they matter for important life outcomes (e.g., leadership), that individuals have agency in the subjective meaning they attach to the categories, and that multiple category memberships do not stand alone but mutually constitute each other.

Part III focuses on cutting-edge research in the social psychology of immigration, including work conducted with a number of different immigrant groups. Taken together, these chapters expose important similarities and differences in how immigrants are received in different contexts and how they negotiate their identities in a new country. In Chapter 7, Victoria M. Esses and her colleagues consider how media portrayals and popular beliefs about refugee claimants in Canada often suggest that they are cheaters, which leads to various psychological consequences, including dehumanization. Susan T. Fiske and Tiane L. Lee complement this finding with research from the United States that extends their stereotype content model to immigration. They show how immigrants, particularly those from Latin America and Africa, are described as more untrustworthy, unskilled, contemptible, disgusting, and worthy of attack and neglect compared to other outgroups. Ying-yi Hong explores how racial–ethnic minority immigrants may construct their identities in different ways, showing how these immigrants' identification processes are linked to their lay theories of race. The chapters repeat some themes raised in Part II, Gender, but also expand on them by considering how immigrants manage their multiple category memberships across situations.

Part IV, Looking Back and Moving Forward, includes two chapters that consider where research on social categories is headed. In Chapter 10, Shaun Wiley and Nida Bikmen consider two themes for the future. They argue that to understand such phenomena as group solidarity, researchers need to consider, first, the diversity *within* and *across* social categories and, second, the way people shape categories in addition to being shaped by them. The concluding chapter in the book is written by Kay Deaux, whose groundbreaking work forms the foundation of many of the chapters. In essence, Deaux gets the last word: She examines what research on gender and immigration has taught us about social categorization as a whole and reflects on the next steps for research and its translation to policy in the future. In the process, Deaux offers a wonderful analysis of the reciprocal dynamic that exists between the actors and the observers in the creation and maintenance of social identities.

Key Themes

In sum, this volume reaches across two categories—gender and immigration—to illustrate several themes about social categories and everyday experience. The first and simplest theme is that social categories matter—particularly when it comes to power and oppression. For example, Eagly's chapter shows how gender creates a labyrinthine path women must follow to become leaders. Esses, Veenvliet, and Medianu show how refugee status—especially as depicted in the media—causes us to see people as less than human and fail to support policies that would treat them with dignity. Fiske and Lee demonstrate how the content of social stereotypes contributes to xenophobia.

The second theme is that categories do not only define us, but people have agency in how they *respond* to others' category-based expectations. For example, Major's chapter demonstrates that the goals people bring to social interactions and the importance of social identities for the self influence how individuals cope with category-based discrimination and stigma. Curtin and Stewart show how two activist women are not defined by the categories they inhabit; instead, they negotiate their gender identities in the context of their many different social roles and embed themselves in their social group memberships in different ways. Their work points not only to the agency people have to define their identities but also to the complicated and multidimensional construct that identity represents.

A third theme is that people have agency in how they *define* social categories. Although there is great ideological and social power in existing social categories, categories are socially constructed. This means that people have the power to remake them. Greenwood emphasizes this point, describing how women from different ethnic groups can develop an alternative interpretation of the social structure to challenge the status quo, even if the public expression of this interpretation invites sanction and is unlikely to be accepted. In a different vein, Wiley and Bikmen explicitly address how consciousness of multiple and intersecting identities can provide a basis for people to reimagine the relations between social groups and challenge the status quo. From a group perspective, having agency means not just taking existing social categories as they are but interrogating the way they vary and change.

The fourth theme of the book is that treating social categories separately—as if they can be examined one at a time—obscures the power differences within a category. Research on social categories has increasingly addressed issues of multiplicity—that we all belong to many groups. For some people, these different group memberships are reflected in a single domain, as is the case for the bicultural people described in Hong's chapter. For others, these different group memberships exist in different categories of gender, race, class, and disability, as demonstrated by Curtin and Stewart's, Greenwood's, and Wiley and Bikmen's treatments of intersectionality.

The final theme of the book is that it is not only which categories we belong to that influences our everyday lives but also how we conceive of them. Hong shows that perceiving intergroup boundaries as rigid prevents bicultural people from freely thinking in terms of their multiple identities and causes them to react against mainstream culture. In contrast, when people see intergroup boundaries as fluid and permeable they are able to move easily among the groups to which they belong, applying appropriate knowledge in appropriate contexts. Wiley and Bikmen also point to the importance of how people perceive the boundaries between their group memberships, in this case for organizing collective action. They argue that groups that emphasize ingroup diversity and outgroup similarity are well positioned to build solidarity across differences and stop recreating social hierarchies according to race, class, or gender within the group.

Social Categories in Everyday Experience uses interrogations of gender and immigration to trace the development of research on social categories over the past 40 years. It puts the psychological meaning in demographic categories and highlights the themes that will move the research forward in the years to come.

References

Cole, E. R. (2009). Intersectionality and research in psychology. *American Psychologist, 64,* 170–180. doi:10.1037/a0014564

Deaux, K. (2006). *To be an immigrant.* New York, NY: Russell Sage Foundation.

Deaux, K., & Major, B. (1987). Putting gender into context: An interactive model of gender-related behavior. *Psychological Review*, *94*, 369–389. doi:10.1037/0033-295X.94.3.369

Dion, K. K., & Dion, K. L. (2001). Gender and cultural adaptation in immigrant families. *Journal of Social Issues*, *57*, 511–521. doi:10.1111/0022-4537.00226

Helms, J. E., Jernigan, M., & Mascher, J. (2005). The meaning of race in psychology and how to change it. *American Psychologist*, *60*, 27–36. doi:10.1037/0003-066X.60.1.27

Mahalingam, R., & Leu, J. (2005). Culture, essentialism, immigration and representations of gender. *Theory & Psychology*, *15*, 839–860. doi:10.1177/0959354305059335

Omi, M., & Winant, H. (1994). Racial formation in the United States: From the 1960s to the 1990s. In P. Rothenberg (Ed.), *Race, class and gender in the United States* (pp. 13–22). New York, NY: Worth.

Purdie-Vaughns, V., & Eibach, R. P. (2008). Intersectional invisibility: The distinctive advantages and disadvantages of multiple subordinate-group identities. *Sex Roles*, *59*(5–6), 377–391. doi:10.1007/s11199-008-9424-4

Waters, M. C. (1999). *Black identities: West Indian immigrant dreams and American realities.* New York, NY: Russell Sage Foundation.

Part I

Theoretical Foundations

1

Self, Social Identity, and Stigma: Through Kay Deaux's Lens

Brenda Major

How do the social categories with which we identify, or to which others assign us, affect our psychological makeup, social behaviors, and life outcomes? Much of Kay Deaux's theoretical and empirical work over the past 30 or more years has centered on this question. Two features of this work stand out. First, Deaux's approach integrates personality, social psychological, and sociological perspectives. To understand behavior, one must attend to person × situation interactions within a larger social context. Second, her perspective emphasizes the importance of people's subjective construals as determinants of their behavior. In this chapter, I reflect on some of the key insights provided by Deaux's theoretical and empirical work on self and social identity and describe how my own work and that of others on responses to stigma has been shaped by this perspective.

Self and Social Identity: Essential Components

Deaux's work on the psychological implications of social categories produced a number of major insights. First, *social categories matter* (e.g., Deaux, 1984). People have expectancies (stereotypes) about individuals based on the social categories to which they belong. These expectancies are communicated in social interaction with others, as well as by larger society. These social representations shape people's behavior toward others as well as targets' self-definition and behavior (Deaux & Major, 1987).

Second, *the self is agentic.* In social interactions, individuals who are *targets* of others' category-based expectancies are not passive victims of those expectancies, but rather are active agents who are motivated to achieve their own goals, goals that are shaped in part by their own self-definitions (e.g., Deaux & Major, 1987; Ethier & Deaux, 1994). The target's goals may include, for example, making a desired impression on others (self-presentation), maintaining a positive self-image (self-enhancement) or maintaining a consistent self-image (self-verification). The goal a target adopts affects whether his or her behavior confirms or disconfirms others' category-based expectancies. Thus, social category membership is not inevitably associated with certain patterns of behavior.

Third, *social identity is an important component of self-definition.* Social identity is fundamentally related to personal identity and is an important component of self-definition (Deaux, 1993; Reid & Deaux, 1996).

> Social identities are those roles or membership categories that a person claims as representative. . . . Personal identity refers to those traits and behaviors that the person finds self-descriptive, characteristics that are typically linked to one or more of the identity categories. . . . Although they can be separated for analysis, each is necessary to give the other meaning. (Deaux, 1993, p. 6)

This perspective implicitly assumes that motives relevant to personal identity (e.g., self-enhancement) are also relevant to social identity (e.g., identity enhancement). The view of social identity exemplified in Deaux's work broke ranks with then dominant approaches that conceptualized social identity as separable from personal identity (Hogg & Abrams, 1988), solely in intergroup terms, as a person's definition of him- or herself as a member of a particular ingroup vis-á-vis an outgroup (e.g., Tajfel, 1981), or as a level of abstraction in self-categorization, distinct from personal identity (Turner, 1987).

Fourth, *social identities are negotiated.* Social identifications can serve a variety of important functions for an individual, such as satisfying needs for self-esteem, for self-coherence, and for belongingness (Ashmore, Deaux, & McLaughlin-Volpe, 2004). Consequently, people are motivated to maintain and manage their identities and engage in "identity work" when their identities are challenged. For example, when people perceive a threat to their social identity (e.g., perceive that others devalue that identity), they may restore a sense of self-worth or self-integrity by negating that social identity (e.g., disidentifying from it) and embracing another favorable identity, or by affirming that identity even more strongly (e.g., Ethier & Deaux, 1994).

Deaux (1993) also asserted that just because a person is assigned by society to a social category does not mean that the person accepts that categorization. Individuals construct their own identities, both in their choice of categories as self-representative and in the meaning they attach to a category. Furthermore, within an individual's identity structure, categories differ in their salience, as well as in their position. Thus, knowing which identities a person claims is not enough to predict his or her behavior. Some social identities are more important, central, valued, and meaningful to an individual than others. These individual differences in social identification have important implications for affect, cognition, and behavior (Deaux, 1993, 1996).

Fifth, *one must consider the person in situation and context.* One cannot understand the psychological impact of social categories without taking into account the *person* in *situation* and in *context* (Deaux & Martin, 2003). Situation and context are not the same. "Situation refers to a particular concrete physical and social setting in which a person is embedded at any one point in time. . . . Context is the surround for situations" (Ashmore et al., 2004, p. 102). How a person experiences or enacts his or her social identity in any given situation depends on the contexts surrounding the person in the situation. Thus, for example, the experience of being a solo member of a social category in a given situation may be quite different depending on the larger social context, such as whether one's social category is in a position of high or low power or social status within society.

These five insights about self and social identity are reflected in Deaux and Major's (1987) interaction-based model of gender-linked social behavior. This model conceptualized gender as a component of ongoing social interactions in which *perceivers* emit expectancies, *targets* (selves) negotiate their own identities, and the context shapes the resultant behavior. Shown in Figure 1.1, the model specifies a dyadic interaction in which a single perceiver has a set of beliefs about a target (Box A) that can be activated by a variety of factors (Box B), influencing the perceiver's behavior toward the target (Box C). Likewise, targets enter situations with a set of beliefs about themselves (Box D), aspects of which may be activated by factors similar to those that affect the perceiver (Box E). After interpreting the perceiver's actions (Box F), the target behaves in accord with his or her interaction goals (Box G) in a manner that may either confirm or disconfirm the perceiver's beliefs. Two general classes of modifying conditions shape the course of the interaction (Box H). These include characteristics of the transmitted expectancy (e.g., the social desirability of the expected behavior, the certainty with which the expectancy is held by the perceiver) and the target's relative concerns with self-presentation versus self-verification. The model also considers the perceiver's interpretation of the target's action (Box I) and the target's interpretations of his or her own actions (Box J).

Although Deaux and Major (1987) presented their model in the form of a dyadic interaction and applied it to gender, their theoretical assumptions apply to larger group contexts as well as to other social identities. Indeed, they suggested that recognizing the importance of others' expectancies, the active identity management of the self, and the importance of context is essential to understand the complexity and variability of social behavior. The perspective outlined in that paper strongly influenced my own subsequent research on the psychological implications of possessing (or being perceived to possess) a stigmatized social identity. In the remainder of this chapter, I briefly describe some of my work in this area, and how it was influenced by the above insights.

Stigma and Self-Esteem

When I began examining the psychological implications of membership in a stigmatized or consensually devalued social category, most social psychologists were studying stigma from the *perpetrator*'s point of view. That is, they were focused on understanding prejudice, stereotyping, and discrimination from the perspective of nonstigmatized or advantaged members of society. Research from this perspective revealed the pervasiveness of prejudice and discrimination against people who are stigmatized and documented stigma's powerful and far-reaching effects on its targets. Prejudice toward and negative stereotypes about the stigmatized limit their access to resources such as education, employment, and quality health care (Clark, Anderson, Clark, & Williams, 1999). Inability to obtain these resources can threaten or compromise the physical well-being of the stigmatized, especially if structural discrimination is

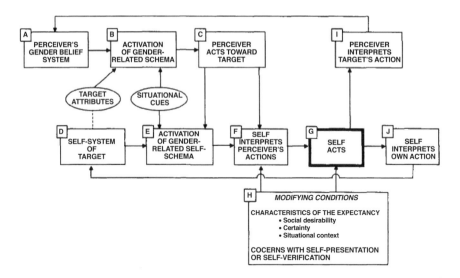

Figure 1.1. A model of social interaction for gender-related behavior. From "Putting Gender Into Context: An Interactive Model of Gender-Related Behavior," by K. Deaux and B. Major, 1987, *Psychological Review, 94,* p. 372. Copyright 1987 by the American Psychological Association.

repeated, pervasive, and severe (Clark et al., 1999). In addition, members of stigmatized groups experience a variety of forms of interpersonal rejection, such as being slighted, ignored, excluded, patronized, belittled, ridiculed, and targeted by violence. Because psychological well-being is at least partly dependent on inclusion by others and the perception that one is valued by others these interpersonal threats can have profoundly negative psychological implications for their targets (Leary, Tambor, Terdal, & Downs, 1995).

Crocker and Major (1989) conducted an extensive review of the literature to examine whether stigma also damages the self-esteem of those who are its targets. At the time of their review, most scholars assumed that prejudice and discrimination inevitably leave a "mark of oppression" on the personalities of their victims (e.g., Allport, 1954/1979; Erikson, 1956). For example, conceptualizations of the "looking glass self" assumed that negative views about certain groups expressed by wider society would be internalized by individuals who belong to those groups (e.g., Mead, 1934). Consequently, it was assumed that stigmatized groups would have lower self-esteem than nonstigmatized groups (e.g., Cartwright, 1950; Clark & Clark, 1947).

Crocker and Major's (1989) review of the empirical evidence on the relationship between membership in a stigmatized or devalued social category and personal self-esteem, however, revealed little support for this view. They found that devalued groups did not reliably have lower self-esteem than members of higher status groups, and some stigmatized groups had levels of self-esteem that were higher than culturally valued groups. Subsequent reviews substantiated these conclusions. For example, African Americans, a group that has faced persistent and severe discrimination for hundreds of years, report levels of self-esteem equal to or greater than European Americans (Twenge & Crocker, 2002). And the vast majority of individuals with disabilities, such as those who are blind, quadriplegic, or developmentally disabled, report positive levels of self-esteem (Diener & Diener, 1996).

Crocker and Major (1989) argued that the stigmatized are not helpless targets (victims) of others' negative beliefs, attitudes, and behaviors, but are *active agents with their own goals and self-relevant motives*. In addition, like Deaux, they argued that the stigmatized engage in *identity negotiation* so as to protect and maintain their personal self-esteem in the face of threats to their social identity. Thus, this perspective emphasized a target's resilience rather than vulnerability to prejudice, and focused on strategies of adaptation and resistance.

Crocker and Major (1989) proposed three cognitive strategies linked to group membership that the stigmatized might use to buffer their self-esteem from devaluation and poor outcomes associated with their social identity. First, they could withdraw their efforts or disengage their personal self-esteem from domains in which their group is negatively stereotyped or disadvantaged. This strategy lessens the sting of negative feedback in these domains. Instead, they could selectively value and invest their self-esteem in domains in which their group is positively stereotyped or advantaged. Subsequent research illustrated that members of stigmatized groups do engage in this strategy when their personal self-esteem is threatened (e.g., Major, Spencer, Schmader, Wolfe, & Crocker, 1998; Steele, 1997). For example, women taking a difficult math test who were exposed to negative gender stereotypes chose to answer fewer math questions and focused instead on answering verbal questions (Davies, Spencer, Quinn, & Gerhardstein, 2002).

A second strategy that stigmatized individuals may use to protect their self-esteem is to make selective social comparisons. That is, stigmatized individuals may selectively compare themselves or their outcomes with members of their own stigmatized group (who are likely to share poor outcomes) and avoid comparing themselves with members of more advantaged groups. They may also selectively construe available comparison information, dismissing the nonstigmatized as too dissimilar from the self, thereby making upward comparisons with them irrelevant. By doing so, the stigmatized can protect themselves from the potentially painful emotional consequences of upward social comparisons. Subsequent work provided evidence that the stigmatized engage in this strategy (e.g., Major, Sciacchitano, & Crocker, 1993).

A third way members of stigmatized groups may protect their personal self-esteem in the face of threats to their social identity is to attribute negative outcomes to the prejudice of others, rather than to internal, stable characteristics of themselves. Crocker and Major (1989) assumed that stigmatized individuals are generally aware that prejudice is a plausible cause of their negative outcomes. Consequently, when they experience such outcomes, the cause is often attributionally ambiguous. That is, when a stigmatized individual experiences a negative outcome, he or she is unsure whether the rejection was his or her own fault, or due to the bigotry of another. Drawing on theories of emotion (e.g., Weiner, 1995), and on Kelley's (1973) discounting hypothesis, they hypothesized that attributing negative events to others' prejudice (a cause external to the self) would protect affect and self-esteem relative to attributing negative events to causes internal to the self (e.g., lack of ability or skill).

The hypothesis that perceiving oneself to be a target of discrimination could buffer self-esteem proved to be most controversial, as well as most heuristic. Branscombe and colleagues (e.g., Branscombe, Schmitt & Harvey, 1999), for example, argued that because social identities are a part of the self-concept, attributions to prejudice are internal, rather than external attributions. Furthermore, they argued that because prejudice signals rejection and exclusion on the part of the dominant group, attributions to prejudice are detrimental to the psychological well-being of the disadvantaged (Branscombe et al., 1999). These criticisms and new data led to refinements and elaborations of the attributional hypothesis in subsequent papers (e.g., Crocker & Major, 1993; Major & Eliezer, 2011; Major, McCoy, Kaiser, & Quinton, 2003; Major, Quinton & McCoy, 2002; Major & Sawyer, 2009).

First, we reconceptualized an attribution to prejudice or discrimination as an attribution of *blame* because it involves attributing responsibility to another person whose actions are unjustified. This definitional clarification is important because attributions to justifiable differential treatment lack the self-protective properties sometimes associated with attributions to discrimination (e.g., Crocker, Cornwell, & Major, 1993). Second, we acknowledged that because attributing outcomes to prejudice implicates an individual's social identity—and social identities are a part of the self—such attributions have a strong internal component. This was consistent with Deaux's claim that personal identity and social identity are interconnected. We then demonstrated experimentally that attributing negative outcomes to discrimination does protect self-esteem relative to blaming internal, stable aspects of the personal self, but does not protect self-esteem relative to blaming other purely external or random causes (Major, Kaiser, & McCoy, 2003). Third, we clarified that attributions to discrimination do not necessarily lead to discounting of personal causes. That is, perceiving that another person is prejudiced does not preclude attributing an outcome to one's own lack of deservingness, or vice versa (McClure, 1998). Consequently, we emphasized the importance of examining *discrimination blame relative to self-blame* when considering the link between attributions to discrimination and self-esteem (e.g., Major et al., 2003; Major, Quinton & Schmader, 2003). Fourth, we emphasized differentiating emotional responses to perceived discrimination. Although attributing outcomes to discrimination may protect against negative self-directed emotions such as depression, shame, and loss of self-esteem, it is unlikely to protect against negative other-directed emotions such as anger and hostility (Major et al., 2002, 2003).

In sum, Deaux's intellectual handprint can be clearly seen in Crocker and Major (1989) as well as in my own and others' subsequent work on the psychological implications of stigma. Following Deaux and Major (1987), current research emphasizes that members of stigmatized groups are not passive targets of others' prejudices and negative stereotypes but are active agents who negotiate their identities, with the goal of maintaining and protecting self-esteem. This approach challenges traditional perspectives on the psychological consequences of membership in a devalued social category.

Stigma-Induced Social Identity Threat

Accumulating research on stigma provided substantial support for the general hypotheses proposed by Crocker and Major (1989). However, it also revealed significant variability in how members of stigmatized groups respond to evidence of prejudice and discrimination against their social groups. These findings confirmed Deaux's insight that *social identities are negotiated* (Ethier & Deaux, 1994). Simply knowing a person's social category membership is not sufficient to predict his or her affective, cognitive, or behavioral response when faced with prejudice and discrimination. Consequently, researchers began to focus on personal, situational, and structural factors that moderate the implications of perceiving and making attributions to discrimination for psychological well-being (for a review, see Major & Sawyer, 2009).

Major and O'Brien (2005) proposed a new model of the psychological impact of stigma that integrated emerging models of stigma that emphasized identity threat and negotiation (e.g., Crocker & Major, 1989; Crocker, Major & Steele, 1998; Steele & Aronson, 1995; Steele, Spencer & Aronson, 2002) with models of how people cope with stressful life events and circumstances in general (e.g., Lazarus & Folkman, 1984). In keeping with Deaux's approach to social category membership, Major and O'Brien's model emphasizes that stigma's effects are mediated through targets' understanding of how others view their social category, their interpretations of immediate situations and larger social contexts, and their personal motives and goals. Their model is top down in emphasizing how people's *subjective construals* of their category membership, environment, and self-relevant motives (e.g., self-esteem protection) shape their emotions, beliefs, and behavior. However, it is also bottom up in assuming that construals emerge from experiences (direct or vicarious) with being a target of negative stereotypes and discrimination. As with models of stress and coping in general, their model assumes that targets' responses to stressors linked to their social category membership are not uniform. Rather, it assumes that responses will vary considerably between targeted groups, within targeted groups, and even within the same individual across contexts. Further, it posits both vulnerability and resilience as common responses to the predicament of stigma, and highlights factors that differentiate these responses.

Major and O'Brien's (2005) model is shown in Figure 1.2. It begins with the assumption that possessing a consensually devalued social identity (a stigma) increases a person's likelihood of being exposed to potentially stressful (identity threatening) situations (see also Miller & Major, 2000). Drawing on theories of stress and coping, it theorizes that how individuals respond to those events depends on their *appraisals* of the event. Appraisals include primary appraisals of the demands posed by a potentially stressful event (e.g., the extent to which it is perceived as self-relevant, dangerous, effortful, creates uncertainty) and secondary appraisals of one's resources to cope with those demands (Lazarus & Folkman, 1984). The model posits that individuals experience *identity threat* when they appraise the demands imposed by a stigma relevant stressor as potentially harmful to their identity, and as exceeding their resources to cope with those demands. Although the model focuses on how stigma may lead to appraisals of identity threat, it notes that stigma may also lead to *identity challenge*. Challenge results when individuals perceive that they have sufficient resources to cope with the demands imposed by a stressor. Thus, someone who perceives himself as a potential target of prejudice might not appraise this as a threat if he feels he has more than sufficient coping resources to meet the demand. For example, Kaiser, Major, and McCoy (2004) showed that people who are dispositionally optimistic report challenge (rather than threat) appraisals when faced with threats to their social identity.

Predictors of Identity Threat

What determines how people appraise events that are potentially identity threatening? The model specifies that the experience of social identity threat is a function of *the person in situation and in context*. Specifically, whether or not people experience identity threat in response to stigma-relevant stressors is a function of their *collective representations* (or context), immediate *situational cues,* and *personal characteristics*. Collectively, these factors shape people's appraisals of events' significance for their well-being and their coping resources, and hence, whether or not they experience identity threat.

COLLECTIVE REPRESENTATIONS. Context is essential for understanding the impact of social categories (Deaux, 2004; Deaux & Philogène, 2001). Deaux defined *context* as "the general and continuing multilayered and interwoven set of material realities, social structures, patterns of social relations, and shared belief systems that surround any given situation" (Ashmore et al., 2004, p. 102). Major and O'Brien (2005) conceptualized context as people's collective representations, or shared understandings, of how groups are viewed in society. For stigmatized groups, these collective representations include awareness that their social identity is devalued in the eyes of others, knowledge of the domi-

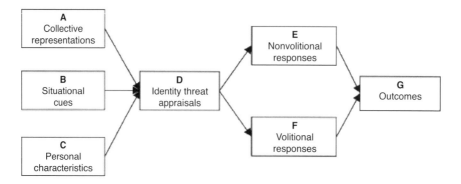

Figure 1.2. An identity-threat model of stigma. From "The Social Psychology of Stigma," by B. Major and L.T. O'Brien, 2005, *Annual Review of Psychology, 56,* p. 398. Copyright 2005 by the American Psychological Association.

nant cultural stereotypes of their stigmatized identity, and recognition that they could be a victim of discrimination (e.g., Crocker et al., 1998). Shared explanations for why different groups occupy the status positions that they do, or status ideologies, are also collective representations (Deaux, Reid, Martin & Bikmen, 2006; Major, Kaiser, O'Brien, & McCoy, 2007). Major and O'Brien (2005) proposed that collective representations can affect a person's appraisals of situations in the absence of obvious forms of discriminatory behavior on the part of others, and even when no other is present in the immediate situation.

IMMEDIATE SITUATIONAL CUES. Characteristics of the immediate situation also determine the impact of social categories (Deaux, 2004; Deaux & Philogène, 2001). Major and O'Brien (2005) assumed that situations differ in the extent to which they signal that an individual is at risk of being devalued, negatively stereotyped, or discriminated against because of his or her social identity and that these situational differences are critical determinants of behavior. A substantial amount of research has provided evidence of this. For example, research on *stereotype threat* effects has shown that for ability-stigmatized groups, such as African Americans or second-generation West Indian immigrants, taking a test described as diagnostic of ability is identity-threatening and leads to poorer performance, compared with taking the same test described as not ability diagnostic (e.g., Deaux et al., 2007; Steele & Aronson, 1995).

Like Deaux (e.g., Deaux et al., 2006), Major and O'Brien (2005) assumed that context (collective representations) can cause the same situation to be perceived and appraised differently by different individuals. For example, McKown and Weinstein (2003) showed that situational cues that increased the relevance of negative group stereotypes lead to social identity threat effects (e.g., impaired performance) among children old enough to be aware of negative stereotypes about their group but not among stigmatized children as yet unaware of group stereotypes. Thus, knowledge of the larger social context influenced how children responded to immediate situational cues. Nonstigmatized and stigmatized groups in particular may react differently to the same immediate situation, in part because they differ in the collective representations they bring to the situation. For example, women's math performance is impaired by solo gender status (i.e., being the only woman in a group of men), but men's math performance is unimpaired by solo gender status (i.e., being the only man in a group of women; e.g., Inzlicht & Ben-Zeev, 2000).

PERSONAL CHARACTERISTICS. Deaux (1993) also emphasized the importance of considering characteristics of the *person* in understanding the impact of social categories. Major and O'Brien's (2005) model likewise posits that people differ in their appraisals of stigma-relevant situations and contexts, and that these individual differences have important consequences for behavior. For example, members of stigmatized groups differ in the extent to which they are stigma conscious or chronically expect that they will be a target of negative stereotypes and prejudice (Mendoza-Denton et al., 2002; Pinel, 1999). These individual differences shape appraisals of potentially identity-threatening situations and events. For example, women high in the expectation that they will be a target of sexist prejudice are more vigilant for identity-related threats in their environment than are women low in the expectation that they will be targets of prejudice. They show higher preconscious attention to identity-threatening words (Kaiser, Vick, & Major, 2006), are quicker to interpret out-group (men's) faces as rejecting (Inzlicht, Kaiser, & Major, 2008), and show a greater increase in the stress hormone cortisol in situations in which their identity is potentially under threat (Townsend, Major, Sawyer, & Mendes, 2010).

Responses to Identity Threat

Major and O'Brien's model (2005) specifies that responses to stigma-induced identity threat can include *involuntary stress responses* as well as *voluntary coping efforts.* Involuntary stress responses are emotional, cognitive, physiological, and behavioral responses that do not serve to regulate or modify stressful experiences (Compas, Connor, Saltzman, Thomsen, & Wadsworth, 1999). Involuntary responses to stigma-induced identity threat include increased anxiety, arousal, blood pressure, and reduced working memory capacity (for a review, see Major & O'Brien, 2005). These involuntary threat responses to stigma-related events illustrate the important point that *social categories matter.*

Schmader and Johns (2003), for example, found that manipulations of stereotype threat (e.g., describing a test as measuring quantitative or intellectual capacity) led to lower working memory capacity among individuals targeted by the stereotype (women and Latinos) but had no effect on individuals not targeted by the stereotype (men and Whites). Another involuntary response to identity threat can be automatic vigilance to threat-related stimuli. Kaiser, Vick, and Major (2006) found that women led to anticipate interacting with a sexist (vs. a nonsexist) man allocated more attention to subliminally presented words that threatened their social identity, as did women who scored high (vs. low) in stigma consciousness. Ironically, people who chronically expect and are vigilant for signs of discrimination may create the rejection they fear by communicating these expectancies to others.

In contrast to involuntary stress responses, voluntary coping efforts are conscious, volitional efforts to regulate emotion, cognition, behavior, physiology, and the environment in response to events or circumstances appraised as stressful (Compas et al., 1999). People can cope with stigma-induced identity threat in a variety of ways. These coping efforts illustrate the important point that *the self is agentic.* Some coping strategies, such as the strategies described by Crocker and Major (1989), are primarily emotion-focused. Their goal is to reduce, avoid, or manage negative emotions. Other strategies are more problem-focused. People may seek to change themselves or their situation to reduce their risk of experiencing identity threat. For example, an overweight person might undergo bariatric surgery to eliminate the stigma of obesity or become an activist to reduce prejudice against his or her group. People also engage in coping strategies that serve both emotion-focused and problem-focused goals (e.g., an overweight person might avoid wearing a bathing suit). Engaging in a particular coping strategy in response to identity threats, however, does not (necessarily) guarantee a positive outcome. Involuntary and voluntary responses to identity threat are distinct from the outcomes of those responses, such as self-esteem, achievement, or health.

Social Identification and Social Identity Threat

Deaux's theoretical and empirical work contributed extensively to contemporary understanding of social identification processes (e.g., Ashmore et al., 2004; Deaux, 1993, 1996). Her work demonstrated that analyses of identity, as manifested in natural group memberships, cannot be conceptualized solely as a cognitive categorization process. One must also consider the personal meanings ascribed to a given category membership. Deaux's position challenged dominant theoretical approaches to social identity at the time (e.g., Turner, 1987). Deaux observed that two people might describe themselves with a common identity (e.g., Hispanic) but associate different meanings with that identity, differ in the importance they accord to that identity in their self-definition, associate different feelings with that identity, and so on (Deaux, 1993, 1996). These differences among people have important implications for behavior.

My own work on social identity and perceived discrimination substantiates these claims. Following in the tradition of some researchers (e.g., Smith & Henry, 1996; Tropp & Wright, 2001), but not others (Ashmore et al., 2004) I define *group* (or *social* or *collective*) *identification* as the importance or centrality of a social identity in the self-concept. I use the term *group* (or *collective*) *self-esteem* to refer to the affective component of one's relationship to the group (liking for the group). I have examined social (group) identification from several different perspectives, including (a) as a predictor of perceived discrimination against the self or ingroup, (b) as a moderator of reactions to perceived discrimination against the group, and (c) as a response to perceived discrimination against the group. Following is a brief description of my work in each of these areas.

Group Identification as a Predictor of Perceived Discrimination

The perception or attribution that oneself or one's group has been a victim of discrimination involves judgments that (a) the individual (or group) was treated unjustly and (b) the treatment was based on social identity or group membership (Major et al., 2002). Accordingly, personal or situational factors that increase the likelihood that outcomes are seen as linked to group membership or are seen as unjust should increase the likelihood that individuals will attribute those outcomes to discrimination. Increased identification with the group changes the interpretation of behavior from the individual to the group level (Tajfel & Turner, 1986), and also increases the likelihood that people make intergroup rather than interpersonal comparisons in ambiguous situations (Gurin, 1985). Based on this reasoning, Major, Quinton, and Schmader (2003) hypothesized that when placed in situations in which there are cues that unjust treatment may have occurred, individuals who are highly identified with their group would more readily make the cognitive leap from judgments of personal injustice to judgments of group-based injustice and make attributions to discrimination.

Reflecting the person × situation perspective outlined by Deaux and Major (1987), Major et al. (2003) also expected group identification to interact with characteristics of the immediate situation to influence perceived discrimination. According to Snyder and Ickes (1985), in *strong* situations where there are salient cues to guide behavior, situational cues are likely to overwhelm the influence of individual differences on behavior. In contrast, in *weak* situations that contain few or no guiding cues to behavior, individual differences are more likely to be influential. Based on this reasoning, Major et al. (2003) predicted that individual differences in group identification would influence attributions to discrimination in attributionally ambiguous situations but not in situations in which cues to prejudice were either blatant or absent.

To test these predictions, they conducted an experiment in which women took a creativity test in mixed gender groups. They were told that a male graduate student would grade the tests and select one of the participants to be the team leader on a second task. The prejudice cue manipulation was introduced while participants were waiting for their tests to be scored. While the experimenter was out of the room participants heard another female participant (a confederate) make one of three statements. In the blatant cue condition, she stated, "You know, I have friends who were in this study and they told me that the guy doing the evaluating is totally prejudiced. He never picks a girl to be team leader—he always picks a guy." In the ambiguous cue condition she stated, "You know, I have friends who were in this study, and they told me that the guy doing the evaluating totally grades guys and girls differently." In the no prejudice cue condition, she stated, "I hope the experiment doesn't last long because I have an appointment across campus." Women in all conditions then received a low score on the creativity test and were rejected as team leader.

As predicted, the extent to which women attributed negative feedback to sex discrimination depended on characteristics of the situation and of the person. In the presence of blatant prejudice cues, women blamed the negative feedback on discrimination, but in the absence of prejudice cues, they did not. There were no effects of gender identification in these two conditions, consistent with Snyder and Ickes's (1985) contention that strong situations overwhelm individual differences. In the attributionally ambiguous condition, however, women who were highly gender identified were significantly more likely to blame negative feedback on sex discrimination than women who were less gender identified. Indeed, highly identified women were as likely to attribute negative feedback to sex discrimination in the ambiguous cue condition as they were in the blatant cue condition. In contrast, low identified women were as unlikely to attribute negative feedback to sex discrimination in the ambiguous condition as they were in the no prejudice condition.

Operario and Fiske (2001, Study 2) observed a similar pattern in a study in which they paired ethnic minority students with a White partner (a confederate) who expressed either antidiversity attitudes (e.g., she was "uncomfortable around different types of people") or prodiversity attitudes (e.g., she "enjoyed being around so many different types of people"). The partner then behaved nonverbally in an unfriendly way during a subsequent interaction with the participant. Thus, for half the participants, the confederate's behavior meshed with her antidiversity attitudes; for the other half, her unfriendly behavior was inconsistent with her prodiversity attitudes. Participants high in ethnic identification were more likely than those low in ethnic identification to rate the partner as prejudiced and blame her behavior on their race, especially when cues to prejudice were ambiguous (i.e., when attitudes and behavior did not mesh).

Collectively, these experiments illustrate that high group identification is associated with increased attributions to discrimination primarily when the prejudice signal is ambiguous. These findings are consistent with the argument that individual differences in social identification change the way that identity-relevant situations are construed (Ashmore et al., 2004; Deaux, 1996).

Group Identification as a Moderator of Reactions to Perceived Discrimination

Individual differences in social identification also moderate how people react to threats against their social identity. Some scholars assert that perceiving discrimination directed against one's group cannot help but lead to psychological distress because discrimination implicates that a core aspect of the self—one's social identity—is devalued (e.g., Branscombe et al., 1999; Schmitt & Branscombe, 2002). This view assumes that threats to social identity and threats to individual identity are experienced as one and the same, and hence will have similar effects on self-esteem and psychological well-being. In contrast, Crocker and Major (1989) proposed that perceptions of bias against the social (collective) self can buffer the individual self from threat. This view assumes that threats to the group and threats to the individual self have different emotional implications.

Neither perspective takes into account individual differences in the extent to which a group identity is incorporated into personal identity. The more important or central group membership is to self-definition, the greater likelihood that negative group-related events will be appraised as self-relevant and identity threatening. Thus, the more central or important a group is to the self-concept the more distressing it should be to perceive discrimination against the group. Several experiments have provided support for this hypothesis.

McCoy and Major (2003, Experiment 1) conducted an experiment in which women, all of whom had previously completed a measure of gender identification, received negative personal feedback from a male evaluator they subsequently learned held either sexist or nonsexist attitudes. Thus, half the women were provided a social identity-linked attribution for their rejection, whereas the other half were not. As predicted, group identification interacted with situational cues to affect women's mood and self-esteem following rejection. Low gender identified women who were rejected by a sexist evaluator, and who could thus attribute their personal rejection to prejudice against their group, reported less depressed mood and higher self-esteem than low gender identified women rejected by a nonsexist evaluator. In contrast, among women high in gender identification, those who were rejected by a sexist evaluator felt as bad as those who were rejected by a nonsexist evaluator.

In a second experiment, McCoy and Major (2003, Experiment 2) assigned Latino American students, all of whom had previously completed a measure of ethnic identification, to read an article describing either the existence of pervasive prejudice against Latinos in the United States or against an unfamiliar and nonself-relevant group (the Inuit in Canada). As predicted, ethnic identification interacted with condition to affect subsequent appraisals of personal threat and depressed mood. Latino Americans who read about prejudice against their own ethnic group reported significantly more feelings of threat and depressed emotion the more strongly they identified with their group. In contrast, Latino Americans in the control group tended to report less threat and depressed emotion the more strongly they identified with their group. Consequently, compared with the control group, exposure to prejudice against the ingroup led to more depressed emotion for participants high in group identification but not for those who were low in group identification. This study thus showed that group identification moderates emotional responses to threats against the group, as well as the individual. This study, as well as the first study by McCoy and Major (2003), found that collective self-esteem (liking for the group) did not moderate emotional responses following either personal or group threat, thereby providing further evidence of the multidimensional nature of social identification (cf. Ashmore et al., 2004).

An experiment by Eliezer, Major, and Mendes (2010) provides further evidence that ingroup prejudice is more threatening for people who are highly identified with their group than for those who are less identified. In this study, women (who had previously completed a measure of gender identification) were randomly assigned to read and then give a videotaped speech summarizing one of two articles. One article described a study showing that sexism in the United States is prevalent, whereas the other described a study showing that sexism is rare. After giving the speech, women completed a distraction task and then sat for a 5-min recovery period. Cardiovascular reactivity (CVR, e.g., changes in blood pressure, heart rate, cardiac output, vascular resistance) was assessed during the speech and again during a postspeech recovery period to index threat experienced on a physiological or automatic level. Self-reported anxiety was measured right after the speech and again after the postspeech recovery period to index threat experienced on a controlled level.

During the speech, women who spoke about prevalent sexism exhibited a pattern of CVR consistent with threat than did those who gave a speech about rare sexism; the former also reported greater anxiety immediately postspeech compared with the latter. These effects occurred regardless of strength of group identification. During the recovery period, however, group identification interacted with condition to predict CVR. Highly identified women in the pervasive sexism condition continued to exhibit a threat pattern of CVR during recovery, whereas low identified women in the prevalent sexism condition (and women in the rare sexism condition) did not. Furthermore, the former reported higher anxiety postrecovery compared with the latter groups. Thus, the effects for group identification were larger when participants had the opportunity to reflect upon discrimination than during the speech. It is likely that the strong situational demands of speaking about pervasive discrimination overwhelmed individual differences during the speech (Snyder & Ickes, 1985). One implication of these findings is that perceiving discrimination against one's social identity may impose not only a heavier psychological burden but also a heavier physiological burden when that identity is an important component of self-definition. This increased burden, if experienced chronically and excessively, may contribute to adverse health outcomes, such as hypertension and cardiovascular disease (McEwen, 2000).

Findings of the studies mentioned here provide strong support for the assertion (Deaux, 1993, 1996) that the position of a social identity in the self-concept affects how people respond to threats associated with that social identity. Social identity and personal identity are distinct for low identified group members. Thus, they do not experience attacks on their social identity as attacks on themselves personally, and attributing negative events to prejudice against their social identity enables them to protect their personal self-esteem. In contrast, for highly identified group members, personal identity and social identity are closely related. They experience an attack on the group as an attack on the self. Thus, attributing rejection to discrimination does not protect their personal self-esteem. Furthermore, when a social identity is a central part of the self-concept, threats to that identity heighten not only psychological distress but also physiological stress.

Group Identification as a Response to Identity Threat

Ethier and Deaux (1994) observed that the need for and expression of social identity is not static, but changes as a function of situation and context. They asked what happens when people leave one context in which their social identity is supported and move to another context in which it is threatened. Social identity theory and self-categorization theory posit that when a group identity is made salient by a change in context, the person will become increasingly identified with his or her group. If the group identity is threatened and is not a source of positive social identity, however, what happens? Some scholars (Allport, 1954/1979; Branscombe et al., 1999) have posited that people identify even more strongly with their group when it is threatened. Groups can provide emotional, informational, and instrumental support, social validation for one's perceptions, social consensus for one's attributions, and a sense of belonging. Other scholars (e.g., Tajfel, 1981), however, have posited that if a social identity does not provide positive self-esteem, the person may attempt to leave the group. With ascribed categories such as race, ethnicity, or gender, however, leaving the group is typically not possible. In these cases, Ethier and Deaux suggested that people may change the meaning or value they associate with an identity. Furthermore, they proposed that strategies of identity negotiation under such circumstances will vary depending on the strength of a person's initial involvement or identification with that identity. Individuals who are highly involved with their identity may increase their identification with the group, whereas those who are weakly involved may decrease their identification with the group.

Ethier and Deaux (1994) found support for this hypothesis in a longitudinal study of identity changes among a small group of Hispanic students during their first year at primarily Anglo universities. They interviewed students at three time points: at the end of their first semester at university, as students returned from holiday break, and as students were completing their year. They measured students' involvement with their ethnic group prior to college, their perceptions of threat to their ethnic identity in the university environment, and changes in their collective self-esteem (affective feelings for their ethnic group), and identification with their ethnic group (importance of their ethnic group in their self-definition).

Ethnic involvement before college predicted changes in identification over time. The stronger students' ethnic background before college, the more they made efforts to maintain their group membership in school, and the more strongly they came to identify with their ethnic group during their first year of college. In contrast, students whose ethnic involvement before college was low showed a different identity path. They perceived the college environment as more threatening to their identity. These perceptions, in turn, were associated with decreases in collective self-esteem (liking for the group) over time, which in turn were associated with decreases in strength of identification over time. This important study was among the first to illustrate the dynamics of identity negotiation over time, in a natural field setting.

Subsequent experiments substantiated Ethier and Deaux's (1994) finding that initial identification predicts social identification changes in response to identity threats (Ellemers, Spears, & Doosje, 2002). McCoy and Major (2003, Experiment 2) assessed Latino American students' ethnic identification before and after reading about pervasive discrimination against their own ethnic group or a nonself-relevant group. Students who had initially reported lower levels of ethnic group identification came to identify even less after reading about pervasive discrimination toward their ethnic group. In contrast, students who had previously reported high ethnic identification reported even stronger ethnic group identification after reading that their group was a victim of pervasive discrimination. Collective self-esteem (liking for the group), in contrast, did not change as a result of the threat manipulation, perhaps because the threat was relatively minor and short-lived.

Conclusion

Deaux's contributions to contemporary understanding of how social category memberships influence affect, cognition, and behavior are substantial. Her work led to a number of major insights that continue to be reflected in and shape work on self, social identity, and stigma. Although once controversial, it is now well established and widely acknowledged that social identity is an important component of self-definition, that individuals differ in the strength and meaning of social identification, and that people negotiate their social identities in response to threats. Furthermore, scholars increasingly recognize the difference between the larger social context and the immediate situation, as well as the importance of taking both into account when trying to predict human behavior. Deaux's writings on social categories and social identity were at the forefront of a body of research that has exploded over the past three decades and shows no signs of abating. Nor has the importance of understanding these issues waned. As evidenced by mounting tensions around the world over immigration, race, religion, and ethnicity, social identities continue to matter to self-definition and intergroup behavior, and understanding their implications is more critical than ever.

References

Allport, G. W. (1954/1979). *The nature of prejudice*. Boston, MA: Addison-Wesley.

Ashmore, R. D., Deaux, K., & McLaughlin-Volpe, T. (2004). An organizing framework for collective identity: Articulation and significance of multidimensionality. *Psychological Bulletin, 130*, 80–114. doi:10.1037/0033-2909.130.1.80

Branscombe, N. R., Schmitt, M. T., & Harvey, R. D. (1999). Perceiving pervasive discrimination among African Americans: Implications for group identification and well-being. *Journal of Personality and Social Psychology, 77*, 135–149. doi:10.1037/0022-3514.77.1.135

Cartwright, D. (1950). Emotional dimensions of group life. In M. L. Raymert (Ed.), *Feelings and emotions* (pp. 439–447). New York, NY: McGraw-Hill.

Clark, R., Anderson, N. B., Clark, V. R., & Williams, D. R. (1999). Racism as a stressor for African Americans: A biopsychosocial model. *American Psychologist, 54*, 805–816. doi:10.1037/0003-066X.54.10.805

Clark, K., & Clark, M. (1947). Racial identification and preference in Negro children. In T. M. Newcomb & E. L. Hartley (Eds.), *Readings in social psychology* (pp. 169–178). New York, NY: Holt.

Compas, B. E., Connor, J. K., Saltzman, H., Thomsen, A., & Wadsworth, M. (1999). Getting specific about coping: Effortful and involuntary responses to stress in development. In M. Lewise & D. Ramsay (Eds.), *Soothing and stress* (pp. 229–256). Mahwah, NJ: Erlbaum.

Crocker, J., Cornwell, B., & Major, B. (1993). The stigma of overweight: The affective consequences of attributional ambiguity. *Journal of Personality and Social Psychology, 64*, 60–70. doi:10.1037/0022-3514.64.1.60

Crocker, J., & Major, B. (1989). Social stigma and self-esteem: The self-protective properties of stigma. *Psychological Review, 96*, 608–630. doi:10.1037/0033-295X.96.4.608

Crocker, J., & Major, B. (1993). Reactions to stigma: The moderating role of justifications. In M. Zanna & J. M. Olson (Eds.), *The psychology of prejudice: The Ontario Symposium* (Vol. 7, pp. 289–314). Hillsdale, NJ: Erlbaum.

Crocker, J., Major, B., & Steele, C. (1998). Social stigma. In S. Fiske, D. Gilbert, & G. Lindzey (Eds.), *Handbook of social psychology* (Vol. 2, pp. 504–553). Boston, MA: McGraw-Hill.

Davies, P. G., Spencer, S. J., Quinn, D. M., & Gerhardstein, R. (2002). Consuming images: How television commercials that elicit stereotype threat can restrain women academically and professionally. *Personality and Social Psychology Bulletin, 28*, 1615–1628. doi:10.1177/014616702237644

Deaux, K. (1984). From individual differences to social categories: Analysis of a decade's research on gender. *American Psychologist, 39*, 105–116. doi:10.1037/0003-066X.39.2.105

Deaux, K. (1993). Reconstructing social identity. *Personality and Social Psychology Bulletin, 19*, 4–12. doi:10.1177/0146167293191001

Deaux, K. (1996). Social identification. In E. T. Higgins & A. W. Kruglanski (Eds.), *Social psychology: Handbook of basic principles* (pp. 777–798). New York, NY: Guilford Press.

Deaux, K. (2004). Immigration and the color line. In G. Philogène (Ed.), *Racial identity in context: The legacy of Kenneth B. Clark* (pp. 197–209). Washington, DC: American Psychological Association. doi:10.1037/10812-011

Deaux, K., Bikmen, N., Gilkes, A., Ventuneac, A., Joseph, Y., Payne, Y. A., & Steele, C. M. (2007). Becoming American: Stereotype threat effects in Afro-Caribbean immigrant groups. *Social Psychology Quarterly, 70*, 384–404. doi:10.1177/019027250707000408

Deaux, K., & Major, B. (1987). Putting gender into context: An interactive model of gender-related behavior. *Psychological Review, 94*, 369–389. doi:10.1037/0033-295X.94.3.369

Deaux, K., & Martin, D. (2003). Interpersonal networks and social categories: Specifying levels of context in identity processes. *Social Psychology Quarterly, 66*, 101–117.

Deaux, K., & Philogène, G. (Eds.) (2001) *Representations of the social.* Oxford, England: Blackwell.

Deaux, K., Reid, A., Martin, D., & Bikmen, N. (2006). Ideologies of diversity and inequality: Predicting collective action in groups varying in ethnicity and immigrant status. *Political Psychology, 27*(1), 123–146. doi:10.1111/j.1467-9221.2006.00452.x

Diener, E., & Diener, C. (1996). Most people are happy. *Psychological Science, 7*, 181–185. doi:10.1111/j.1467-9280.1996.tb00354.x

Eliezer, D., Major, B., & Mendes, W. B. (2010). The costs of caring: Gender identification increases threat following exposure to sexism. *Journal of Experimental Social Psychology, 46*, 159–165. doi:10.1016/j.jesp.2009.09.015

Ellemers, N., Spears, R., & Doosje, B. (2002). Self and social identity. *Annual Review of Psychology, 53*, 161–186. doi:10.1146/annurev.psych.53.100901.135228

Erikson, E. (1956). The problem of ego-identity. *Journal of the American Psychoanalytic Association, 4*, 56–121.

Ethier, K., & Deaux, K. (1994). Negotiating social identity when contexts change: Maintaining identification and responding to threat. *Journal of Personality and Social Psychology, 67*, 243–251. doi:10.1037/0022-3514.67.2.243

Gurin, P. (1985). Women's gender consciousness. *Public Opinion Quarterly, 49*, 143–163. doi:10.1086/268911

Hogg, M. A., & Abrams, D. (1988). *Social identifications: A social psychology of intergroup relations and group processes.* New York, NY: Routledge.

Inzlicht, M., & Ben-Zeev, T. (2000). A threatening intellectual environment: Why females are susceptible to experiencing problem-solving deficits in the presence of males. *Psychological Science, 11*, 365–371. doi:10.1111/1467-9280.00272

Inzlicht, M., Kaiser, C., & Major, B. (2008). The face of chauvinism: How prejudice scripts shape perceptions of facial affect. *Journal of Experimental Social Psychology, 44*, 758–766. doi:10.1016/j.jesp.2007.06.004

Kaiser, C. R., Major, B., & McCoy, S. K. (2004). Expectations about the future and the emotional consequences of perceiving prejudice. *Personality and Social Psychology Bulletin, 30*, 173–184. doi:10.1177/0146167203259927

Kaiser, C. R., Vick, S. B., & Major, B. (2006). Prejudice expectations moderate preconscious attention to cues that are threatening to social identity. *Psychological Science, 17*, 332–338. doi:10.1111/j.1467-9280.2006.01707.x

Kelley, H. H. (1973). The process of causal attribution. *American Psychologist, 28*, 107–128. doi:10.1037/h0034225

Lazarus, R. S., & Folkman, S. (1984). *Stress, appraisal, and coping.* New York, NY: Springer-Verlag.

Leary, M. R., Tambor, E. S., Terdal, S. K., & Downs, D. L. (1995). Self-esteem as an interpersonal monitor: The sociometer hypothesis. *Journal of Personality and Social Psychology, 68*, 518–530. doi:10.1037/0022-3514.68.3.518

Major, B., & Eliezer, D. (2011). Attributions to discrimination as a self-protective strategy: Evaluating the evidence. In M. D. Alicke & C. Sedikides (Eds.), *Handbook of self-enhancement and self-protection* (pp. 320–337). New York, NY: Guilford Press.

Major, B., Kaiser, C. R., O'Brien, L., & McCoy, S. (2007). Perceived discrimination as worldview threat or worldview confirmation: Implications for self-esteem. *Journal of Personality and Social Psychology, 92*, 1068–1086. doi:10.1037/0022-3514.92.6.1068

Major, B., McCoy, S. K., Kaiser, C. R., & Quinton, W. J. (2003). Prejudice and self-esteem: A transactional model. *European Review of Social Psychology, 14*, 77–104. doi:10.1080/10463280340000027

Major, B., & O'Brien, L. T. (2005). The social psychology of stigma. *Annual Review of Psychology, 56*, 393–421. doi:10.1146/annurev.psych.56.091103.070137

Major, B., Quinton, W., & McCoy, S. (2002). Antecedents and consequences of attributions to discrimination: Theoretical and empirical advances. In M. P. Zanna (Ed.), *Advances in experimental social psychology* (Vol. 34, pp. 251–329). San Diego, CA: Academic Press.

Major, B., Quinton, W. J., & Schmader, T. (2003). Attributions to discrimination and self-esteem: Impact of group identification and situational ambiguity. *Journal of Experimental Social Psychology, 39*, 220–231.

Major, B., & Sawyer, P. J. (2009). Attributions to discrimination: Antecedents and consequences. In T. D. Nelson (Ed.), *Handbook of prejudice, stereotyping and discrimination* (pp. 89–110). New York, NY: Psychology Press.

Major, B., Sciacchitano, A. M., & Crocker, J. (1993). Ingroup/outgroup comparisons and self-esteem. *Personality and Social Psychology Bulletin, 19*, 711–721. doi:10.1177/0146167293196006

Major, B., Spencer, S., Schmader, T., Wolfe, C., & Crocker, J. (1998). Coping with negative stereotypes about intellectual performance: The role of psychological disengagement. *Personality and Social Psychology Bulletin, 24*, 34–50.

McClure, J. (1998). Discounting causes of behavior: Are two reasons better than one? *Journal of Personality and Social Psychology, 74*, 7–20. doi:10.1037/0022-3514.74.1.7

McCoy, S. K., & Major, B. (2003). Group identification moderates emotional responses to perceived prejudice. *Personality and Social Psychology Bulletin, 29*, 1005–1017. doi:10.1177/0146167203253466

McEwen, B. S. (2000). The neurobiology of stress: From serendipity to clinical relevance. *Brain Research, 886*, 172–189. doi:10.1016/S0006-8993(00)02950-4

McKown, C., & Weinstein, R. S. (2003). The development and consequences of stereotype consciousness in middle childhood. *Child Development, 74*, 498–515. doi:10.1111/1467-8624.7402012

Mead, G. H. (1934). *Mind, self and society: From the standpoint of a social behaviorist.* C. W. Morris, (Ed.). Oxford, England: University of Chicago.

Mendoza-Denton, R., Downey, G., Purdie, V. J., Davis, A. & Pietrzak, J. (2002). Sensitivity to status-based rejection: Implications for African American students' college experience. *Journal of Personality and Social Psychology, 83*, 896–918.

Miller, C. T., & Major, B. (2000). Coping with stigma and prejudice. In T. Heatherton, R. Kleck, M. R. Hebl, & J. G. Hall (Eds.), *The social psychology of stigma* (pp. 243–272). New York, NY: Guilford Press.

Operario, D., & Fiske, S. T. (2001). Ethnic identity moderates perceptions of prejudice: Judgments of personal versus group discrimination and subtle versus blatant bias. *Personality and Social Psychology Bulletin, 27*, 550–561. doi: 10.1177/0146167201275004

Pinel, E. C. (1999). Stigma consciousness: The psychological legacy of social stereotypes. *Journal of Personality and Social Psychology, 76*, 114–128. doi:10.1037/0022-3514.76.1.114

Reid, A., & Deaux, K. (1996). Relationship between social and personal identities: Segregation or integration. *Journal of Personality and Social Psychology, 71*, 1084–1091. sdoi:10.1037/0022-3514.71.6.1084

Schmader, T., & Johns, M. (2003). Converging evidence that stereotype threat reduces working memory capacity. *Journal of Personality and Social Psychology, 85*, 440–452. doi:10.1037/0022-3514.85.3.440

Schmitt, M. T., & Branscombe, N. R. (2002). The meaning and consequences of perceived discrimination in disadvantaged and privileged social groups. *European Review of Social Psychology, 12*, 167–199. doi:10.1080/14792772143000058

Smith, E. R., & Henry, S. (1996). An ingroup becomes part of the self: Response time evidence. *Personality and Social Psychology Bulletin, 22*, 635–642. doi:10.1177/0146167296226008

Snyder, M., & Ickes, W. (1985). Personality and social behavior. In G. Lindzey & E. Aronson (Eds.), *Handbook of social psychology* (3rd ed., Vol. 2, pp. 883–947). New York, NY: Random House.

Steele, C. M. (1997). A threat in the air: How stereotypes shape intellectual identity and performance. *American Psychologist, 52*, 613–629. doi:10.1037/0003-066X.52.6.613

Steele, C. M., & Aronson, J. (1995). Stereotype threat and the intellectual test performance of African Americans. *Journal of Personality and Social Psychology, 69*, 797–811. doi:10.1037/0022-3514.69.5.797

Steele, C. M., Spencer, S. J., & Aronson, J. (2002). Contending with group image: The psychology of stereotype and social identity threat. In M. P. Zanna (Ed.), *Advances in experimental social psychology* (Vol. 34, pp. 379–440). San Diego, CA: Academic Press.

Tajfel, H. (1981). *Human groups and social categories.* Cambridge, England: Cambridge University Press.

Tajfel, H., & Turner, J. C. (1986). The social identity theory of intergroup behavior. In S. Worchel & W. G. Austin (Eds.), *The psychology of intergroup relations* (pp. 7–24). Chicago, IL: Nelson-Hall.

Townsend, S. S. M., Major, B., Sawyer, P. J., & Mendes, W. B. (2010). Can the absence of prejudice be more threatening than its presence? It depends on one's worldview. *Journal of Personality and Social Psychology, 99,* 933–947. doi: 10.1037/a0020434

Tropp, L. R., & Wright, S. C. (2001). Ingroup identification as the inclusion of ingroup in the self. *Personality and Social Psychology Bulletin, 27,* 585–600. doi:10.1177/0146167201275007

Turner, J. C. (1987). *Rediscovering the social group: A self-categorization theory.* Oxford, England: Blackwell.

Twenge, J. M., & Crocker, J. (2002). Race, ethnicity, and self-esteem: Meta-analyses comparing Whites, Blacks, Hispanics, Asians, and Native Americans, including a commentary on Gray-Little and Hafdahl. *Psychological Bulletin, 128,* 371–408. doi:10.1037/0033-2909.128.3.371

Weiner, B. (1995). *Judgments of responsibility: A foundation for a theory of social conduct.* New York, NY: Guilford Press.

2

Understanding Social Categories: An Epistemological Journey

Gina Philogène

When social psychologists take on the difficult task of analyzing social categorization and identity, they go through a certain progression in their conceptual thinking about how the individual is embedded in his or her social context. They realize that their methods and theories must be more relational, viewing meaning as emerging from the relation of the individual to his or her environment (Gibson, 1977, 1986). They also realize that they should address these issues by reaching across the typical divisions of the social sciences. Each discipline has developed its own rich tradition of the dynamic between the individual and his or her environment, and we are well advised to draw from each other. Social psychology, at its best, can and should bridge these disciplinary boundaries because of its uniquely positioned focus on the individual–social nexus at the very core of the discipline.

In this chapter, I illustrate how our discipline has shown its enormous potential in that regard by tracing its epistemological journey from social categorization and identity via cross categorization and intersectionality to social representations and positioning. These are all different facets of a complex web that allows us to grasp how social categories shape our everyday experience. Throughout its evolution, social psychology has benefited from key theorists recognizing the need for multiple frames of reference to understand how the individual gets embedded in the social. Kay Deaux is one example of such theorists. She has consistently proven that she understands the depth of contextualization of individuals in the broader cultural, economic, political, and social facets of contemporary societies.

Kay Deaux's theoretical orientation is complex; it cannot be traced in linear fashion. Shaped by her own experience of gender discrimination, Deaux set out in the early 1970s to explore the misconceptions about gender differences and their reification in the social world. Motivated by a political pursuit, she brought sexism and discrimination toward women into the open (Deaux, 1978). But Deaux's career transcended the strictures of one fixed social category, that of gender, to focus on other systemic manifestations of inequality and discrimination. She showed herself open to the pleas of others as they struggled to establish better concepts of self and influence the society in which they evolved (Deaux & Ethier, 1998; Ethier & Deaux, 1994; Kite & Deaux, 1986; Kite, Deaux, & Miele, 1991), as in her more recent research on immigration (Deaux, 2004, 2008; Deaux et al., 2007; Deaux, Reid, Martin, & Bikmen, 2006; Tormala & Deaux, 2006). Her conceptual model of multiple dimensions of identity has placed her work within the same spirited tradition of activism found already among Kurt Lewin and followers of his participatory action research. Long before research in psychology started paying attention to the socially constructed nature of identities, Deaux had already stressed the importance of the multifaceted characteristics of social categories. By looking at their ramifications in the social context, Deaux pointed out early how the meanings given to these categories serve as tautological validation of their existence, a sort of self-fulfilling prophecy, as, for example, her work on gender-role norms and attribution.

On the study of social categories, a central concept in psychology, Deaux and others realized in the 1980s that they had to go beyond a fixed view of identity to reconstruct the individual as an array of multiple forces that in their interaction with one another provide meaning for one's identity (Deaux & Major, 1987). This multiplicity of influences underpinning the formation of identity in a social context first became recognized around the idea of defining individuals and their relations to others by means of two interacting categories, which may magnify or neutralize intragroup solidarity and intergroup distance. Research then extrapolated from such combining of two categories to the simultaneous coexistence of several categories defining the individual in his or her social context, putting emphasis on the intersectionality of these categories. In the 1990s, social theorists recognized that the individual has a certain agency in shaping how relevant categories intersect and what comes of these intersections (see, e.g., Collins, 2000). But it is also clear that this process of social positioning, whereby individuals seek to influence processes and outcomes related to identification, does not occur in isolation. Rather, it is part of a broader and deeper embeddedness of individuals within a system of collectively elaborated beliefs, shared understandings, and communicated representations engulfing all of us and shaping how we think about the world (Clémence, 2001).

This chapter has two objectives. One, it traces the epistemological development of the notion of social categories to highlight how social psychologists have progressed in their understanding of this concept. The field has gone through major transformations concerning its recognition and understanding of social categories. Of the reasons for this transformation, at least four are crucial. To begin with, we have come to recognize much more profoundly that categories are social constructs and what that means. Social psychologists have begun to explore more systematically how social objects develop in a social context, engaging in the process in more observational research such as field studies or the kind of work done in liberation psychology or action research. The field has also responded to a need to bridge psychological forms of social psychology with sociological ones. Finally, we have benefited from the push for interdisciplinary research, which has allowed us to see given concepts in a fluid and relational sense.

This chapter then explores how social categories, once created and becoming real, get concretized through their interplay to allow individuals to take positions concerning important issues in everyday lives. Such actualizations provide a structuring framework through which individuals make sense of the world around them and, at the same time, use to legitimize their own point of view. It is when we take positions about important matters that we engage in relations with others, both to share and to differentiate, as a matter of reaffirming who we are and validating what we think. A full understanding of social categories requires an appreciation of the notion of social positioning to see how collectively constructed categories become real and serve a purpose in the lives of social actors.

The Human Drive for Social Categorization

Humans have a strong need to create cognitive and social order by means of social categorization. We tend to project people as members of specific groups in order to simplify as well as easily recall knowledge about them, and so shape our social interactions with them. How do these social categories come about? We create a social category by structuring common features supposedly shared by all members of that category. In and of themselves, such social categories are abstract and devoid of meaning. However, because they are socially produced, they get endowed with meaning so they can be applied effectively to specific combinations of people. These individuals are turned into members through an interdependence in which they share common features strictly ascribed to that particular category. The power of such categories resides in the salience with which they get applied and, once named, how quickly they become points of reference in our everyday lives. After being immersed in the cultural fabric and therefore made meaningful, social categories serve as identification markers and thereby turned into elements of one's identity. This process of socially categorizing is fundamental to our cognitive capacities and our relation to culture.

The centrality of social categories in the interplay between the individual and the social has led to the development of divergent perspectives within social psychology. Although sociologists ranging from Durkheim to Bourdieu have emphasized our systemic classificatory impulses, social psychological approaches have looked at these abstract notions from the point of view of the processes by which they come into being (Turner, Hogg, Oakes, Reicher, & Wetherell, 1987).

A prominent theoretical perspective in social psychology on categories derived from the work of Henri Tajfel in social identity theory, particularly his "minimal group" experiments. In these studies, Tajfel (1970) put his subjects into two different groups in a laboratory setting on the basis of specious, even irrelevant characteristics. Although the participating individuals did not know each other and had no expectation of staying connected in any fashion beyond the confines of the study, they began soon after being grouped to express ingroup bias. At the same time, subjects nourished negative intergroup sentiments defining boundaries between two (entirely arbitrarily composed) groups, thus giving either group meaning as vectors of emotional attachment and cognitive discrimination. In other words, when people are arbitrarily placed in one of two groups in a laboratory setting, with no history of animosity and nothing at stake, identification ends up nourishing intragroup solidarity and perhaps even intergroup negative discrimination (Brewer & Hewstone, 2004; Tajfel, 1981).

Although we appreciate that social identity and self-categorization require a cultural and structural setting (Reicher, 2004), it is nonetheless amazing how little it takes for individuals to group together in contradistinction to each other. What Tajfel's minimal group studies demonstrated so effectively was that humans tend to internalize social categories, no matter how arbitrarily defined and ascribed. They vest themselves both affectively and cognitively in those categories to figure out who they are in relation to others, either *in* or *out*. Identity gets built around the adoption of social categories to define *me* as part of *us* and against the *other* (Ashmore, Deaux, & McLaughlin-Volpe, 2004).

Apart from their arbitrary and abstract nature, social categories do not exist in isolation. Individuals are not just defined by one category alone but are the result of a complex interplay among different categories. A person embodies more than one category at any one time. As Reid (1993) pointed out, the emphasis of early social psychological research on a single defining category could never fully grasp the complexity and multidimensional nature of one's identity. People integrate more than one category in their own sense of self and then let such multiplicity define their social relations with others. An important study by Deschamps and Doise (1978) shed light on this complexity. The two found that when people composed groups combining two different characteristics in such a way that those cut across each other (e.g., Black females and White females), intergroup bias between them would be reduced. These *crossed-categorizations* proved that people in their multidimensional complexity are capable of sharing and excluding at the same time. We have plenty of additional evidence of reducing intergroup bias when crossing category memberships (Brewer, Ho, Lee, & Miller, 1987; Crisp & Hewstone, 2006; Dovidio et al., 2006).

Empirical studies following that perspective have, in particular, examined the consequences of convergence of simultaneously salient categories, such as religion and nationality (Hewstone, Islam, & Judd, 1993), gender and age (Klauer, Ehrenberg, & Wegener, 2003), or race and gender (Abrams & Hogg, 1990). They all show how social categories are mutually constitutive, which means that one category of identity takes its meaning from another category. The improved understanding of the relational dynamics of categories with one another, which crossed-categorization research has provided us, helps us appreciate better the intrinsically fluid and flexible nature of categories (Urban & Miller, 1998).

The Propagation of Intersectionality

In recent years people have looked more intensely at the coconstruction of social identities resulting from the complex amalgamation of different categories. The influential incorporation of intersectionality as a theoretical model is an important advance in social psychology, made possible by the contributions of feminist theorists exploring the full context of gender (McCall, 2005; Shields, 2008a). It is in that work, which began with the academic emergence of women's studies a generation ago, that we can see the possibility of going beyond the cross-categorization literature to analyze the interaction of several determinant social categories for a more meaningful analysis of social identity and a more dynamic understanding of the complexities involved in social relations (Pastrana, 2010).

In the 1970s and 1980s, feminists returned to the age-old question of what it means to be a woman in order to better understand what divides women and keeps them apart. This was an utterly political question posited from within an emerging social movement that was seeking to address the issue of discrimination and oppression on the basis of gender. Going back to Sojourner Truth's piercing poem "Ain't I a Woman?," a new generation of feminists recognized that the struggles of the 19th century against slavery and for women's suffrage had already faced the same questions about what it meant to be a woman and what it would take to transform society, notably the role of women in it. Rather than just focusing on social class as the primary variable of differentiation, the feminist theorists stressed the crucial role of other categories, in particular that of race, in recognition of Black women's unique experiences of oppression (hooks, 1981). This work lent itself well to examining the interrelations between racism, sexuality, gender, and class.

Looking at multiple social (economic, political, cultural) as well as individual (psychic, subjective, experiential) axes of differentiation put interactively into a specific historical context, these writers gave birth to the intersectionality perspective. That approach respects the complexities of multi-faceted social identities, which it analyzes in terms of how individuals are socially stratified within a web of oppression, thereby putting emphasis on the operation of power relations among individuals in a group structured by those identity markers (Shields, 2008b).

Before intersectionality gradually established itself in psychology it had already taken root in sociology, gender studies, ethnic studies, and even literature. Although it has been a challenge to cope epistemologically as well as methodologically with such complex, fluid, and multidimensional phenomena, especially those grounded in the social, intersectionality has had the advantage of reinforcing psychology's growing openness toward capturing the dynamic, interactive, and constantly changing nature of social identity. It no longer holds the notion that identity facets can be separated, rejecting more and more the sequential analysis of single social category dimensions in favor of a more holistic analysis of where and how they intersect (Warner, 2008).

Cole (2009) made an important attempt to embed the intersectionality perspective in psychology. Cole argued that one of the virtues of intersectionality is that it forces psychologists to reconceptualize the meaning and significance of social categories as they interact with each other, rather than as they simply coexist alongside each other. According to Cole, psychological inquiry has to ask how social categories jointly shape outcomes and experiences. In pursuit of that objective it may be useful for psychological research to focus on three inter-related questions about social categories defining an individual's identity. The question of who is to be included in any given category puts the focus on the diversity within any given category to understand better how categories depend on one another for meaning. The second question pertains to the presence of inequality within social categories to analyze their qualities of structuring hierarchies of power and privilege shaping our lives. The final question would look at the similarities between otherwise clearly different categories to identify where they overlap, how they interact, and under what conditions they motivate action for change.

From her early work on gender and gender difference, Deaux has brought to social psychology a socially defined perspective in which the individual exists in a relational engagement to a broader context of intragroup similarities and intergroup relations. Deaux's qualitative study of women occupying hitherto male-dominated jobs in the steel industry (Deaux & Ullman, 1983) used social psychological methodologies of empirical research to shed light on a major public policy issue of the time, the impact of affirmative action programs. Although this study did not generate the kind of response it deserved in social psychology, it remains a classic in employment studies and in the use of social sciences for assessments of public policy. Apart from drawing the important empirical conclusion that the success of affirmative action programs depends on rising employment opportunities, the study stands out as an example of intersectionality itself in taking account of the multiplicity of identities embodied in an individual.

Her activist academic agenda and political engagement have allowed Kay Deaux to connect to the experience of many different social groups on the basis of profound similarities they share in the inequity linked to their social status. She thus continues a long-standing tradition of feminist social scientists who have gone beyond the monolithic influence of a single category to the intersectionality of multiple categories with which to take proper account of the complexities of women's lives under conditions of oppression. Her appreciation of multiple experiences of oppression connecting different social categories has led Kay Deaux to a quest for understanding the fundamental processes underlying identity formation. From the point of view of the questions she asked it is clear that her work takes account of the target perspective. In addition, from a methodological perspective her fluidity in both quantitative as well as qualitative approaches has led her to integrate into her work a sociological perspective on social psychology stemming from European traditions, such as Tajfel's and Turner's social identity theory, Harré and Billig's discourse analysis, and Moscovici's social representation theory (Deaux & Philogène, 2001; Farr, 1996).

Meaning Making: The Influence of Social Representations

Identity only makes sense if one has a holistic interpretation of the different social categories, how they interact with one another to create new combinations, and how they can change over time to reconfigure the identity in question. This task requires us to move beyond a primary focus on the centrality of the individual into his or her broader social context.

Identity, in the sense of Tajfel and Turner's (1979) social identity theory, moves from the individual out into their web of in- and outgroup relations whereby the object of that identity, the individual as social actor, becomes collectively represented. We can look at the whole sequencing from single social category via the model of cross-categorization to intersectionality and beyond that to social positioning to highlight an interactive process of identity formation as a socially communicated and collectively represented sense of who you are for yourself and in the eyes of others. You only become who you are by reference to how others see you. From that perspective, the significance of an identity as an amalgam of different social categories presumes shared knowledge, which gets elaborated in a given societal context as points of reference (e.g., God, America), clusters of meaning (e.g., religion, patriotism), and carriers of action galvanizing individuals (e.g., the political activism of the Tea Party in response to President Obama's health care reform initiatives). The contents of identity, including what it means to be socially identified by others (Moloney & Walker, 2007), are constructed by means of social representations. This implies that identities are *social representations*, providing a filtering lens through which we see the world around us (Breakwell & Lyons, 1996).

Social representations are the products of social thinking. They structure beliefs and knowledge about phenomena considered significant for a given community and, as such, become the processes by which we construct our social reality (Moscovici, 1984). Their power resides in the social psychological mechanisms by which they shape how we think and talk about events and objects. Social representations allow us to make images in order to crystallize figuratively, and thereby concretize, objects in the external world that we need to understand. They help us articulate concepts that capture our abstract thought and reasoning in a way that we can all agree on, even if we disagree on the details. For instance, most of us have a sense of global warming as an impending reality, yet we disagree vehemently as to why it is happening and what to do about it.

Social representations acquire a crucial role in our daily cognitive activity when facing the unfamiliar, which we need to render familiar. That activity never takes place in a vacuum but is a collectively elaborated process—a major part of our communicative interaction, built into our language, giving substance to what we communicate to each other and how we talk about topics of common interest. In his groundbreaking study of the propagation of psychoanalysis in postwar France, which gave social representation theory its birth, Moscovici (1961/1976, 2008) evoked two processes by which the unfamiliar is rendered familiar and made part of our reality. We anchor a new phenomenon—for example, a relation, practice, or event—by integrating this unfamiliar object into our familiar, well-established worldviews. We objectify the new phenomenon by turning the initially abstract object into something concrete enough to imagine, name, give meaning to, and then reliably evoke as reference whenever we need to. These two processes combine to turn something new into something real, something from the level of idea to the level of reality, as a social process of elaboration.

Social representations can take root to the extent they are built on shared knowledge of our common social reality. Any interaction, whether between two individuals or two groups of individuals, presupposes commonly shared and collectively elaborated social representations through which we make sense of the world and communicate that sense to each other. These representations originate quite naturally in daily life in the course of interindividual communication as proof of our fundamentally social existence. When we create and elaborate them, we turn these social representations into collective points of reference that enable us to name the world around us, classify the various aspects of that reality, and guide our relationship to them.

The study of social representations involves examining society in all its dynamic expressions by focusing on the social nature of thought and the ways in which people change their society. As proof of our fundamentally social existence, these representations emphasize the interplay between internal mechanisms manifesting themselves through an interpretative individual and the constantly changing social world, collectively elaborated. This process is actualized through the interconnectedness of individuals, helping them make sense of the world and communicate that sense to each other. Because these representations are collectively elaborated and are part of our everyday discourse, we let them become deeply embedded in our cultural fabric (Jodelet, 1991; Philogène, 2001).

When we create social representations we give meaning to concepts within specific social groups as a process of social negotiation and communication making those groups. In that sense it is fair to say that social representations are an interpretative frame to see how social categories really work. Categories defining group membership and shaping inter- or intragroup relations only come alive when activated as social representations. It is through this process that individuals can and do take a stand on common points of reference. Bringing into the social space of everyday life a salient mix of social categories that get activated in the course of interaction as social representations in a multidimensional dynamic of clustering compels one by this activation process to take positions about represented and categorized objects of relevance.

Kay Deaux's seminal work on immigrants (Deaux, 2006), one of the first comprehensive social psychological analyses of American immigration, not only managed to incorporate psychological insights about patterns of immigrant behavior but also clarified how representations of immigrants, both social and cultural, have shaped their social identity. In contrast to sociologists' emphasis on demographic patterns, political scientists' focus on public policy, and other objective indicators, Deaux brought to bear the role of social representations as the structuring element of attitudes, beliefs, and images that a community holds about immigrants and immigration. In framing her analysis, she envisioned an agenda for a social psychology that would integrate findings from other fields of immigration research, thereby moving us beyond the disciplinary divisions towards a multidimensional and multidisciplinary level of analysis of this identity. This work is reflective of the idea that the social identities of immigrants have to be understood through their representational manifestations, which are assumed in a specific social context. As Deaux has shown, social representation theory can be seen as a key perspective that not only emphasizes our socially constructed world but also ultimately connects individuals' interpretations of that world and their social production of knowledge about it.

Social Positioning

Positioning theory is a perspective that seeks to articulate an alternative way of interpreting and understanding the dynamic of human relations within a social constructionist paradigm (Haslanger, 2003). It provides a framework to understand how social categories are anchored through the processes of categorization and actualized through a process by which individuals take a position about a network of significations. This perspective requires a shift in our analysis away from the metaphorical notion of *role* to the more dynamic metaphor of *position*. The concept of role is criticized as being a relatively static concept to describe the way these social categories are actually experienced and enacted by their participants. The concept of position, on the other hand, is characterized more dynamically in terms of relation processes, which constitute interaction between individuals. This connection of the positioning concept to the discursive construction of personal narrations offers a great deal of flexibility, given that one's position is ever-changing, even if only by degrees.

Positioning theory is an interactionist approach, introduced by Harré and others (Van Langenhove & Harré, 1995) as a metaphor to identify ways in which individuals are situated or positioned within a social sphere. Conceived as a discursive model, *positioning*, according to Harré, refers to the use of rhetorical devices by which actors communicating with each other are presented as standing in various kinds of relations to each other (e.g., relations of power, knowledge, ignorance, dominance, submission) and thereby accentuating their identity as a confluence of different social categories.

The confluence of social categories provides individuals with their social position in their respective society and culture. In other words, these categories place the person in a social field that is structured (e.g., by occupation, race, nationality) and hierarchized. Depending on the prevailing constellation of intersecting categories, the individual concerned positions him- or herself socially within that structure. That positioning is both internal, a matter of the individual's own drive, and external, a function of how others place that individual. Thus, when I make up my mind on a controversial issue, such as abortion, it provides a basis for a display of my social belonging as well as my group membership affiliations. Not all social categories that one embodies are activated, but some decisive ones are made salient for the positioning activities to run their course.

The notion of social positioning has the advantage of giving individuals greater agency, thus endowing them with the possibility of affecting change, whereas other approaches typically imply a less active view of individuals as carriers of an amalgam of social categories whose interplay molds them. Deaux's adoption of a target perspective, endowing individuals with the power to determine their own uniqueness through self-description and self-classification, fits into the broader tradition of social positioning discussed above in which individuals have agency to shape who they are and how they are seen by others. Complementing methodological emphasis on the self as a psychological construct that is key to one's unique identity, Deaux also sought to examine the relational and collective determinants of social identification. In Deaux, Reid, Mizrahi, and Ethier (1995), she found five types of social identity: personal relationships, vocations, political affiliations, ethnic or religious groups, and stigmatized groups. How these work together depends, on the one hand, on their relative proximity and saliency within a hierarchical structure. On the other hand, their interaction with each other is mediated by the individual's engagement with the outside world as shaped by these five elements. Once again, and this time from the point of view of one's social context, social positioning serves as a useful mechanism of connecting individuals to their social context.

The difference between social positioning and other perspectives on categorization is that the former implies individuals negotiating—within themselves, with others sharing relevant categories, as well as with outsiders not sharing those categories—their identity, status, and influence. Theorists of social positioning (Clémence, 2001; Doise, 1987) have emphasized the usefulness of this concept in giving coherence to the different categories embodied within the individual. People have to shape the multiplicity and intersections of their respective categories to make sense of who they are and to structure how they are seen by others. Positioning engulfs both intraindividual ordering of categories and interindividual situational contexts into a dialectical resolution by placing individuals as actors in a relational web, a social field of interactions, and a network of significations.

Social positioning presupposes a field of categories within which individuals can be placed (or place themselves) relative to others. Such positioning puts individuals as social actors into a field of categories that structure vectors of identity which help them assimilate, classify, and organize knowledge about the world. Depending on ascribed differences in socioeconomic status, gender, sexuality, ethnicity, and so on, one's positioning within that web of categories will shape how one connects to others. That can only be the case, because these preexisting categorical differentiations that position one have been reified and are thus recognized by others on the basis of shared experiences, beliefs, and representations. In other words, social positioning occurs through a common frame of reference around which groups get formed. It structures knowledge shared between members of the same group. In this context, the categories are above all a social process of activation and elaboration. They do not reside a priori within the individual, but converge onto the individual from an external network of assignments.

Conclusion

This chapter's exploration of key social psychological paradigms starts with a fundamental concept shaping the lives of individuals, that of social category, which we internalize as identity-shaping facet of our existence and reference of orientation. Social categories are, in this sense, crucial bridges from our individual selves to the social world within which we live. Categories embody the social in us, and as such they have been subject to rethinking and deepening as psychologists have tried to get a better handle on what it means to be a social being. In the first paradigm, centered on the symbolic interactionists around Mead, a major step toward capturing a sense of the social in us was taken with the emphasis on one's role to be played in the social settings of one's daily existence. Any role was at that point seen as connected to a specific underlying category. Here we bring social representation theory into view for the first time to explore this connection more systematically. We anchor in the categorization process salient categories as social representations to make them real to us. And then we objectify these representations as roles we play to let the category become part of our identity, through which we see ourselves and are seen by others.

The link between category and role, connected through the anchoring and objectification of social representations through which we make a social category our reality as part of our identity, is still a static one. It ignores the fact that we each comprise a variety of categories. Moreover, it underestimates our desire for change and our ability to let identity turn us into actors for societal change. Modern social psychology has worked hard over the last couple of decades to respond to these criticisms with a better approach. For one, we in the field have come to recognize the complexity of one's identity being inexorably tied to the inescapable coexistence of several simultaneous categories defining and determining who we are. We let this realization take us into a more dynamic, meaning more relationally oriented, theoretical framework. We have moved on rapidly from looking at the interaction of two categories, as exemplified best in the cross-categorization research of Deschamps and Doise (1978), to analyzing the intersectionalities of several social categories in recognition that anyone's fully developed social identity is composed of multiple dimensions (Cole, 2009; Deaux, 2004, 2008; Deaux & Ethier, 1998).

The more dynamic approach in social identity theory also wanted to give the socially defined individual a more active existence as an agent of change in connection with others. Both cross-categorization and intersectionality research begot a parallel advance from role to position, an epistemological advance in which Willem Doise once again played an important role. His theory of social positioning, with its dialectical tension between intraindividual ordering of categories and interindividual situational contexts, posits individuals as actors in a social setting subject to change.

Once again, it is social representation theory that helps establish the link between these two parallel conceptual developments, from single category to intersectionality and from role to position. As we form social representations, we anchor in the process the mixture of categories that will motivate our positioning. In return, by taking such a position vis-à-vis a relevant object, we objectify those categories in their interaction as identity facets to reaffirm our belonging and affiliations to several category memberships. Social representation theory is therefore crucial to understand the important place social categories occupy in our reality, by providing a broader context for social identity to be actualized in the positions and positioning of individuals.

References

Abrams, D. & Hogg, M. A. (1990). Social identification, self-categorization, and social influence. *European Review of Social Psychology*, *1*, 195–228. doi:10.1080/14792779108401862

Ashmore, R. D., Deaux, K., & McLaughlin-Volpe, T. (2004). An organizing framework for collective identity: Articulation and significance of multidimensionality. *Psychological Bulletin*, *130*, 80–114. doi:10.1037/0033-2909.130.1.80

Breakwell, G. M., & Lyons, E. (1996). *Changing European identities: Social psychological analyses of social change*. Oxford, England: Butterworth-Heinemann.

Brewer, M. B., & Hewstone, M. (Eds.). (2004). *Self and social identity*. Oxford, England, and Malden, MA: Blackwell.

Brewer, M. B., Ho, H. K., Lee, J. Y., & Miller, N. (1987). Social identity and social distance among Hong Kong school children. *Personality and Social Psychology Bulletin*, *13*, 156–165. doi:10.1177/0146167287132002

Clémence, A. (2001). Social positioning and social representations. In K. Deaux & G. Philogène (Eds.), *Representations of the social* (pp. 83–95). New York, NY: Blackwell.

Cole, E. R. (2009). Intersectionality and research in psychology. *American Psychologist, 64*, 170–180. doi:10.1037/a0014564

Collins, P. H. (2000). *Black feminist thought: Knowledge, consciousness, and the politics of empowerment*. New York, NY: Routledge.

Crisp, R. J., & Hewstone, M. (2006). *Multiple social categorization*. London, England: Psychology Press.

Deaux, K. (1978). The power of feminist thinking. *Contemporary Psychology, 23*, 295–296.

Deaux, K. (2004). Immigration and the color line. In G. Philogène (Ed.), *Racial identity in context: The legacy of Kenneth B. Clark* (pp. 197–209). Washington, DC: American Psychological Association. doi:10.1037/10812-011

Deaux, K. (2006). A nation of immigrants: Living our legacy. *Journal of Social Issues, 62*, 633–651.

Deaux, K. (2008). To be an American: Immigration, hyphenation, and incorporation. *Journal of Social Issues, 64*, 925–943. doi:10.1111/j.1540-4560.2008.00596.x

Deaux, K., Bikmen, N., Gilkes, A., Ventuneac, A., Joseph, Y., Payne, R., & Steele, C. (2007). Becoming American: Stereotype threat effects in Black immigrant groups. *Social Psychology Quarterly, 70*, 384–404. doi:10.1177/019027250707000408

Deaux, K., & Ethier, K. A. (1998). Negotiating social identity. In J. K. Swim & C. Stangor (Eds.), *Prejudice: The target's perspective* (pp. 301–323). San Diego, CA: Academic Press.

Deaux, K., & Major, B. (1987). Putting gender into context: An interactive model of gender-related behavior. *Psychological Review, 94*, 369–389. doi:10.1037/0033-295X.94.3.369

Deaux, K., & Philogène, G. (2001). *Representations of the social*. New York, NY: Blackwell.

Deaux, K., Reid, A., Martin, D., & Bikmen, N. (2006). Ideologies of diversity and inequality: Predicting collective action in groups varying in ethnicity and immigrant status. *Political Psychology, 27*, 123–146. doi:10.1111/j.1467-9221.2006.00452.x

Deaux, K., Reid, A., Mizrahi, K., & Ethier, K. A. (1995). Parameters of social identity. *Journal of Personality and Social Psychology, 68*, 280–291. doi:10.1037/0022-3514.68.2.280

Deaux, K., & Ullman, J. (1983). *Women of steel: Female blue-collar workers in the basic steel industry*. New York, NY: Praeger.

Deschamps, J. C., & Doise, W. (1978). Crossed-category membership in intergroup relations. In H. Tajfel (Ed.), *Differentiation between social groups: Studies in the social psychology of intergroup relations* (pp. 141–158). London, England: Academic Press.

Doise, W. (1987). Idées nouvelles et notions anciennes [New ideas and ancient notions]. In J. L. Beauvois, R. V. Joule, & J. M. Monteil (Eds.), *Perspectives Cognitives et Conduites Sociales* [Cognitive Perspectives and Social Conduct] (pp. 229–243). Suisse, Cousset, Del Val.

Dovidio, J., Gaertner, S. L., Hodson, G., Riek, B. M., Johnson, K. M., & Houlette, M. (2006). Recategorization and crossed-categorization: The implications of group salience and representations for reducing bias. In R. J. Crisp & M. Hewstone (Eds.), *Multiple social categorization: Processes, models and application* (pp. 65–89). London, England: Psychology Press.

Ethier, K. A., & Deaux, K. (1994). Negotiating social identity in a changing context: Maintaining identification and responding to threat. *Journal of Personality and Social Psychology, 67*, 243–251. doi:10.1037/0022-3514.67.2.243

Farr, R. (1996). *The roots of modern social psychology: 1872–1954*. London, England: Wiley Blackwell.

Gibson, J. J. (1977). The theory of affordances. In R. Shaw & J. Bransford (Eds.), *Perceiving, acting, and knowing: Toward an ecological psychology* (pp. 67–82). Mahwah, NJ: Erlbaum.

Gibson, J. J. (1986). *The ecological approach to visual perception*. London, England: Psychology Press.

Haslanger, S. (2003). Social construction: The "debunking" project. In F. F. Schmitt (Ed.), *Socializing metaphysics: The nature of social reality* (pp. 301–325). Lanham, MD: Rowman and Littlefield.

Hewstone, M., Islam, M. R., & Judd, C. M. (1993). Models of crossed-categorization and intergroup relations. *Journal of Personality and Social Psychology, 64*, 779–793. doi:10.1037/0022-3514.64.5.779

hooks, b. (1981). *Ain't I a woman: Black women and feminism*. Boston, MA: South End Press.

Jodelet, D. (1991). *Madness and social representations*. London, England: Harvester/Wheatsheaf.

Kite, M. E., & Deaux, K. (1986). Attitudes toward homosexuality: Assessment and behavioral consequences. *Basic and Applied Social Psychology*, *7*, 137–162. doi:10.1207/s15324834basp0702_4

Kite, M. E., Deaux, K., & Miele, M. (1991). Stereotypes of young and old: Does age outweigh gender? *Psychology and Aging*, *6*, 19–27. doi:10.1037/0882-7974.6.1.19

Klauer, K. C., Ehrenberg, K., & Wegener, I. (2003). Crossed-categorization and stereotyping: Structural analyses, effect patterns, and dissociative effects of context relevance. *Journal of Experimental Social Psychology*, *39*, 332–354. doi:10.1016/S0022-1031(03)00017-9

McCall, L. (2005). The complexity of intersectionality. *Signs: Journal of Women in Culture and Society*, *30*, 1771–1800. doi:10.1086/426800

Moloney, G., & Walker, I. (2007). *Social representations and identity: Content, process and power*. London, England: Palgrave-Macmillan. doi:10.1057/9780230609181

Moscovici, S. (1961/1976). *La psychoanalyse, son image et son public* [Psychoanalysis: Its image and its public]. Paris, France: P.U.F.

Moscovici, S. (1984). The phenomenon of social representations. In R. M. Farr & S. Moscovici (Eds.), *Social representations* (pp. 3–70). Cambridge, England: Cambridge University Press.

Moscovici, S. (2008). *Psychoanalysis: Its image and its public*. Malden, MA: Polity.

Pastrana, A. (2010). Privileging oppression: Contradictions in intersectional politics. *The Western Journal of Black Studies*, *34*, 53–63.

Philogène, G. (2001). Theory of methods. In K. Deaux & G. Philogène (Eds.), *Representations of the social* (pp. 39–41). New York, NY: Blackwell.

Reicher, S. (2004). The context of social identity: Domination, resistance, and change. *Political Psychology*, *25*, 921–945. doi:10.1111/j.1467-9221.2004.00403.x

Reid, P. T. (1993). Poor women in psychological research: Shut up and shut out. *Psychology of Women Quarterly*, *17*, 133–150. doi:10.1111/j.1471-6402.1993.tb00440.x

Shields, S. A. (2008a). Gender: An internationality perspective. *Sex Roles*, *59*, 301–311. doi:10.1007/s11199-008-9501-8

Shields, S. A. (Ed.). (2008b, September). Intersectionality of social identities: A gender perspective [Special issue]. *Sex Roles*, *59*(5–6).

Tajfel, H. (1970). Experiments in intergroup discrimination. *Scientific American*, *223*, 96–102. doi:10.1038/scientificamerican1170-96

Tajfel, H. (1981). *Human groups and social categories*. Cambridge, England: Cambridge University Press.

Tajfel, H., & Turner, J. C. (1979). An integrative theory of intergroup conflict. In W. G. Austin & S. Worchel (Eds.), *The social psychology of intergroup relations* (pp. 33–47). Monterey, CA: Brooks/Cole.

Tormala, T. T., & Deaux, K. (2006). Black immigrants to the United States: Confronting and constructing ethnicity and race. In R. Mahalingam (Ed.), *Cultural psychology of immigration* (pp. 131–150). Mahwah, NJ: Erlbaum.

Turner, J. C., Hogg, M. A., Oakes, P. J., Reicher, S., & Wetherell, M. S. (1987). *Rediscovering the social group: A self-categorization theory*. Oxford, England: Blackwell.

Urban, L. M., & Miller, N. (1998). A theoretical analysis of crossed-categorization effects: A meta-analysis. *Journal of Personality and Social Psychology*, *74*, 894–908. doi:10.1037/0022-3514.74.4.894

Van Langenhove, L., & Harré, R. (1995). Telling your life: Autobiographical talk and positioning. In N. Coupland & J. Nussbaum (Eds.), *Discourse and life-span development* (pp. 81–91). London, England: Sage.

Warner, L. R. (2008). A best practices guide to intersectional approaches in psychological research. *Sex Roles*, *59*, 454–463. doi:10.1007/s11199-008-9504-5

3

Extraordinary Takes on "Ordinary Life": Categories of Sex, Gender, and Identity in the Work of Kay Deaux

Frances Cherry

The purpose of this chapter is to contextualize the relevance of social categories—sex, gender, and identity—in the social psychological writings of Kay Deaux. This entails both a reflection on changes in social psychology as well as changes in the culture in which social psychology is embedded. Up to the mid-20th century, social categories of gender and culture were coded, understood, and lived more rigidly as sex and race (Pickren & Rutherford, 2010; Winston, 2004). Theories of human nature were grounded in the biological determinism of the late 19th century in which sex and race had relatively well-prescribed legal, psychological, and cultural consequences.

The transformation of these social categories in the post–World War II period represents accomplishments through research, legal action, and social movements. For social psychologists such as Kay Deaux, this has meant important contributions to a better understanding of the fluid nature of gendered and racialized categories. By negotiating a new vocabulary for the changing experiences of women, minorities, and immigrants, among others, Deaux (2006a) connected earlier traditions in the human sciences to the newer sensibilities of the 21st century.

The new vocabulary of gender and culture began appearing in textbooks of social psychology in the 1970s, partly as a reflection of the growing inclusion of women and minorities in graduate psychology programs. Through the scholarship of Kay Deaux from the 1960s to the present, it is possible to better understand the transformation in social psychology from fixed and nonoverlapping social categorizations to fluid and intersectional ones. Some of this transformation is best understood as the way in which lived identities and experiences can serve to shape the trajectory of an academic discipline and how, in turn, we ourselves are reshaped by that discipline. This chapter probes larger epistemological themes of disciplinary identity and interdisciplinarity across 5 decades of an extraordinary social psychologist's takes on ordinary life. Following a brief summary of Deaux's academic formation, several themes central to her work are explored: social categories as ranges of possibilities; the desire to bridge psychological and sociological social psychology;

the personal, professional, and historical relevance of sex, gender, and place; the role of intersecting identities in "ordinary life," particularly in the case of immigrant groups; and categories of sex, gender, and identity in the work of Kay Deaux.

By the time she received her undergraduate degree at Northwestern University in 1963, Deaux (2001) had discovered "the pleasures of concentrated, independent work" (p. 205). Through several hands-on research experiences in her formative undergraduate years, she became a strong advocate of an apprenticeship model of how to do social psychology. Kay (Kujala) spent the summer of 1963 working with Donald Campbell and his colleagues in what turned out to be their classic volume, *Unobtrusive Measures: Nonreactive Research in the Social Sciences* (Webb, Campbell, Schwartz, & Sechrest, 1966). It was that summer job that gave her "a glimpse of creative thinking and an appreciation for the multiple paths that a scientific approach might take" (Deaux, 2001, p. 205). It should be said that in the early 1960s, psychological social psychology was not held in particularly high esteem in many departments of psychology, and most departments were still dominated by memory and learning theorists. Nonetheless, reflecting back on this period, Deaux (2001) wrote, "In some inchoate way, I defined myself as a social psychologist" (p. 205).

After a slight detour to Columbia University, where her intentions were to research social issues and get a doctorate in social work, Deaux returned to psychology at Brooklyn College. There she developed her research skills further as an assistant to James Bieri, whose work focused on social perception and cognition. Bieri had been a student of personal construct theorist George Kelly and introduced notions of cognitive simplicity and complexity into the psychological literature (Bieri, 1955). When Bieri moved to the University of Texas, Deaux moved to Austin to complete her PhD under his supervision, which she did in 1967.

Categories as Ranges of Possibilities

One of the central themes in Deaux's approach to social psychology emerged in her early work with Bieri, namely, a sense that perceptions, cognitions, traits, and attitudes are fluid rather than static and that attitudinal positions are best represented by a range of positions rather than a rigidly fixed point (Atkins, Deaux & Bieri, 1967; Bieri, Deaux & Atkins, 1966; Deaux, 1968a; Deaux & Bieri, 1967). Reflecting years later on the topic of fixed or fluid notions of self, Deaux (2009) said that the "idea that there are ranges of possibilities within which behavior unfolds, is fundamental to the way I think." Using the concept of latitude of acceptance, Deaux and Bieri (1967) explored the way in which self-conceptions of one's masculinity and femininity might shift in response to social dynamics. However, Deaux claimed no strong sense that this work was either a conscious or enlightened attempt to make sex differences a central focus of her early work. Rather, her work with Bieri reflects a percolating interest in the social categories that were beginning to change along with women's changing circumstances in the mid to late 1960s.

Bridging Sociological and Psychological Social Psychology

Deaux entered graduate school at a time when psychological and sociological social psychology were drifting apart (Oishi, Kesebir, & Snyder, 2009). She was part of a relatively large contingent of social psychologists in a department of psychology at the University of Texas in which learning psychology was predominant. In 1967, and very close to obtaining her PhD, she attended a conference on graduate education in social psychology, convened at Case Western Reserve University (Lundstedt, 1968). Speaking to an audience that included many luminaries in both sociological and psychological social psychology, Deaux (1968b) presented her thoughts on the future of graduate education in social psychology and her view that the splitting off of social psychology in two directions and departments wasn't "necessarily the most desirable solution" (Deaux, 1968b, p. 210) for either. Although she did not claim to have a full historical perspective for understanding all the dimensions of the rift, she expressed the view that psychological social psychologists' foray into the "purer air of the experimental laboratory" (Deaux, 1968b, p. 211) did not have to be a permanent outcome.

Perhaps drawing on her early work in association with Donald Campbell, Deaux expressed a prescient sense of later critiques of an exclusively laboratory-based social psychology. Her earliest work has a finely honed sense of the trade-offs between internal and external validity and the importance of considering the generalizations of laboratory work to real social groups, organizations, and other collectivities. Students working with her both in laboratory and field research knew firsthand about the methodological sophistication one could gain by learning the tools of rigorous experimentation and statistical analysis. Her broader goal, at least from a disciplinary perspective, was to "blend the methodological rigor and laboratory findings of psychology with parallel developments in sociology and anthropology" (Deaux, 1968b, p. 211). As a graduate student, she was surprised to find her own work already cited by sociologists (something that has continued to the present). One constant theme that emerges from the tension between internal and external validity is expressed in the importance Deaux has always ascribed to the project of bridging psychological and sociological social psychology.

Changing Categories and Being Changed by Them

A third theme for those who began changing the vocabulary of social psychology in the mid-1960s is the reflexive relationship between the researcher and his or her objects of scientific investigation—the way in which our own identities are inextricably entangled in our subject matter. Deaux's percolating interest in masculinity–femininity is an apt way of describing the kind of subterranean force that was about to erupt in psychology in the mid-1970s. For example, Deaux remembered being asked by a member of her doctoral thesis committee why she had chosen attitudes toward women being drafted into the military as her dimension of interest over a more salient local issue, such as raising tuition fees (Deaux, 2009). Keeping in mind that this was the Vietnam War era and that a military draft was in place, what could have been more obviously salient than attitudes toward drafting women into the military? However, it was still unusual for a woman to be in the predominantly male world of graduate school in psychology. The "nonconscious ideology" of women's place in society and psychology's historical role in giving scientific authority to that place was only just being questioned in the writings of that period (Bem & Bem, 1970; Maccoby & Jacklin,1974; Shields, 1975; Weisstein, 1971).

Deaux took up her first academic appointment as an assistant professor of psychology at Wright State University from 1967 to 1970 and moved to Purdue University in 1970. She remarked that her "work on gender issues began in earnest at Purdue" (Deaux, 2001, p. 207). At some point in the late 1960s and early 1970s, the personal became both political and scientific. Ellen Berscheid (1992) observed that "in 1965 few people . . . and few institutions were aware that the word sex had been inserted at the last minute into Title VII of the 1964 Civil Rights Act" (p. 526). In fact, that seemingly small change in legislation had significant consequences for women's participation rates in higher education and ultimately for the way in which academic psychology would begin the process of retheorizing women's lives (Pickren & Rutherford, 2010). Berscheid also reflected on the way in which women experienced a personal connection to sex differences research: "One spontaneously remembers the sighs of recognition that greeted the Deaux and Emswiller (1974) article, whose subtitle, 'What is Skill for the Male is Luck for the Female,' said it all for many of us" (p. 527).

Berscheid (1992) argued that women entering social psychology in the 1960s were less "ghettoized" than in other fields of inquiry precisely because they had access to established frameworks and could begin the work of assessing the relevance of sex differences. This may have been the case in Deaux's early work in which she was exploring the differences evoked for evaluating men's and women's achievement. Deaux's (1972) pratfall study "To Err is Humanizing: But Sex Makes a Difference" is a superb example of the precise way in which her work began to show the limitations of generalization when sex was at issue. In this early period, Deaux tested out various hypotheses relevant to social judgment and attitude change using several of the social psychological frameworks that had become established throughout the 1950s and 1960s: a theory of social (in)equality relevant to real-world settings (Adams, 1963), authoritarianism as a personality measure interacting with social situations (Adorno, Frenkel-Brunswik, Levinson, & Sanford, 1950), theories of social communication and cognitive processes relevant to attitude change (Festinger, 1954, 1957; Sherif & Hovland, 1961; Sherif, Sherif, & Nebergall, 1965), as well as theories of social attribution (Heider, 1958; Weiner et al., 1971).

At Purdue University, Deaux moved through the professorial ranks, directed the social-personality program (1978–1981 and 1984–1986) and established a women's studies program with political scientist Irene Diamond. She mentored her first cohort of students (Janet Taynor, Fran Cherry, Tim Emswiller, Elizabeth Farris, Arie Nadler, Brenda Major, and Laurie Lewis) interested in the social psychology of sex differences and sex stereotyping. In that 15-year span, Deaux published some of the best-known studies of the way in which women's achievement was undervalued and attributed to factors other than ability, often by women themselves. Although these findings occurred with "depressing regularity" (Deaux & Emswiller, 1974, p. 80), they also provided the empirical evidence that ultimately transformed the vocabulary of the field from sex to gender.

Sex to Gender

The distinction between *sex* and *gender*, articulated in Rhoda Unger's (1979) classic paper, "Towards a Redefinition of Sex and Gender," pointed the field toward the socially constructed nature of masculinity and femininity and toward sex differences that could be explained by the situational pressures in women's lives. Pickren and Rutherford (2010) wrote of the significance of this shift: "It became possible to talk about how people and processes became gendered, rather than seeing masculinity and femininity as some essential, unchangeable quality of being biologically male or female" (p. 270).

As the vocabulary of social psychology shifted from sex to gender, it is important to note that feminist historians of psychology had also begun the process of reclaiming women's history in psychology (Scarborough & Furumoto, 1987; Shields, 1975). Of particular interest to this project was Mary Whiton Calkins, a student of William James and an advocate of psychology as the science of the social and relational self. Whether consciously or otherwise, feminist social psychologists were part of a larger project in psychology: They were reflexively reclaiming themselves through their choice to study the limits of sex differences and the shift to gender and they were becoming part of the return of a much older project involving the scientific study of the social self.

By the mid-1980s there was a substantial infrastructure of academic courses, representation in professional organizations, and journals and conferences focused on the psychology of women and sex roles. Deaux's early work provided the textbook for new courses on the social psychology of sex roles (Deaux, 1976a), a missing chapter on sex roles in mainstream social psychology textbooks (Deaux, in Wrightsman, 1977, a well-known textbook which she later coauthored and then first-authored), and even a flirtation with the popular press (Deaux, 1976b). Deaux could look back on more than a decade of scholarly activity and begin to integrate some of the basic findings on sex differences and sex role stereotyping in the context of social perception and social judgment.

In much of her work up to the mid-1980s, earlier themes emerge. For example, Deaux was able to bring her own insights in what was still a nontraditional occupation for women to her work in the steel industry (Deaux & Ullman, 1982, 1983). Research with women in blue-collar employment also revealed continuing concerns for the importance of balancing laboratory and field research and her earlier suggestion that sociological and psychological levels of analysis need not be permanently separated. It also foreshadows later work that reconnects to the Lewinian tradition in social psychology of bringing sound laboratory and field research to bear on social change through legal and social policy avenues (Cherry & Deaux, 2006; Deaux, 2006b; Fiske, Bersoff, Borgida, Deaux, & Heilman, 1991).

By the mid-1980s Deaux's work was starting to capture a greater sense of the fluidity of social categories and shifting the field from sex to gender. For example, in 1984 Deaux and Lewis published an examination of the gender stereotype, arguing for the notion that "common conceptions of male and female are much more diverse" (p. 992) than the descriptive content associated with the labels. Stereotypical thinking involves the interaction of independent components of "traits, role behaviors, occupations, and physical appearance" (p. 992).

This shift away from the study of enduring sex differences in social psychology and a recognition of the malleability of gender was strongly voiced in Deaux and Major's *Psychological Review* article, "Putting Gender Into Context: An Interactive Model of Gender-related Behavior" (1987). The article opens with the assertion that sex differences are often elusive and then proceeds to set out a different course for the social psychology of sex and gender. True to an earlier theme of pluralism in Deaux's work, this article shifts the vocabulary for understanding gendered behavior from reactive to enactive and negotiated, and from passive to active; there is a strong emphasis on the notion of performing gender in ways that differ across situations. Coauthor Brenda Major (K. Deaux, personal communication, August 26, 2010) remembered her own enthusiasm in the collaboration in the following way:

> There was new work emerging on the Self that was very exciting coming out in the 1980s—Marcus, Swann, Tesser, and Steele all published papers in the 1980s on self-processes—and Carver & Scheier—great stuff on self-presentation—a virtual explosion of work on the self. And it changed my/our thinking about social interaction processes—it emphasized the self (target) as active.

Major recalled that the emphasis up to that point had been on sex differences or on how societal expectations and stereotypes shaped men's and women's behavior. Their paper followed a conference on sex and gender in May 1985 and shifted the language Deaux was using to understand gender-related behavior (Deaux, 1985).

In keeping with Deaux's earlier concern for bridging sociological and psychological social psychology, Deaux and Major (1987) drew more heavily on sociological social psychology in which the tradition of self-presentation has figured prominently as well as a newer strand of self-theory, namely *self-verification*. Gender was enacted or negotiated within a context of social interaction in which all parties have agency and goals for their interaction. Actors are conceptualized as constructing "their behaviors to meet the demands of the immediate situation . . . people may assume different identities in different situations and at different times" (Deaux & Major, 1987, p. 370). Gender is understood in this work as a process rather than a fixed outcome for all time and all situations. Deaux (personal communication, August 27, 2010) reflected on the article's place in her intellectual history:

> I really think it was quite pivotal. In many respects, it represented a culmination of my thinking on gender to that point, continuing a theme that in some ways started with *The Behavior of Women and Men*, but also incorporating work that I had done on stereotypes, attributions. It also marked a transition to my work on identity more generally. In the paper, Brenda and I talk about gender as being just one of many possible identities that someone might have and that might be salient in any particular situation. As we developed that theme, I began to think about what some of the other identities might be, which led me to the social identity literature.

Gender to Social and Intersecting Identities

Deaux moved in the mid-1980s from West Lafayette, Indiana, a small Midwestern college town, to the densely populated and multicultural New York City to take up a position at the Graduate Center, City University of New York (GC/CUNY). She described the way her work was directly affected by the move to the Graduate Center:

> Certainly the move . . . changed the way I did research. At Purdue, as at many major research universities, one has lab space, subject pools, under-graduate research assistants . . . The Graduate Center had/has little to none of that: No undergraduates at the institution at all, either as participants or assistants to research. I had one room for my research when the Graduate Center was in its original building (on 42nd Street) but after the move to the 365 Fifth Avenue address . . . there were no dedicated research rooms. Necessarily, then, one could not do experiments in the way that I had known, and one needed to find other ways to ask questions and get answers. (K. Deaux, personal communication, August 29, 2010)

There were also ways in which her students and her colleagues differed. Her students in New York were "much more diverse than I had known in my previous academic experience, in a lot of respects: ethnic diversity, past experience, future ambitions" (K. Deaux, personal communication, August 29, 2010). And her colleagues also offered a greater scope for understanding how complex identities are negotiated across a diverse array of situations. Of her new colleagues and new setting, she noted:

> Interdisciplinary perspectives are much easier to gain at the Graduate Center than at many other institutions, due to the unusual structure of doctoral programs, particularly in psychology. As a result of the structure, most fields of psychology were not represented in my immediate situation, while other fields of social science were readily accessible. Colleagues in psychology at the Graduate Center exposed me to alternative perspectives and methodologies, particularly in the later years that I was there. The program faculty is a very heterogeneous group in terms of their background and training, professional reference groups, and ways of doing research. (It is far from a typical social-personality psychology program!) Certainly I became much more familiar with and appreciative of some qualitative approaches to research (though I remain more quantitative in my own work). (K. Deaux, personal communication, August 29, 2010)

Deaux spent 1986 to 1987 at the Center for Applied Behavioral Sciences (CABS) in Palo Alto and was part of a working group on self and identity that was balanced between sociologists (Shel Stryker, Roberta Simmons, and George Bohrnstedt) and psychologists (Tory Higgins, Dan Olweus, and Robbie Case). In these years, experimental social psychologists like Deaux were finding a way to disconnect from an individualistic understanding of women's lives and take up the historically older notion of a social self in relation to others. In so doing, they were taking seriously aspects of the critique of the 1970s and 1980s that psychological social psychology reflected—in both theory and method—the individualism of North American culture to the detriment of understanding historical and collective aspects of social life (see, e.g., Greenwood, 2004; Jost & Kruglanski, 2002; Markus and Kitayama, 1994).

In fact, Deaux's work from the mid-1980s on reflects the reconciliation between experimentalists and social constructionists for which Jost and Kruglanski (2002) argued. These authors emphasized the importance to both paradigms of a dynamic interplay among levels of analysis; of the self as constructed in multiple levels of history, culture, and social group; and of the fluidity of group identifications and categorizations. Jost and Kruglanski made reference to social identity and social representation (Deaux & Philogène, 2000) as two of several areas that held promise for integrating empirical and constructivist approaches in social psychology.

It is impossible to do justice to the wealth of writings on self and social identity that Deaux produced following her year at CABS. However, some themes emerge. There are continuing preoccupations with social categories as ranges of possibilities and reconnections to sociological social psychology. There are also themes of integration and conversation across levels of analysis without requiring either an abandonment of quantitative techniques or the use of experimental tools of inquiry.

In the mid-1980s the conversation about the category of social identity was relatively new to American psychological social psychology. In fact, Deaux remembered how difficult it was to prepare a syllabus for an identity research seminar at CUNY that she offered for the first time in the spring of 1988. The situation is reminiscent of how little material there was when Deaux offered a psychology of sex roles course in the early 1970s. In the case of identity, there was European research by Henri Tajfel (1981) on collective aspects of identity, social identification, and categorization. And there was a strand of sociological social psychology sympathetic to the relationship among self, identity, and society (e.g., Stryker, 1989). Deaux's first seminar on social identity continued beyond that first year, and in 1999 it became a joint seminar with Bill Cross when he joined the Graduate Center faculty. Earlier in the decade, Cross (1991) had published *Shades of Black*, differentiating personal and group identities historically, theoretically, and empirically in the lives of African Americans. Throughout the 1990s, Deaux published a series of lucid and rigorous takes on the negotiations of self and identity, several of which addressed aspects of diversity for social identities other than gender (for example, Deaux, 1991, 1992; Deaux, Reid, Mizrahi, & Cotting, 1999; Deaux, Reid, Mizrahi, & Ethier, 1995; Ethier & Deaux, 1990, 1994).

Deaux's work on self, social, and collective identity forged new connections to developmental and personality psychology and furthered the links to sociological social psychology. For example, she cofounded a social identity working group with Diane Ruble and Jacqueline Eccles that was funded for a 5-year period (2000–2005) by the Russell Sage Foundation. The working group brought together about 20 people, primarily developmental and social psychologists using a variety of theoretical and methodological approaches, who met twice yearly and at other times to begin conversations about social identity. In an interview with Kay Deaux (2009), she described the collaboration with her coauthors in a paper that grew out of that working group initiative. The *Psychological Bulletin* paper, "An Organizing Framework for Collective

Identity: Articulation and Significance of Multidimensionality" (Ashmore, Deaux, & McLaughlin-Volpe, 2004), took shape over a period of years, with the three authors reading extensively and meeting to discuss and revise the paper that was ultimately published. The result was so highly collaborative that a footnote indicates authorship is alphabetical. This is the process that engaged Deaux when she was attempting to bring conceptual clarity to an ill-defined area. Furthermore, the paper has become part of the discussion of an intersectionality perspective in which feminist identity is dynamically performed in relation to other identities (Shields, 2008).

In April 1996, her colleagues in sociology at Indiana University–Purdue University at Indianapolis held a 2½- day conference on self, social identity, and social movements (Stryker, Owens, & White, 2000). Kay Deaux and Anne Reid presented a paper, "Contemplating Collectivism," that signaled an emerging theme in the work of psychological social psychologists, namely, a turn from individualism to collectivism. However, for this paper, Deaux and Reid (2000) claimed the middle ground—the *meso* or midrange level of analysis of social groups, "a unit of analysis larger than an individual but smaller than a country" (p. 175). Deaux's contribution to the midrange level of analysis avoids the dangers of both essentializing culture and asocializing individuals. In another piece, "The Kaleidosopic Self," Deaux and Perkins (2001) integrated the individual, relational, and collective levels of representations of the self. Again, the metaphor of the kaleidoscope does justice to distinguishing the three representations of self, the dynamic "overlap and interplay" among them, and the viewer's angle of observation.

Social Identity to Immigration

In the preceding commentary, there are references to intellectual, disciplinary, and societal changes that would explain the kinds of categories Deaux was drawn to pursue in her work. However, it does not explain why Deaux took up the field of the social psychology of immigration. To be sure, her work in this relatively new field for psychological social psychologists is reminiscent of the early days of studying both gender and social identity; she begins with conversations intended to bring conceptual clarity to a field that is ill-defined.

There is another element worthy of mention, one that does not lend itself to easy articulation and is only rarely offered in histories of scientific inquiry. Geographer David Livingstone, in an effort to bring geographers and historians of science together, asked questions relevant to my understanding of Deaux's turn to studying immigration and the role that living in New York may have played in that turn. Livingstone (2003) questioned the role of place in his opening chapter in *Putting Science in its Place*: *Geographies of Scientific Knowledge*: "Scientific knowledge is made in a lot of different places. Does it matter where? Can the location of scientific endeavor make any difference to the conduct of science? And even more important, can it affect the content of science?" (p. 1). Livingstone answered in the affirmative, recognizing that this goes "against the grain" that science is not responsive to local conditions (p. 1).

I would argue that place is of some significance in Deaux's work, and that New York City has been reflexively woven into the direction her work took in the late 1990s. One of the premier novelists of the city, E. L. Doctorow (2000), captured those influences in his turn of the 20th century novel, *City of God*, through the words of his protagonist:

> I can stop on any corner at the intersection of two busy streets, and before me are thousands of lives headed in all four directions . . . and how can I not know I am momentarily part of the most spectacular phenomenon in the unnatural world? . . . For all the wariness or indifference with which we negotiate our public spaces, we rely on the masses around us to delineate ourselves. The city may begin from a marketplace, a trading post, the confluence of waters, but it secretly depends on the human need to walk among strangers. . . Not that you shouldn't watch your pocketbook, lady (p. 11).

These "strangers" in the "unnatural world" of New York City and the fascination with their possibilities for pro- and antisocial behavior have been of enormous heuristic value for novelists and social psychologists alike. One can think of the possibilities for new social relations resulting from changes in housing legislation in the 1950s: see, for example, integrated housing studies by Morton Deutsch and Mary Evans Collins (1951), and Marie Jahoda and Patricia Salter West (1951); Kenneth Clark's research with youth in Central Harlem in the early 1960s (Harlem Youth Opportunities Unlimited, Inc., 1964); Bibb Latane and John Darley's earliest thinking about bystander intervention (Cherry, 1995); studies of helping on the subways of New York (Piliavin, Piliavin, & Rodin, 1975; Piliavin, Rodin, & Piliavin, 1969) and finally, Stanley Milgram's (1977) explorations of urban life in general, but New York in particular. These are but a few examples of how the "ordinary life" of New York has inspired and been inscribed in social psychological theory and practice.

In reflecting on what drew Kay Deaux to study the social psychology of immigration, she claimed that

> the presence of some first-rate scholars of immigration in the sociology department (of the Graduate Center) was a wonderful asset; a year (2001–2002) as a visiting scholar at the Russell Sage Foundation (located in New York City) solidified both my interest in immigration and my interdisciplinary perspective. (K. Deaux, personal communication, August 29, 2010)

The identity seminar at the Graduate Center did, in fact, morph in the late 1990s into the Immigration Research Group, and the centrality of place is, I would argue, heuristic in subsequent writings on immigration. Her work has always had a situated sensibility and an evocation of place. When asked specifically about New York City and its relationship to her work, she stated: "My research interests, which had begun to shift to more general questions of identity, were certainly shaped by the New York experience. When one looks at ethnic identity in New York City, one is looking at patterns of immigration" (K. Deaux, personal communication, August 27, 2010).

In 2000, Deaux published an interestingly titled article, "Surveying the Landscape of Immigration: Social Psychological Perspectives," setting forth some of the intellectual terrain in what has become a vibrant area of research for social psychologists. She draws attention to the social comparison processes immigrant group members used to establish their value in any given society and the complex negotiation processes by which multiple identities are forged and enacted daily. Exploring the "landscape of identity work" (Deaux, 2000, p. 428) is as importantly social and psychological as it is physical. Deaux's work on immigration builds substantially on earlier research with Kathleen Ethier on Hispanic students entering elite U.S. colleges (Deaux & Ethier, 1998; Ethier & Deaux, 1994) in which they introduced the process of *remooring*. Combining change and movement with social and psychological aspects of identity, Deaux (2000) brought spatial metaphor of remooring to the context of immigration: "Immigration involves leaving one domain in which identity has been enacted and supported, and coming to a new domain in which identity must be resituated and often redefined" (p. 429).

To understand any number of processes relevant to remooring, such as choosing to blend or alternate identities, it seems important to have some familiarity with an immigrant's country of origin as well as country of residence. Deaux's social psychology of immigration is not explicitly tied to any one location; however, running throughout *To Be an Immigrant* (2006b) is a sense that place matters. For example, the Haitian immigrant to New York has a vastly different reception from that of the Haitian immigrant to Miami.

In many of the published writings of the past decade, Deaux and her collaborators have referred to situated identity in a way that evokes the importance of understanding local cultures (e.g., Deaux, 2006a; Deaux, Reid, Martin & Bikman, 2006; Deaux & Wiley, 2007; Tormala & Deaux, 2006; Wiley & Deaux, 2010; Wiley, Perkins, & Deaux, 2008). Deaux began working explicitly with multilevel models much earlier; however, her work on immigration develops the connections among micro-, meso-, and macrolevels of understanding more fully in terms of framework and data. Deaux has always been less inclined to test hypotheses than to map the terrain of uncharted areas of social life. Her recent writings fill in the contours of the landscape of immigrant social identities: There are connections between those identities and societal representations of race; there are connections between stereotypic portrayals of immigrants and group relevant performance. All of Deaux's writings seek to imbue demographic labels with social and psychological significance. In any specific case, she wrote of the importance of "historical circumstances, the current attitudinal climate, the situational demands, and the concerns and negotiations of the immigrants" (Deaux, 2006a, p. 201).

The Distance Travelled

From sex to gender to identity is a distance travelled in its own right. One can see reflected in Deaux's work some of the major changes in social psychology stemming from the post-World War II period. The key elements are a preoccupation with the multiplicity and intersectionality of social categories and a search for a better understanding of their structure and function in social relations. For Deaux, this requires all of the available tools of empirical social science; primarily, but not exclusively, quantitative. Deaux is a disciplinary bridge builder to the core, adamant about the importance of agency, and certain that social policy should be grounded in rigorous research. The concepts that have attracted Deaux are as personal as they are professional. Remooring captures her own reconnections to sociological understanding; the kaleidoscopic self captures her own multifaceted and ever changing conversations with generations of students and colleagues.

References

Adams, J. S. (1963). Toward an understanding of inequity. *The Journal of Abnormal and Social Psychology*, *67*, 422–436. doi:10.1037/h0040968

Adorno, T. W., Frenkel-Brunswik, E., Levinson, D. J., & Sanford, R. N. (1950). *The authoritarian personality*. New York, NY: Harper.

Ashmore, R.D., Deaux, K., & McLaughlin-Volpe, T. (2004). An organizing framework for collective identity: Articulation and significance of multidimensionality. *Psychological Bulletin, 130*, 80–114. doi:10.1037/0033-2909.130.1.80

Atkins, A. L., Deaux, K. K., & Bieri, J. (1967). Latitude of acceptance and attitude change: Empirical evidence for a reformulation. *Journal of Personality and Social Psychology*, *6*, 47–54. doi:10.1037/h0024527

Bem, S. L., & Bem, D. J. (1970). Case study of a nonconscious ideology: Training the woman to know her place. In D. J. Bem (Ed.), *Beliefs, attitudes, and human affairs* (pp. 80–99). Belmont, CA: Brooks/Cole.

Berscheid, E. (1992). A glance back at a quarter century of social psychology. *Journal of Personality and Social Psychology*, *63*, 525–533. doi:10.1037/0022-3514.63.4.525

Bieri, J. (1955). Cognitive complexity–simplicity and predictive behavior. *The Journal of Abnormal and Social Psychology*, *51*, 263–268. doi:10.1037/h0043308

Bieri, J., Deaux, K. K., & Atkins, A. L. (1966). Stimulus saliency and anchoring: Temporal and end stimulus effects. *Psychonomic Science*, *6*, 145–146.

Cherry, F. (1995). *The "stubborn particulars" of social psychology: Essays on the research process*. London, England: Routledge.

Cherry, F., & Deaux, K. (2006). The Lewinian legacy in the Society of the [sic] Psychological Study of Social Issues. In J. Trempala, A. Pepitone, & B. H. Raven (Eds.), *Lewinian psychology* (pp. 56–65). Bydgoszcz, Poland: Kazimierz Wielki University Press.

Cross, W. E. (1991). *Shades of black: Diversity in African American identity*. Philadelphia, PA: Temple University Press.

Deaux, K. (1968a). Variations in warning, information preference, and anticipatory attitude change. *Journal of Personality and Social Psychology*, *9*, 157–161. doi:10.1037/h0021247

Deaux, K. (1968b). Graduate education: Final rehearsal for a career. In S. Lundstedt (Ed.), *Higher education in social psychology* (pp. 210–217). Cleveland, OH: Case Western Reserve University Press.

Deaux, K. (1972). To err is humanizing: But sex makes a difference. *Representative Research in Social Psychology*, *3*, 20–28.

Deaux, K. (1976a). *The behavior of women and men*. Monterey, CA: Brooks/Cole.

Deaux, K. (1976b). Ahhh, she was lucky. *Psychology Today*, *10*, 70–75.

Deaux, K. (1985). Sex and gender. *Annual Review of Psychology, 36*, 49–81.

Deaux, K. (1991). Social identities: Thoughts on structure and change. In R. C. Curtis (Ed.), *The relational self: Theoretical convergences in psychoanalysis and social psychology* (pp. 77–93). New York, NY: Guilford Press.

Deaux, K. (1992). Personalizing identity and socializing self. In G. M. Breakwell (Ed.), *Social psychology of identity and the self-concept* (pp. 9–33). London, England: Academic Press.

Deaux, K. (2000). Surveying the landscape of immigration: Social psychological perspectives. *Journal of Community & Applied Social Psychology*, 10, 421–431.

Deaux, K. (2001). Kay Deaux. In A. N. O'Connell (Ed.), *Models of achievement: Reflections of eminent women in psychology* (Vol. 3, pp. 201–218). Mahwah, NJ: Erlbaum.

Deaux, K. (2006a). A nation of immigrants: Living our legacy. *Journal of Social Issues, 62,* 633–651. doi:10.1111/j.1540-4560.2006.00480.x

Deaux, K. (2006b). *To be an immigrant.* New York, NY: Russell Sage Foundation.

Deaux, K. (2009, August 9). Interview with Kay Deaux at the annual meeting of the American Psychological Association, Toronto, Canada.

Deaux, K., & Bieri, J. (1967). Latitude of acceptance in judgments of masculinity–femininity. *Journal of Personality, 35,* 109–117. doi:10.1111/j.1467-6494.1967.tb01418.x

Deaux, K., & Emswiller, T. (1974). Explanations of successful performance in sex-linked asks: What is skill for the male is luck for the female. *Journal of Personality and Social Psychology, 29,* 80–85. doi:10.1037/h0035733

Deaux, K., & Ethier, K. A. (1998). Negotiating social identity. In J. K. Swim & C. Stangor, (Eds.), *Prejudice: The target's perspective* (pp. 301–323). San Diego, CA: Academic Press.

Deaux, K., & Lewis, L. L. (1984). The structure of gender stereotypes: Interrelationships among component and gender label. *Journal of Personality and Social Psychology, 46,* 991–1004. doi:10.1037/0022-3514.46.5.991

Deaux, K., & Major, B. (1987). Putting gender into context: An interactive model of gender-related behavior. *Psychological Review, 94,* 369–389. doi:10.1037/0033-295X.94.3.369

Deaux, K., & Perkins, T. S. (2001). The kaleidoscopic self. In C. Sedikides & M. B. Brewer (Eds.), *Individual self, relational self, collective self* (pp. 299–313). Philadelphia, PA: Taylor & Francis.

Deaux, K., & Philogene, G. (Eds.). (2001). *Representations of the social: Bridging theoretical traditions.* Oxford, England: Blackwell.

Deaux, K., & Reid, A. (2000). Contemplating collectivism. In S. Stryker, T. J. Owens, & R. W. White (Eds.), *Self, identity, and social movements* (pp. 172–190). Minneapolis, MN: University of Minnesota Press.

Deaux, K., Reid, A., Martin, D., & Bikmen, N. (2006). Ideologies of diversity and inequality: Predicting collective action in groups varying in ethnicity and immigrant status. *Political Psychology, 27,* 123–146. doi:10.1111/j.1467-9221.2006.00452.x

Deaux, K., Reid, A., Mizrahi, K. & Cotting, D. (1999). Connecting the person to the social: The functions of social identification. In T. R. Tyler, R. Kramer & O. John (Eds.), *The psychology of the social self* (pp. 91–113). Hillsdale, NJ: Erlbaum.

Deaux, K., Reid, A., Mizrahi, K., & Ethier, K. A. (1995). Parameters of social identity. *Journal of Personality and Social Psychology, 68,* 280–291. doi:10.1037/0022-3514.68.2.280

Deaux, K., & Ullman, J. C. (1982). Hard-hatted women: Reflections on blue-collar employment. In J. Bernardin (Ed.), *Women in the work force* (pp. 29–47). New York, NY: Praeger.

Deaux, K., & Ullman, J. C. (1983). *Women of steel: Female blue-collar workers in the basic steel industry.* New York, NY: Praeger.

Deaux, K., & Wiley, S. (2007). Moving people and shifting representations: Making immigrant identities. In G. Moloney & I. Walker (Eds.), *Social representations and identity: Content, process, and power* (pp. 9–30). New York, NY: Palgrave Macmillan.

Deutsch, M., & Collins, M. E. (1951). *Interracial housing: A psychological evaluation of a social experiment.* New York, NY: Russell.

Doctorow, E. L. (2000). *City of God.* New York, NY: Plume Penguin.

Ethier, K. A., & Deaux, K. (1990). Hispanics in Ivy: Assessing identity and perceived threat. *Sex Roles, 22,* 427–440. doi:10.1007/BF00288162

Ethier, K. A., & Deaux, K. (1994). Negotiating social identity in a changing context: Maintaining identification and responding to threat. *Journal of Personality and Social Psychology, 67,* 243–251. doi:10.1037/0022-3514.67.2.243

Festinger, L. (1954). A theory of social comparison processes. *Human Relations, 7,* 117–140. doi:10.1177/001872675400700202

Festinger, L. (1957). *A theory of cognitive dissonance.* Evanston, IL: Row.

Fiske, S. T., Bersoff, D. N., Borgida, E., Deaux, K., & Heilman, M. E. (1991). Social science research on trial. The use of sex stereotyping research in Price Waterhouse v. Hopkins. *American Psychologist, 46,* 1049–1060. doi:10.1037/0003-066X.46.10.1049

Greenwood, J. D. (2004). *The disappearance of the social in American social psychology.* Cambridge, England: Cambridge University Press.

Harlem Youth Opportunities Unlimited, Inc. (1964). *Youth in the ghetto: A study of the consequences of powerlessness and a blueprint for change.* New York, NY: Author.

Heider, F. (1958). *The psychology of interpersonal relations.* New York, NY: Wiley. doi:10.1037/10628-000

Jahoda, M., & West, P. S. (1951). Race relations in public housing. *Journal of Social Issues, 7,* 132–139. doi:10.1111/j.1540-4560.1951.tb02227.x

Jost, J. T., & Kruglanski, A. W. (2002). The estrangement of social constructionism and experimental social psychology: History of the rift and prospects for reconciliation. *Personality and Social Psychology Review, 6,* 168–187. doi:10.1207/S15327957PSPR0603_1

Livingstone, D. (2003). *Putting science in its place: Geographies of social knowledge.* Chicago, IL: University of Chicago Press.

Lundstedt, S. (1968). *Higher education in social psychology.* Oxford, England: Press of Case Western Reserve U.

Maccoby, E. E., & Jacklin, C. N. (1974). *The psychology of sex differences.* Stanford, CA: Stanford University Press.

Markus, H. R., & Kitayama, S. (1994). A collective fear of the collective: Implications for selves and theories of selves. *Personality and Social Psychology Bulletin, 20,* 568–579. doi:10.1177/0146167294205013

Milgram, S. (1977). *The individual in a social world: Essays and experiments.* Reading, MA: Addison-Wesley.

Oishi, S., Kesebir, S., & Snyder, B. H. (2009). Sociology: A lost connection in social psychology. *Personality and Social Psychology Review, 13,* 334–353. doi:10.1177/1088868309347835

Pickren, W. E., & Rutherford, A. (2010). *A history of modern psychology in context.* New York, NY: Wiley.

Piliavin, I. M., Piliavin, J. A., & Rodin, J. (1975). Costs, diffusion, and the stigmatized victim. *Journal of Personality and Social Psychology, 32,* 429–438. doi:10.1037/h0077092

Piliavin, I. M., Rodin, J., & Piliavin, J. A. (1969). Good Samaritanism: An underground phenomenon. *Journal of Personality and Social Psychology, 13,* 289–299. doi:10.1037/h0028433

Scarborough, E., & Furumoto, L. (1987). *Untold lives: The first generation of American women psychologists.* New York, NY: Columbia University Press.

Sherif, C., Sherif, M., & Nebergall, R. (1965). *Attitude and attitude change: The social judgment–involvement approach.* Philadelphia, PA: Saunders.

Sherif, M., & Hovland, C. I. (1961). *Social judgment: Assimilation and contrast effects in communication and attitude change.* New Haven, CT: Yale University Press.

Shields, S. A. (1975). Functionalism, Darwinism, and the psychology of women. *American Psychologist, 30,* 739–754. doi:10.1037/h0076948

Shields, S. A. (2008). Gender: An intersectionality perspective. *Sex Roles, 59,* 301–311. doi:10.1007/s11199-008-9501-8

Stryker, S. (1989). The two psychologies: Additional thoughts. *Social Forces, 68,* 45–54. doi:10.2307/2579219

Stryker, S., Owens, T. J., & White, R. W. (Eds.) (2000). *Self, social identity and social movements.* Minneapolis, MN: University of Minnesota Press.

Tajfel, H. (1981). *Human groups and social categories.* Cambridge, England: Cambridge University Press.

Tormala, T. T., & Deaux, K. (2006). Black immigrants to the United States: Confronting and constructing ethnicity and race. In R. Mahalingam (Ed.), *Cultural psychology of immigration* (pp. 131–150). Mahwah, NJ: Erlbaum.

Unger, R. K. (1979). Toward a redefinition of sex and gender. *American Psychologist, 34,* 1085–1094. doi:10.1037/0003-066X.34.11.1085

Webb, E. J., Campbell, D. T., Schwartz, R. D., & Sechrest, L. (1966). *Unobtrusive measures: Nonreactive research in the social sciences.* Chicago, IL: Rand McNally.

Weiner, B., Frieze, I., Kukla, A., Reed, L., Rest, S., & Rosenbaum, R. M. (1971). *Perceiving the causes of success and failure.* Morristown, NJ: General Learning Press.

Weisstein, N. (1971). Psychology constructs the female; or, the fantasy life of the male psychologist (with some attention to the fantasies of his friends, the male biologist and the male anthropologist). *The Journal of Special Education, 35,* 362–373.

Wiley, S., & Deaux, K. (2010). The bicultural identity performance of immigrants. In A. Azzi, X. Chryssochoou, B. Klandermans, & B. Simon (Eds.), *Identity and participation in culturally diverse societies: A multidisciplinary perspective* (pp. 49–68). West Sussex, England: Wiley-Blackwell. doi:10.1002/9781444328158.ch3

Wiley, S., Perkins, K., & Deaux, K. (2008). Through the looking glass: Ethnic and generational patterns of immigrant identity. *International Journal of Intercultural Relations, 32,* 385–398. doi:10.1016/j.ijintrel.2008.04.002

Winston, A. (Ed.). (2004). *Defining difference: Race and racism in the history of psychology.* Washington, DC: American Psychological Association. doi:10.1037/10625-000

Wrightsman, L. S. (1977). *Social psychology.* Monterey, CA: Brooks/Cole.

Part II———————————————

Gender

4

Women as Leaders: Progress Through the Labyrinth

Alice H. Eagly

A focus on leadership exposes the patriarchal structure of society. Consider that exactly 12, or 2%, of the CEOs of the *Fortune* 500 and only 14% of the corporate officers and 16% of the board members are women (Catalyst, 2011). In political leadership roles, women remain underrepresented throughout the world (UNIFEM, 2010), especially in the most powerful elected positions. The United States has never had a woman president or vice-president, and women constitute only 17% of its senators, 16% of congressional representatives, 12% of state governors, and 24% of state legislators (Center for American Women and Politics, 2011). Despite the quotas that exist for women's parliamentary representation in many nations, the world average is only 19% (Inter-Parliamentary Union, 2011). In the United States, women have risen somewhat faster in some nonelective positions, comprising 31% of the Senior Executive Service of the federal government, the highest executive branch positions not appointed by the president (U.S. Office of Personnel Management, 2010). Women also are better represented among chief executives when all organizations are taken into account, now constituting 26% of these individuals (U.S. Bureau of Labor Statistics, 2011).

This small sampling of statistics on leadership makes clear that relative to their proportion of the population, women are underrepresented in roles that provide substantial authority and dramatically underrepresented at the very highest levels of authority. It is not that women lack workplace prestige—they are well represented in many high-status professional occupations (e.g., physicians, professors, teachers, pharmacists; see Magnusson, 2009). In fact, women constitute 52% of all managers and professionals in the United States (U.S. Bureau of Labor Statistics, 2011). However, men more often than women occupy positions conferring decision-making authority and the ability to influence others' pay or promotions (Smith, 2002). This lack of authority in part reflects lack of access to managerial positions and in part the lesser authority of women than men even when rank and tenure in organizations are held constant (e.g., Lyness & Thompson, 2000; Smith, 2002). Even in female-dominated organizations and professions, men ascend to leadership faster than women—a phenomenon known as the *glass escalator* (e.g., Maume, 1999; C. L. Williams, 1995).

It is clear that even after two 20th century feminist movements dedicated to promoting gender equality, no nation has achieved the political and social equality of women and men. Many nations have moved further toward gender equality than the United States, which ranks 37th in gender equality among the nations of the world, as indexed by the Gender Inequality Index, which is produced by the United Nations Development Programme (2011). One reason for this unfavorable ranking of the United States is the low representation of women in Congress, as parliamentary representation is much higher for women in most other industrialized nations, due in part to voluntary or legislated quota for the representation of women (Quota Project, 2011). In addition, Norway, Spain, France, and Iceland have imposed legislated quotas for women on the governing boards of publically listed corporations (Worldcrunch, 2011). In the individualist and strongly democratic culture of the United States, such quotas are not politically feasible, despite moderate public support for "special efforts to hire and promote qualified women" (Kane & Whipkey, 2009, p. 244).

Answering the question "Why not gender equality?" lies in the province of social scientists, but also of many others, including journalists and politicians. The analysis that floats about in the popular culture is symbolized by the *glass ceiling*, a metaphor offered by journalists in 1986 and readily grasped by a public that wanted answers (Hymowitz & Schellhardt, 1986). What does the glass ceiling symbolize? It connotes a nearly impenetrable barrier that remains hidden from aspiring women through its glasslike quality of invisibility. Women naively bump their heads against this unseen and unanticipated barrier just as high positions are almost within their grasp and clearly visible through that ceiling. It follows from the glass ceiling symbolism that only occasionally, by dint of extreme effort, exceptional merit, or dumb luck, a woman shatters this barrier to achieve a high position.

Although the glass ceiling idea has had wide appeal, deconstruction of its meaning reveals that it is far from an apt metaphor for representing women's restricted access to high positions. Most obviously, women are not impeded in their careers only at very high levels—that is, right at the door of organizations' "C-suites," occupied by officers whose titles contain the word *chief*. Instead, at all career stages from very junior to very senior, women encounter challenges not faced to the same extent by men. At all points along career ladders, women drop out more often than men. Yet, because men commonly switch among different organizations to further their careers, the quit rates of women and men are approximately equal (Eagly & Carli, 2007). Women more often than men quit to devote themselves to their families. When more women than men drop out at all levels of career paths, they inevitably are rare at the highest level. Consistent with the glass ceiling metaphor, might it nonetheless be true that the obstacles for women are more difficult at higher than lower levels of pay and authority? Formal tests of this idea have produced inconsistent results (e.g., Baxter & Wright, 2000; Cotter, Hermsen, Ovadia, & Vanneman, 2001). Regardless of whether barriers may be sometimes more severe at higher levels, the glass ceiling is simplistic in suggesting that there exists a single, homogeneous barrier that shuts women out only from high-level positions. This image, easily brought to mind because of its frequent repetition in media and everyday conversation, ignores the complexity and variety of the obstacles that women leaders can face, even as they begin their careers. Moreover, the invisibility of the glass barrier implies that women neither anticipate nor understand the special challenges that they face in ascending to higher positions.

To symbolize the varied causes that have produced the relative paucity of women in positions of higher authority and power, a different metaphor is essential—an alternative that can shape thinking in a more accurate and productive direction. Therefore, Eagly and Carli (2007) proposed *labyrinth* to represent the varied challenges that women encounter in their career paths. Labyrinths are puzzles that challenge the mind. Women's paths to high positions are varied and often discontinuous and progress sometimes requires pausing, backing up, and continuing in a different direction. By anticipating the twists and turns in labyrinths, some women overcome challenges and meet their goals. As the years have passed, more women have successfully pursued their aspirations and fulfilled their desires to lead, reaching the sought-after goal at the labyrinth's center.

Because the intersection of gender and leadership has been widely studied by social scientists, they are uniquely positioned to illuminate the challenges that women face. Research by psychologists, sociologists, political scientists, and economists has identified causality in three broad domains: the family division of labor, cultural stereotypes that produce prejudice and discrimination, and impediments embedded in organizational cultures and structures that fit men's lives far better than women's lives. In this chapter, I briefly review all these considerations but concentrate on a social psychological analysis that views discrimination against women leaders as embedded in cultural stereotypes about women, men, and leaders.

Family Division of Labor

One of the fundamental causes of women's lesser power and authority is that they typically have greater family responsibilities than men, and these time-consuming responsibilities limit their careers by decreasing the time and effort that they can devote to a career. It is true that the family division of labor has moderated somewhat in the United States. Men spend more time in child care than in the past, but women do as well (Bianchi, Robinson, & Milkie, 2006; Bond, Thompson, Galinsky, & Prottas, 2002). Even with the smaller families that now prevail, both men and women spend more time in one-on-one interaction with children than they did in the middle of the 1960s (Bianchi et al., 2006). Nevertheless, even according to the most recent data from time diary studies, women spend substantially more time than men on both housework and child care (U.S. Bureau of Labor Statistics, 2010a). Because much of women's domestic work (e.g., child care, laundry, cooking) is obligatory, they cannot easily opt out of these responsibilities because of time constraints or employment obligations. Employed women generally sacrifice personal time to be with their children and, as a result, have less leisure time than men (U.S. Bureau of Labor Statistics, 2010a). Yet women, especially mothers, often cut back on employment if their circumstances allow this choice. For example, one U.S. study of women with strong educational credentials showed that 37% voluntarily dropped out of employment at some point, compared with 24% of similarly qualified men (Hewlett & Luce, 2005). Among women with one or more children, this percentage rose to 43%. The main reason that these women gave up their employment was for "family time," but for men it was to change careers.

Women experience long-term cumulative losses in income and promotions not only from time away from employment but also from part-time employment (Rose & Hartmann, 2004). More employed women than men work part time (27% vs. 13% of men; U.S. Bureau of Labor Statistics, 2010b). Even women in traditionally male-dominated, high-status professions are more likely than their male counterparts to accommodate family responsibilities by reducing their employment hours (Boulis, 2004; Noonan & Corcoran, 2004). In sum, there is validity to the claim that on average men have more on-the-job experience. This fact decreases women's chances for promotion to higher ranks.

Cultural Stereotypes and Discrimination
Against Women as Leaders

Despite men's greater job experience, this factor does not fully account for disparities in the access of men and women to leadership. Workplace discrimination also lessens women's opportunities and is especially strong in relation to women who are mothers (Correll, Benard, & Paik, 2007; Heilman & Okimoto, 2008). This discrimination follows, at least in part, from bosses' beliefs that women employees' greater work–family conflict makes them less suitable for promotion to higher positions (Hoobler, Wayne, & Lemmon, 2009). To examine potential discrimination, economists and sociologists have conducted many studies of gender gaps that take into account the effects of human capital variables, including job experience on hiring, wages, and promotion. Such factors account only partially for female–male differences in earnings and promotions (Blau & Kahn, 2006). The gender gaps that remain unexplained even when women and men are statistically equated in multiple regression equations suggest the presence of discrimination in wages and promotions. Yet these correlational analyses are inevitably ambiguous because of the possibility that social scientists were not able to access all of the causally relevant variables for their analyses.

Additional evidence of discrimination emerges from experiments that compared participants' evaluations of identical job applications or resumes from women and men. In particularly strong demonstrations of discrimination, field experiments known as *audit studies* present persons responsible for personnel selection with job applications or resumes (or sometimes phone calls or in-person applicants) by means of the normal channels through which the organizations received job applications. These inadvertent research participants did not know they were providing data for a research project or that certain applications they received were constructed to differ only in sex or other attributes (e.g., race, age) to meet the requirements of an experimental design (see Pager, 2007). A portion of these field experiments examined sex discrimination.

The findings of these experiments reveal substantial discrimination against women in the more senior jobs that yield higher status and wages and against both sexes when they apply for jobs dominated by the other sex (see the review by Riach & Rich, 2002). These conclusions are echoed by the somewhat less naturalistic experiments that involve simulations of hiring situations, with students or employees serving as research participants and receiving resumes varying only in applicant sex (see the meta-analysis by Davison & Burke, 2000). In addition, a meta-analysis of experiments comparing the evaluations of male and female leaders whose performances had been experimentally equated found that for the identical performances, female leaders overall received somewhat lower evaluations than male leaders, especially in masculine settings or male-dominated roles (Eagly, Makhijani, & Klonsky, 1992).

Field studies are also consistent with the presence of sex discrimination in evaluating leaders. For example, examining archival organizational data from managers of a large financial services organization, Lyness and Heilman (2006) compared evaluations of women and men after controlling for demographic and organizational variables. The results showed that women in line jobs, which were male-dominated, received lower performance ratings than women in staff jobs, more commonly held by women, or than men in either line or staff jobs. Moreover, a meta-analysis of 96 studies of leaders' effectiveness, as assessed mainly by performance evaluations in organizational field studies, found that men fared better than women in male-dominated leadership roles or culturally masculine settings but that women surpassed men in settings that were less male-dominated or less culturally masculine (Eagly, Karau, & Makhijani, 1995). In summary, for many leadership positions especially those dominated by men, discrimination against women prevails, as shown by corroborating evidence from field and laboratory experiments and correlational field studies (see also Heilman & Eagly, 2008).

Psychology of Prejudice Toward Women as Leaders

Understanding discrimination toward women as leaders demands a nontraditional understanding of the nature of prejudice. Psychologists conventionally defined prejudice as a negative attitude toward a social group, which negatively biases judgments of individuals and produces inequitable treatment (e.g., Allport, 1954/1979). Straightforward application of this type of analysis to understand discrimination against women as leaders suggests that people disparage women and therefore believe them inadequate to be leaders. The flaw in this analysis is that research has found that women as a social group are evaluated on the whole quite favorably, often more favorably than men. Even though both favorable and unfavorable qualities are ascribed to both sexes, totaling up all of these qualities for both sexes reveals that women are somewhat more favorably regarded in most tests—that is, women are perceived as the nicer, kinder, friendlier sex. This "women-are-wonderful" effect (Eagly & Mladinic, 1994) has challenged the understanding of prejudice as following from an overall negative attitude toward a target group. Instead, prejudice should be understood as contextual (see Deaux & Major, 1987). Prejudice arises at the intersection of groups and roles—that is, in relation to certain groups of people occupying certain types of roles, regardless of the overall evaluation of the group. The fact that women are regarded as the nicer, kinder sex qualifies them for social roles believed to reward such qualities—particularly for the domestic role and paid employment in service and other jobs that reward cooperative social interaction (e.g., social worker, store clerk, teacher). However, the positive attributes on which women excel are not regarded as the most important qualifications for leadership roles.

Discrimination against female leaders occurs because many people believe that women lack the capacity to be effective leaders, especially at higher levels—that is, that women have less leadership ability than men. From a social psychological perspective, this bias against women as leaders is a consequence of cultural stereotyping that produces prejudicial reactions in predictable circumstances (Eagly & Diekman, 2005). In general, stereotypes about social groups often bias our judgments of individual group members (e.g., Darley & Gross, 1983; von Hippel, Sekaquaptewa, & Vargas, 1995). Stereotypes can be elicited automatically and are generally resistant to change because people tend to seek out and attend to information that confirms their stereotypes and to disregard contradictory information (Hart et al., 2009).

The potential for prejudice exists when social perceivers hold a stereotype about a group that is incongruent with the attributes they think are required for success in certain classes of social roles. When a group member and an incongruent social role become joined in the mind of a perceiver, often because some group members seek to occupy the role, this inconsistency generally lowers the evaluation of the group member as an occupant of the role.

Consistent with this idea that prejudice emerges at the intersection of a group's stereotype and the requirements of a social role, Eagly and Karau (2002) proposed a role incongruity theory of prejudice toward female leaders. Prejudice against women as leaders flows from the incongruity that people often perceive between the characteristics typical of women and the requirements of leader roles (see Heilman, 1983, 2001, for a related analysis). This analysis emphasizes gender roles, defined as consensual beliefs about the attributes of women and men. These beliefs comprise two kinds of expectations, or norms: *descriptive beliefs* (or stereotypes), which are consensual expectations about what members of a social group actually do; and *injunctive (or prescriptive) beliefs*, which are consensual expectations about what group members ought to do or ideally would do (Cialdini & Trost, 1998). The term *gender role* thus refers to the descriptive and injunctive expectations associated with women and men.

According to research in the United States and many other nations, people expect men to be *agentic*—assertive, dominant, competent, and authoritative, and women to be *communal*—warm, supportive, kind, and helpful (Newport, 2001; J. Williams & Best, 1990; see Kite, Deaux, & Haines, 2008, for a review). The inconsistency follows from the predominantly agentic qualities that people believe are necessary to succeed as a leader—that is, qualities that are more like men than women. Even when an individual woman actually has the qualities thought necessary for leadership, people may believe that she does not "have what it takes" for success as a leader, merely on the basis of her gender. These meanings ascribed to women and men form a constant backdrop to social interaction, coloring the judgments made about people encountered in organizations and other contexts (Deaux & LaFrance, 1998). Because leadership evokes mainly masculine associations, it is not consistent with typical mental associations about women. Prejudice and discrimination thus follow from the ways that people observe and interpret everyday social interaction (Eagly & Diekman, 2005).

There are many empirical demonstrations that beliefs about leaders are more similar to beliefs about men than about women. In the best-known research, the "think manager–think male" studies that were first conducted by Schein (1973), participants rated men, women, or successful leaders (or managers) on gender-stereotypical traits. Researchers then conducted a correlational analysis on these data to determine whether the leader traits were more similar to the traits ascribed to men or women. In another paradigm (Powell & Butterfield, 1979), participants rated leaders on agentic and communal traits, and the ratings were analyzed to test whether leaders were perceived as more agentic than communal. Similarly, other researchers assessed gender stereotypes ascribed to leaders by having participants rate occupations that involve leadership (e.g., manager, executive, senator) on a single bipolar scale assessing masculinity versus femininity (Shinar, 1975).

In a meta-analysis that encompassed studies implementing all three of these methods of investigating the perceived masculinity of leaders, Koenig, Eagly, Mitchell, and Ristikari (2010) established that leadership is culturally masculine. Depending on the paradigm, leaders were viewed as more similar to men than women, more agentic than communal, or more masculine than feminine. The implications for women of this cultural masculinity of leadership are clear-cut: Women do not typically impress people as especially qualified to lead. Even those women who objectively possess outstanding qualifications for leadership have the burden of overcoming preconceptions that they are not well equipped to lead. Not only do the descriptive aspects of stereotyping make it difficult for women to gain access to leader roles, but the prescriptive aspects of stereotyping produce conflicting expectations concerning how female leaders should behave–that is, that they should be agentic to fulfill the leader role but communal to fulfill the female gender role (Eagly & Karau, 2002).

Doubt concerning women's ability to lead is common even in young children. Specifically, researchers asked children ages 5 to 10 years the reasons why no woman has served as president of the United States (Bigler, Arthur, Hughes, & Patterson, 2008). In open-ended responses, children noted women's deficiencies (e.g., "Men have courage and responsibility. Who knows what women would do?") slightly more often than they blamed discrimination (e.g., "People think girls can't be good rulers"; Bigler et al., 2008, p. 93). Thus, even young children construct beliefs about women's personal attributes to explain the observed correlation between sex and occupancy of leader roles.

Public opinion polls have corroborated preferences for male leaders. For example, pollsters asked people what they think about personally having a job in which a woman or a man has authority over them. The specific Gallup Poll question was, "If you were taking a new job and had your choice of a boss, would you prefer to work for a man or woman?" (Carroll, 2006). The responses obtained from Americans from the first administration of this question in 1953 through the most recent administration in 2006 have shown a preference for male bosses over female bosses, although this differential in favor of men has decreased over the years. An especially sharp drop in men's advantage occurred from 2000 to 2002 but was followed by a modest increase in favor of men from 2002 to 2006 (Carroll, 2006). Despite an erosion of the huge preference for male bosses that existed in the middle of the 20th century, men still retained a clear advantage in 2006, with 37% of respondents preferring a male boss compared with 19% preferring a female boss. However, the most popular response in recent polls, given by 43% of the respondents in 2006, is an apparently more egalitarian "no preference" or "it doesn't matter" answer, which requires that the respondent spontaneously decide to depart from the man versus woman response format of the question.

Consequences of Role Incongruity

Given the prevalence of gender and leader stereotypes, they have pervasive effects. Merely classifying persons as male or female automatically evokes the ascription of masculine and feminine qualities to them (e.g., Banaji & Hardin, 1996; Ito & Urland, 2003). These mental associations, or stereotypes, can be influential even when people are unaware of their presence (e.g., Sczesny & Kühnen, 2004). Perceived as deficient in essential leader qualities, women have reduced access to leadership, particularly in contexts in which leadership has an especially agentic definition.

The descriptive gender stereotypes that disadvantage women as leaders may emerge quite early during the encoding stage of information processing (Scott & Brown, 2006; see also Foti, Knee, & Backert, 2008). Specifically, participants in experiments had difficulty encoding leadership behaviors into the underlying prototypical leadership trait of assertiveness when the behaviors were enacted by a woman. This phenomenon would make it difficult for women to be perceived as possessing the qualifications for leader roles.

The descriptive aspects of stereotypes can also act as self-fulfilling prophecies. Realization that others hold certain expectations about one's behavior can trigger confirmation of these expectations (see the review by Geis, 1993). Therefore, if a colleague at work believes that a woman is not assertive enough to be an effective manager, these stereotyped expectancies can trigger anxiety and influence her behavior in a stereotype-confirming direction. Moreover, these descriptive stereotypes can undermine women's willingness to put themselves forward as potential leaders. Such an effect appeared in research on stereotype threat in which presenting participants with gender-stereotypical portrayals of women prior to a group task caused the women (but not the men) to indicate less interest in being the group leader and more interest in taking a follower role (Davies, Spencer, & Steele, 2005).

The prescriptive aspects of gender stereotypes are important because they often place competing demands on women leaders, who face a double bind (Eagly & Carli, 2007). The cultural prescriptions for women emphasize being especially communal, and the prescriptions for most leadership roles emphasize being especially agentic. The resulting dilemma is that communal female leaders may be criticized for not being agentic enough and not properly taking charge, and agentic female leaders may be criticized for lacking communion and not being nice enough. Such reactions can place female leaders in a lose–lose situation. If their behavior confirms the gender stereotype, they are not thought to be acting as a proper leader, but if their behavior confirms the leader stereotype, they are not thought to be acting as a good woman. Violating either of these stereotypes can lower evaluations of women and their performance (e.g., Cuddy, Fiske, & Glick, 2004; Eagly & Karau, 2002; Heilman, Wallen, Fuchs, & Tamkins, 2004). Female leaders can alleviate this dilemma to some extent by exhibiting both agentic and communal behavior (Johnson, Murphy, Zewdie, & Reichard, 2008; see also Eagly & Carli, 2007).

Demonstrating the devaluation of especially assertive women, a meta-analysis of experiments that varied the sex of leaders while holding other attributes constant showed that the devaluation of women's leader behaviors is particularly pronounced when these behaviors are stereotypically masculine, especially when they are autocratic or directive (mean $d = 0.30$; Eagly et al., 1992). Thus, a male manager who acts in a forceful manner is generally perceived as behaving appropriately and displaying leadership, whereas a female leader who behaves in exactly the same way is vulnerable to being regarded as unacceptably pushy and not at all nice. Male managers, in contrast, apparently suffer no penalty when they manifest the more culturally feminine collaborative and democratic leadership styles (Eagly et al., 1992).

Given this double bind whereby women can be criticized for being both like and unlike leaders, they can find leadership challenging. These difficulties are especially apparent when women endeavor to exert influence. Being influential—that is, affecting the beliefs or behaviors of others—is essential to effective leadership. Because of the double bind, people may resist a woman's influence, particularly in masculine settings. Sometimes they resist her because they think she lacks communion, so she just doesn't seem all that likable. Sometimes they resist her because they think she lacks agency and competence, so she just doesn't seem able to take charge and therefore is not respected as a leader. Yet people have greater influence when they appear both agentically competent and warm. So for women to gain the double bind requires a skillful balancing act (Eagly & Carli, 2007).

Leading in the Androgynous Middle Ground

Given the double bind of cross-pressures from leadership roles and the female gender role, it is not surprising that female leaders report that achieving an appropriate and effective leadership style is one of their greatest challenges. Demonstrating this concern, a study of *Fortune* 1000 women executives found that 96% rated as *critical* or *fairly important* that they develop a style with which male managers are comfortable (Catalyst, 2000).

Many people wonder whether men and women typically differ in leadership style. To address this issue, meta-analyses of relevant studies have compared the leadership styles of men and women who occupy the same or similar leadership roles. The first of these projects reviewed the classic literature on leadership style, which emphasized the distinction between task-oriented and relationship-oriented styles and between autocratic and democratic styles (Eagly & Johnson, 1990; see also van Engen & Willemsen, 2004). Except for college students recruited for laboratory experiments, the findings failed to confirm the gender-stereotypical expectation that women lead in an interpersonally oriented style and men in a task-oriented style. Yet female leaders tended on average to adopt a somewhat more democratic or participative style and a less autocratic or directive style than male leaders did (mean $d = 0.22$). This relatively small average difference became especially small in male-dominated leadership roles. Apparently, without a critical mass of other women to affirm the legitimacy of a more collaborative, participative style, women leaders tend to opt for styles that are typical of their male colleagues.

In most settings, women are usually more readily accepted as leaders when they share power by being at least somewhat participative and collaborative. However, such a style is not necessarily better than a more directive one. The effectiveness of autocratic and democratic styles is contingent on various features of group and organizational environments (see meta-analyses by Foels, Driskell, Mullen, & Salas, 2000; Gastil, 1994). Under some circumstances, democratic and participative styles are effective, and under other circumstances, autocratic and directive styles are more effective.

Another meta-analysis examined the more recent research literature on *transformational* and *transactional* leadership styles (Eagly, Johannesen-Schmidt, & van Engen, 2003). Transformational leadership is widely accepted as a model of contemporary good managerial practices (see Avolio, 1999; Bass, 1998) and is in fact correlated with leaders' effectiveness (see the meta-analysis by Judge & Piccolo, 2004). Such leadership involves establishing oneself as a role model by gaining followers' trust and confidence. Transformational leaders state future goals, develop plans to achieve them, and innovate even when their organization is generally successful. They mentor and empower followers by encouraging them to develop their full potential. As this description of transformational leadership suggests, it is neither masculine nor feminine when considered in its entirety but instead culturally androgynous. Yet because one of its elements, the mentoring and empowering of subordinates, is culturally feminine (Hackman, Furniss, Hills, & Paterson, 1992), transformational leadership may be slightly more aligned with the female than the male gender role (Duehr & Bono, 2006; Kark, 2004).

Transformational leadership differs from transactional leadership, which is embedded in give-and-take relationships that appeal to subordinates' self-interest. One aspect of transactional leadership that is quite effective is rewarding good performance by followers (Judge & Piccolo, 2004). In contrast, reprimanding or otherwise sanctioning followers for their mistakes and failures is not as effective. Yet another potential leadership style, labeled *laissez-faire*, involves a general failure to take responsibility for managing. This approach is quite ineffective (Judge & Piccolo, 2004).

A meta-analysis of 45 studies examined all available research that had assessed leadership styles of women and men according to these distinctions between transformational, transactional, and laissez faire leadership (Eagly et al., 2003). This analysis established small sex-related differences, such that women were generally more transformational in leadership style (mean $d = -0.10$) and also more transactional in terms of providing rewards for satisfactory performance (mean $d = -0.13$). Women's transformational leadership was especially evident in their focus on developing and mentoring followers and attending to their individual needs (mean $d = -0.19$). In contrast, men were more likely than women to emphasize followers' mistakes and failures (mean $d = 0.12$). In addition, men were more likely than women to wait until problems become severe before intervening (mean $d = 0.27$) and to avoid taking responsibility for managing (mean $d = 0.16$). Although these negative and ineffective styles were more common among men than women, they were relatively uncommon among leaders of both sexes.

Given men's greater access to leadership, it is startling to obtain these particular meta-analytic findings, even though they are only small average differences. One way of summarizing the findings is that women received higher ratings than men on the components of leadership style that relate positively to effectiveness, and men received higher ratings than women on the components of style that do not enhance effectiveness. The implications of these findings for effectiveness were corroborated by the somewhat better performance of female than male managers on the effectiveness measures used in the studies included in the meta-analysis (Eagly et al., 2003).

The causes of these differences in women's and men's leadership may lie in several factors (Eagly et al., 2003). One possibility is that the transformational repertoire (and rewarding behaviors) resolves some of the typical incongruity between leadership roles and the female gender role because these behaviors are not distinctively masculine. Another possibility is that gender roles influence women's leadership by means of the spillover and internalization of gender-specific norms, thereby facilitating the somewhat feminine aspects of transformational leadership. A third possibility is that a double standard for entering into managerial roles produces more highly skilled female than male leaders. Although it seems likely that all three factors contribute to the demonstrated sex differences in leadership style, additional research is required to resolve these causal issues.

Women's manifestation of effective styles of leadership suggests that women might be even more skilled as leaders than men are. One way to explore this idea is to examine the relation between the percentages of women in executive positions in organizations and how well those organizations perform financially. Such studies have been conducted examining *Fortune* 1000 and other large U.S. companies. Results show that the higher the percentage of women in executive positions or on boards of directors, the better the financial outcomes for the companies (e.g., Carter, Simkins, & Simpson, 2003; Erhardt, Werbel, & Shrader, 2003; Krishnan & Park, 2005). A similar study of European-based companies compared the financial performance of organizations having the greatest gender diversity in top management with the average performance of companies in their economic sector. This analysis also showed that companies with greater gender diversity performed better (Desvaux, Devillard-Hoellinger, & Baumgarten, 2007). Despite the ambiguity of these correlational associations, these data suggest that women executives are a corporate asset.

Other studies have examined leaders' effectiveness by having research participants rate how effective individual managers are as leaders. These effectiveness ratings may be contaminated by gender bias but nevertheless have some validity because leaders can be effective only if their leadership is endorsed and accepted by others. In a meta-analysis of 96 studies comparing the effectiveness of male and female leaders holding comparable leadership roles, no overall difference was found between these women and men (Eagly et al., 1995). However, this finding was overshadowed by findings showing that some contexts favored men, and some favored women: In masculine settings, such as the military, men received higher ratings of effectiveness than women, whereas in less masculine settings, such as in education, women received somewhat higher effectiveness ratings than men (Eagly et al., 1995). These findings suggest that effectiveness may well be influenced by gender stereotypes. In male-dominated settings, people are most likely to equate good leadership with stereotypically masculine behaviors, creating doubt about women's effectiveness as leaders and greater challenges in becoming effective. Yet women who do manage to be successful in very high-status roles may be perceived as highly competent (Rosette & Tost, 2010). The reason for this perception appears to be that people assume a double standard whereby such women had to overcome especially difficult challenges. In view of the varying perceptions of female competence in different settings, the meaning of the overall finding in Eagly et al.'s (1995) meta-analysis of no effectiveness difference between male and female managers remains ambiguous because it is a product of the distributions of settings in the individual studies that the meta-analysis included.

Organizational Challenges Faced by Women Leaders

Organizations often present impediments to women's advancement, even though these challenges and difficulties were rarely designed to block women and may appear on the surface to be gender-neutral, not favoring men or women (e.g., Acker, 1990; Martin, 2003). One major impediment is that organizations have become increasingly demanding of their professional workforce by requiring long work hours, constant availability, and many personal sacrifices. Therefore, the implicit model of an ideal employee is a person who has few outside responsibilities and is totally devoted to the organization (Acker, 1990; J. Williams, 2000). Demands for such commitment are especially clear for those in high-status executive positions (e.g., Judge, Cable, Boudreau, & Bretz, 1995). Research has confirmed that people employed in management and related fields usually work longer than average hours (Brett & Stroh, 2003; Jacobs & Gerson, 2004). Compared with other employees, professionals and managers are also are more likely to have personal digital assistants (PDAs) and cell phones, which are often used to continue paid work in the evenings, on weekends, and during vacations. Employees become always available to the organization (Towers, Duxbury, Higgins, & Thomas, 2006).

These extreme time demands produce obvious difficulties for people with heavy family responsibilities. Because men have fewer domestic duties and more leisure time than women, they find it easier to commit to extreme hours on the job and experience less conflict over these demands. Executive men are generally advantaged by their stay-at-home wives, who accept the bulk of home management and domestic tasks. A study of senior executives revealed that

75% of the men had stay-at-home wives, whereas 74% of the women had employed spouses (Galinsky et al., 2003).

Women's time-consuming family and work responsibilities can undermine their ability to network and thereby create social capital in the workplace. Studies indicate that women have less access to powerful career networks than men do (Burt, 1998; Dreher & Cox, 1996). In general, possessing mentors and networks within and outside of one's own organization is associated with increased salary and promotions (Ng, Eby, Sorensen, & Feldman, 2005; Wolff & Moser, 2009). Thus, women's relative lack of social capital impedes their access to leadership opportunities (see Timberlake, 2005).

The social capital that women do amass is generally less effective in promoting their careers than the social capital amassed by men. One reason for this effect is that networks generally are sex-segregated because people tend to affiliate with others who are similar to themselves (McPherson, Smith-Lovin, & Cook, 2001). Because men hold the bulk of leadership positions, the most powerful networks tend to be dominated by men, with women decidedly underrepresented. Men thus benefit more than women do from having connections with colleagues and mentors (Dreher & Cox, 1996; Forret & Dougherty, 2004). Consistent with LeVine and Campbell's (1972) realistic group conflict theory and Kanter's (1977) concept of homosocial reproduction, men and women are to some extent in competition for power and influence, especially at the tops of hierarchies where men have more to lose from women's advancement. Thus, even though connections with powerful men can be helpful to women's careers (Burt, 1998; Dreher & Cox, 1996; Huffman & Torres, 2002), such connections can be difficult for women to form.

In addition to lack of access to important networks, women face other challenges from traditional male corporate cultures. Female executives and professionals have reported they have difficulty fitting in with the culture of their organizations and obtaining the demanding responsibilities, complex challenges, and international travel opportunities that can yield credentials for promotion to higher positions (e.g., Lyness & Thompson, 1997, 2000; Ohlott, Ruderman, & McCauley, 1994). Women also receive relatively fewer line management positions, which entail profit-and-loss responsibility, and more staff management positions than their male counterparts (Catalyst, 2004; Galinsky et al., 2003). In addition, women are more likely to be given highly risky assignments that can easily result in failure, a phenomenon known as the *glass cliff* (see Haslam & Ryan, 2008). Based on archival research on firms in the United Kingdom (Ryan & Haslam, 2005), women had a higher probability of being appointed to a leadership position than men when the companies were experiencing financial downturns. However, this relation apparently holds only for subjective indicators of firm value such as stock prices and not for accountancy-based measures such as return on assets or equity (see Adams, Gupta, & Leeth, 2009; Haslam, Ryan, Kulich, Trojanowski, & Atkins, 2010). All in all, women do not have equal access to the desirable assignments that are likely to lead to advancement and instead receive less desirable assignments that are either too easy or too risky.

In conclusion, organizational structure and culture implicitly favor men. Because men generally lack the extensive domestic duties that are typical for women, they can more easily satisfy demands for long work hours and continuous availability. Corporate cultures and male networks are often unwelcoming to women, thereby undermining their ability to create social capital on the job. And women have difficulty obtaining good assignments that have advancement potential. These obstacles inherent in the structure and culture of many modern organizations disadvantage women and contribute to their relative absence from higher-level leadership positions.

Are There Ways Through the Labyrinth?

In this chapter, I explained that women's access to leadership in society is limited by multiple factors. Still, women's situation has changed considerably in recent decades: Women no longer face roadblocks that completely obstruct their access to positions of authority. The meta-analysis on the masculinity of leader stereotypes indicates that in all three of the research paradigms that have investigated this stereotype, it has changed to become less masculine (Koenig et al., 2010). This shift toward greater androgyny gives evidence that leadership roles have become generally more hospitable to women. Nevertheless, women have a long way to go before their power and authority are equal to those of men. Viewing this situation, some see the glass as half empty, with women having made only very slow and limited progress. Others see the glass as half full, with women having made progress that is very substantial, even amazing. Interpretations of the pace of change differ because change is uneven, faster in some organizations and sectors of the economy than in others, and much faster in some nations than in others.

The fact of change raises questions about how some women make their way through the labyrinth and how organizations and societies move toward the inclusion of women in positions of authority. As Eagly and Carli (2007) argued, individual women generally gain from blending agency and communion in their everyday workplace behavior. By so doing, they address both sides of the double bind: They show that they are sufficiently directive and assertive to be leaders but that this agency does not undermine the warmth and sociability that women are expected to display. Manifesting behavior that has both clearly agentic and clearly communal elements is not necessarily easy but it is no doubt a wise strategy in many contexts. This behavioral strategy can also help women build workplace social capital. Career success requires being welcomed in networks and included in relationships that foster advancement.

Women who advance in their careers also finesse work–life problems. Attaining a successful career along with a successful family life requires negotiating competing demands of work and family. Doing this skillfully is perhaps life's greatest challenge for many women, and good outcomes can be especially elusive for women who do not share domestic responsibilities equitably with their life partners or have considerable access to paid help.

Negotiating the labyrinth of career challenges is often regarded as women's problem, but it is also the problem of the organizations that present impediments to women that are more difficult than those faced by men. There are many sensible organizational innovations that foster progressive change

(Eagly & Carli, 2007). Unbiased performance evaluations are essential. Flexibility in the timing and mode of meeting workplace demands is extremely helpful as are family supports such as on-site child care. As managerial roles are in flux because of broader changes in the economy and society, the present is a favorable time for organizations to experiment with innovations that can make organizations as welcoming to women as to men.

Change toward gender equality is not a continuous march on a straight road. Instead, social change requires individual commitment and collective struggle. As women gain greater equality some people resent these changes, producing backlash. Ideologically traditional individuals can long for familiar arrangements in which men provided for their families and women tended to domestic matters. With the ebbing of the activism of the feminist movement and a degree of backlash against the changes that have occurred, the collective march toward gender equality appears to have paused on many fronts (see Blau, Brinton, & Grusky, 2006). In this situation, individual women are under pressure to find their own way through the labyrinth without the guidance once provided by feminist ideology and advocacy. Research on gender and leadership can help fill this void. It provides important insight into the causes and consequences of gender inequality. These insights can guide women who are thoughtfully and persistently making their way through the labyrinth.

References

Acker, J. (1990). Hierarchies, jobs, bodies: A theory of gendered organizations. *Gender & Society, 4,* 139–158. doi:10.1177/089124390004002002

Adams, S. M., Gupta, A., & Leeth, J. D. (2009). Are female executives overrepresented in precarious leadership positions? *British Journal of Management, 20,* 1–12. doi:10.1111/j.1467-8551.2007.00549.x

Allport, G. W. (1954/1979). *The nature of prejudice.* Cambridge, MA: Perseus Books.

Avolio, B. J. (1999). *Full leadership development: Building the vital forces in organizations.* Thousand Oaks, CA: Sage.

Banaji, M. R., & Hardin, C. D. (1996). Automatic stereotyping. *Psychological Science, 7,* 136–141. doi:10.1111/j.1467-9280.1996.tb00346.x

Bass, B. M. (1998). *Transformational leadership: Industrial, military, and educational impact.* Mahwah, NJ: Erlbaum.

Baxter, J., & Wright, E. O. (2000). The glass ceiling hypothesis: A comparative study of the United States, Sweden, and Australia. *Gender & Society, 14,* 275–294. doi:10.1177/089124300014002004

Bianchi, S. M., Robinson, J. P., & Milkie, M. A. (2006). *Changing rhythms of American family life.* New York, NY: Russell Sage Foundation.

Bigler, R. S., Arthur, A. E., Hughes, J. M., & Patterson, M. M. (2008). The politics of race and gender: Children's perceptions of discrimination and the U.S. presidency. *Analyses of Social Issues and Public Policy (ASAP), 8,* 83–112. doi:10.1111/j.1530-2415.2008.00161.x

Blau, F. D., Brinton, M. C., & Grusky, D. B. (2006). *The declining significance of gender?* New York, NY: Russell Sage Foundation.

Blau, F. D., & Kahn, L. M. (2006). The U.S. gender pay gap in the 1990s: Slow convergence. *Industrial & Labor Relations Review, 60,* 45–66.

Bond, J., Thompson, T. C., Galinsky, E., & Prottas, D. (2002). *Highlights of the national study of the changing workforce.* New York, NY: Families and Work Institute.

Boulis, A. (2004). The evolution of gender and motherhood in contemporary medicine. *The Annals of the American Academy of Political and Social Science, 596,* 172–206. doi:10.1177/0002716204268923

Brett, J. M., & Stroh, L. K. (2003). Working 61 hours a week: Why do managers do it? *Journal of Applied Psychology, 88*, 67–78. doi:10.1037/0021-9010.88.1.67

Burt, R. S. (1998). The gender of social capital. *Rationality and Society, 10*, 5–46. doi:10.1177/104346398010001001

Carroll, J. (2006, September 1). *Americans prefer male boss to a female boss.* Retrieved from http://www.gallup.com

Carter, D. A., Simkins, B. J., & Simpson, W. G. (2003). Corporate governance, board diversity, and firm value. *Financial Review, 38*, 33–53. doi:10.1111/1540-6288.00034

Catalyst. (2000). *Across three cultures Catalyst finds top barriers to women's professional advancement.* Retrieved from https://www.catalyst.org/press-release/29/across-three-cultures-catalyst-finds-top-barriers-to-womens-professional-advancement

Catalyst. (2004). *Women and men in U.S. corporate leadership: Same workplace, different realities?* Retrieved from http://catalyst.org/file/74/women%20and%20men% 20in%20u.s.%20corporate %20leadership%20same%20workplace,%20different%20realities.pdf

Catalyst. (2011). *U.S. women in business: Pyramids* (May 2011). Retrieved from http://www.catalyst.org/publication/132/us-women-in-business

Center for American Women and Politics. (2011). *Women in elective office 2011: Fast Facts* (6/10). Retrieved from http://www.cawp.rutgers.edu/fast_facts/levels_of_office/documents/elective.pdf

Cialdini, R. B., & Trost, M. R. (1998). Social influence: Social norms, conformity and compliance. In D. T. Gilbert, S. T. Fiske, & G. Lindzey (Eds.), *The handbook of social psychology* (4th ed., Vol. 2, pp. 151–192). Boston, MA: McGraw-Hill.

Correll, S. J., Benard, S., & Paik, I. (2007). Getting a job: Is there a motherhood penalty? *American Journal of Sociology, 112*, 1297–1339. doi:10.1086/511799

Cotter, D. A., Hermsen, J. M., Ovadia, S., & Vanneman, R. (2001). The glass ceiling effect. *Social Forces, 80*, 655–682. doi:10.1353/sof.2001.0091

Cuddy, A. J. C., Fiske, S. T., & Glick, P. (2004). When professionals become mothers, warmth doesn't cut the ice. *Journal of Social Issues, 60*, 701–718. doi:10.1111/j.0022-4537.2004.00381.x

Darley, J. M., & Gross, P. H. (1983). A hypothesis-confirming bias in labeling effects. *Journal of Personality and Social Psychology, 44*, 20–33. doi:10.1037/0022-3514.44.1.20

Davies, P. G., Spencer, S. J., & Steele, C. M. (2005). Clearing the air: Identity safety moderates the effects of stereotype threat on women's leadership aspirations. *Journal of Personality and Social Psychology, 88*, 276–287. doi:10.1037/0022-3514.88.2.276

Davison, H. K., & Burke, M. J. (2000). Sex discrimination in simulated employment contexts: A meta-analytic investigation. *Journal of Vocational Behavior, 56*, 225–248. doi:10.1006/jvbe.1999.1711

Deaux, K., & LaFrance, M. (1998). Gender. In D. T. Gilbert, S. T. Fiske, & G. Lindzey (Eds.), *The handbook of social psychology* (4th ed., Vol. 1, pp. 788–827). New York, NY: McGraw-Hill.

Deaux, K., & Major, B. (1987). Putting gender into context: An interactive model of gender-related behavior. *Psychological Review, 94*, 369–389. doi:10.1037/0033-295X.94.3.369

Desvaux, G., Devillard-Hoellinger, S., & Baumgarten, P. (2007). *Women matter: Gender diversity, a corporate performance driver.* Paris, France: McKinsey & Company.

Dreher, G. F., & Cox, T. H., Jr. (1996). Race, gender, and opportunity: A study of compensation attainment and establishment of mentoring relationships. *Journal of Applied Psychology, 81*, 297–308. doi:10.1037/0021-9010.81.3.297

Duehr, E. E., & Bono, J. E. (2006). Men, women, and managers: Are stereotypes finally changing? *Personnel Psychology, 59*, 815–846. doi:10.1111/j.1744-6570.2006.00055.x

Eagly, A. H., & Carli, L. L. (2007). *Through the labyrinth: The truth about how women become leaders.* Cambridge, MA: Harvard Business School Press.

Eagly, A. H., & Diekman, A. B. (2005). What is the problem? Prejudice as an attitude-in-context. In J. F. Dovidio, P. Glick, & L. Rudman (Eds.), *On the nature of prejudice: Fifty years after Allport* (pp. 19–35). Malden, MA: Blackwell.

Eagly, A. H., Johannesen-Schmidt, M. C., & van Engen, M. L. (2003). Transformational, transactional, and laissez-faire leadership styles: A meta-analysis comparing women and men. *Psychological Bulletin, 129*, 569–591. doi:10.1037/0033-2909.129.4.569

Eagly, A. H., & Johnson, B. (1990). Gender and leadership style: A meta-analysis. *Psychological Bulletin, 108*, 233–256. doi:10.1037/0033-2909.108.2.233

Eagly, A. H., & Karau, S. J. (2002). Role congruity theory of prejudice toward female leaders. *Psychological Review, 109*, 573–598. doi:10.1037/0033-295X.109.3.573

Eagly, A. H., Karau, S. J., & Makhijani, M. G. (1995). Gender and the effectiveness of leaders: A meta-analysis. *Psychological Bulletin, 117*, 125–145. doi:10.1037/0033-2909.117.1.125

Eagly, A. H., Makhijani, M. G., & Klonsky, B. G. (1992). Gender and the evaluation of leaders: A meta-analysis. *Psychological Bulletin, 111*, 3–22. doi:10.1037/0033-2909.111.1.3

Eagly, A. H., & Mladinic, A. (1994). Are people prejudiced against women? Some answers from research on attitudes, gender stereotypes, and judgment of competence. In W. Stroebe & M. Hewstone (Eds.), *European review of social psychology* (Vol. 5, pp. 1–35). New York, NY: Wiley.

Erhardt, N. L., Werbel, J. D., & Shrader, C. B. (2003). Board of director diversity and firm financial performance. *Corporate Governance, 11*, 102–111. doi:10.1111/1467-8683.00011

Foels, R., Driskell, J. E., Mullen, B., & Salas, E. (2000). The effects of democratic leadership on group member satisfaction: An integration. *Small Group Research, 31*, 676–701. doi:10.1177/1046496400031006003

Forret, M. L., & Dougherty, T. W. (2004). Networking behaviors and career outcomes: Differences for men and women? *Journal of Organizational Behavior, 25*, 419–437. doi:10.1002/job.253

Foti, R. J., Knee, R. E., Jr., & Backert, R. S. G. (2008). Multilevel implications of framing leadership perceptions as a dynamic process. *The Leadership Quarterly, 19*, 178–194. doi:10.1016/j.leaqua.2008.01.007

Galinsky, E., Salmond, K., Bond, J. T., Kropf, M. B., Moore, M., & Harrington, B. (2003). *Leaders in a global economy: A study of executive women and men.* New York, NY: Families and Work Institute.

Gastil, J. (1994). A meta-analytic review of the productivity and satisfaction of democratic and autocratic leadership. *Small Group Research, 25*, 384–410. doi:10.1177/1046496494253003

Geis, F. L. (1993). Self-fulfilling prophecies: A social psychological view of gender. In A. E. Beall & R. J. Sternberg (Eds.), *The psychology of gender* (pp. 9–54). New York, NY: Guilford Press.

Hackman, M. Z., Furniss, A. H., Hills, M. J., & Paterson, T. J. (1992). Perceptions of gender-role characteristics and transformational and transactional leadership behaviors. *Perceptual and Motor Skills, 75*, 311–319. doi:10.2466/PMS.75.4.311-319

Hart, W., Albarracin, D., Eagly, A. H., Lindberg, M., Merrill, L., Brechan, I., & Lee, K. H. (2009). Feeling validated versus being correct: A meta-analysis of selective exposure to information. *Psychological Bulletin, 135*, 555–588. doi:10.1037/a0015701

Haslam, S. A., & Ryan, M. K. (2008). The road to the glass cliff: Differences in the perceived suitability of men and women for leadership positions in succeeding and failing organizations. *The Leadership Quarterly, 19*, 530–546. doi:10.1016/j.leaqua.2008.07.011

Haslam, S. A., Ryan, M. K., Kulich, C., Trojanowski, G., & Atkins, C. (2010). Investing with prejudice: The relationship between women's presence on company boards and objective and subjective measures of company performance. *British Journal of Management, 21*, 484–497.

Heilman, M. E. (1983). Sex bias in work settings: The lack of fit model. *Research in Organizational Behavior, 5*, 269–298.

Heilman, M. E. (2001). Description and prescription: How gender stereotypes prevent women's ascent up the organizational ladder. *Journal of Social Issues, 57*, 657–674. doi:10.1111/0022-4537.00234

Heilman, M. E., & Eagly, A. H. (2008). Gender stereotypes are alive, well, and busy producing workplace discrimination. *Industrial and Organizational Psychology: Perspectives on Science and Practice, 1*, 393–398. doi:10.1111/j.1754-9434.2008.00072.x

Heilman, M. E., & Okimoto, T. G. (2008). Motherhood: A potential source of bias in employment decisions. *Journal of Applied Psychology, 93*, 189–198. doi:10.1037/0021-9010.93.1.189

Heilman, M. E., Wallen, A. S., Fuchs, D., & Tamkins, M. M. (2004). Penalties for success: Reactions to women who succeed at male gender-typed tasks. *Journal of Applied Psychology, 89*, 416–427. doi:10.1037/0021-9010.89.3.416

Hewlett, S. A., & Luce, C. B. (2005). Off-ramps and on-ramps: Keeping talented women on the road to success. *Harvard Business Review, 83*, 43–54.

Hoobler, J. M., Wayne, S. J., & Lemmon, G. (2009). Bosses' perceptions of family–work conflict and women's promotability: Glass ceiling effects. *Academy of Management Journal, 52*, 939–957. doi:10.5465/AMJ.2009.44633700

Huffman, M. L., & Torres, L. (2002). It's not only "who you know" that matters: Gender, personal contacts, and job lead quality. *Gender & Society, 16*, 793–813. doi:10.1177/089124302237889

Hymowitz, C., & Schellhardt, T. C. (1986). The glass ceiling: Why women can't seem to break the invisible barrier that blocks them from top jobs. *Wall Street Journal*, March 24, special supplement, 1, 4.

Inter-Parliamentary Union. (2011). *Women in national parliaments* (situation as of June 30, 2010). Retrieved from http://www.ipu.org/wmn-e/world.htm

Ito, T. A., & Urland, G. R. (2003). Race and gender on the brain: Electrocortical measures of attention to the race and gender of multiply categorizable individuals. *Journal of Personality and Social Psychology, 85*, 616–626. doi:10.1037/0022-3514.85.4.616

Jacobs, J. A., & Gerson, K. (2004). *The time divide: Work, family, and gender inequality.* Cambridge, MA: Harvard University Press.

Johnson, S. K., Murphy, S. E., Zewdie, S., & Reichard, R. J. (2008). The strong, sensitive type: Effects of gender stereotypes and leadership prototypes on the evaluation of male and female leaders. *Organizational Behavior and Human Decision Processes, 106*, 39–60. doi:10.1016/j.obhdp.2007.12.002

Judge, T. A., Cable, D. M., Boudreau, J. W., & Bretz, R. D., Jr. (1995). An empirical investigation of the predictors of executive career success. *Personnel Psychology, 48*, 485–519. doi:10.1111/j.1744-6570.1995.tb01767.x

Judge, T. A., & Piccolo, R. F. (2004). Transformational and transactional leadership: A meta-analytic test of their relative validity. *Journal of Applied Psychology, 89*, 755–768. doi:10.1037/0021-9010.89.5.755

Kane, E. W., & Whipkey, K. J. (2009). Predictors of public support for gender-related affirmative action: Interests, gender attitudes, and stratification beliefs. *Public Opinion Quarterly, 73*, 233–254. doi:10.1093/poq/nfp019

Kanter, R. M. (1977). *Men and women of the corporation.* New York, NY: Basic Books.

Kark, R. (2004). The transformational leader: Who is (s)he? A feminist perspective. *Journal of Organizational Change Management, 17*, 160–176. doi:10.1108/09534810410530593

Kite, M. E., Deaux, K., & Haines, E. L. (2008). Gender stereotypes. In F. L. Denmark & M. A. Paludi (Eds.), *Psychology of women: A handbook of issues and theories* (2nd ed., pp. 205–236). Westport, CT: Praeger.

Koenig, A. M., Eagly, A. H., Mitchell, A. A., & Ristikari, T. (2010). *Are leader stereotypes masculine? A meta-analysis of three research paradigms.* Manuscript submitted for publication.

Krishnan, H. A., & Park, D. (2005). A few good women—on top management teams. *Journal of Business Research, 58*, 1712–1720. doi:10.1016/j.jbusres.2004.09.003

LeVine, R. A., & Campbell, D. T. (1972). *Ethnocentrism.* New York, NY: Wiley.

Lyness, K. S., & Heilman, M. E. (2006). When fit is fundamental: Performance evaluations and promotions of upper-level female and male managers. *Journal of Applied Psychology, 91*, 777–785. doi:10.1037/0021-9010.91.4.777

Lyness, K. S., & Thompson, D. E. (1997). Above the glass ceiling? A comparison of matched samples of female and male executives. *Journal of Applied Psychology, 82*, 359–375. doi:10.1037/0021-9010.82.3.359

Lyness, K. S., & Thompson, D. E. (2000). Climbing the corporate ladder: Do female and male executives follow the same route? *Journal of Applied Psychology, 85*, 86–101. doi:10.1037/0021-9010.85.1.86

Magnusson, C. (2009). Gender, occupational prestige, and wages: A test of devaluation theory. *European Sociological Review, 25*, 87–101. doi:10.1093/esr/jcn035

Martin, P. Y. (2003). "Said and done" versus "saying and doing": Gender practices, practicing gender at work. *Gender & Society, 17*, 342–366. doi:10.1177/0891243203017003002

Maume, D. J., Jr. (1999). Occupational segregation and the career mobility of White men and women. *Social Forces, 77*, 1433–1459. doi:10.2307/3005882

McPherson, M., Smith-Lovin, L., & Cook, J. M. (2001). Birds of a feather: Homophily in social networks. *Annual Review of Sociology, 27*, 415–444. doi:10.1146/annurev.soc.27.1.415

Newport, F. (2001, February 21). *Americans see women as emotional and affectionate, men as more aggressive: Gender specific stereotypes persist in recent Gallup poll.* Retrieved from http://www.gallup.com

Ng, T. W. H., Eby, L. T., Sorensen, K. L., & Feldman, D. C. (2005). Predictors of objective and subjective career success: A meta-analysis. *Personnel Psychology, 58*, 367–408. doi:10.1111/j.1744-
6570.2005.00515.x

Noonan, M. C., & Corcoran, M. E. (2004). The mommy track and partnership: Temporary delay or
dead end? *The Annals of the American Academy of Political and Social Science, 596*, 130–150.
doi:10.1177/0002716204268773

Ohlott, P. J., Ruderman, M. N., & McCauley, C. D. (1994). Gender differences in managers' developmental job experiences. *Academy of Management Journal, 37*, 46–67. doi:10.2307/256769

Pager, D. (2007). The use of field experiments for studies of employment discrimination:
Contributions, critiques, and directions for the future. *Annals of the American Academy of
Political and Social Science, 609*, 104–133. doi:10.1177/0002716206294796

Powell, G. N., & Butterfield, D. A. (1979). The "good manager": Masculine or androgynous?
Academy of Management Journal, 22, 395–403. doi:10.2307/255597

Quota Project. (2011). *Global database of quotas for women: Country overview*. Retrieved from
http://www.quotaproject.org/

Riach, P. A., & Rich, J. (2002). Field experiments of discrimination in the market place. *The
Economic Journal, 112*, F480–F518. doi:10.1111/1468-0297.00080

Rose, S. J., & Hartmann, H. I. (2004). *Still a man's labor market: The long-term earnings gap*.
Washington, DC: Institute for Women's Policy Research. Retrieved from http://www.iwpr.
org/pdf/C355.pdf

Rosette, A. S., & Tost, L. P. (2010). Agentic women and communal leadership: How role prescriptions confer advantage to top women leaders. *Journal of Applied Psychology, 95*, 221–235.
doi:10.1037/a0018204

Ryan, M. K., & Haslam, S. A. (2005). The glass cliff: Evidence that women are overrepresented in
precarious leadership positions. *British Journal of Management, 16*, 81–90. doi:10.1111/
j.1467-8551.2005.00433.x

Schein, V. E. (1973). The relationship between sex role stereotypes and requisite management
characteristics. *Journal of Applied Psychology, 57*, 95–100. doi:10.1037/h0037128

Scott, K. A., & Brown, D. J. (2006). Female first, leader second? Gender bias in the encoding of leadership behavior. *Organizational Behavior and Human Decision Processes, 101*, 230–242.
doi:10.1016/j.obhdp.2006.06.002

Sczesny, S., & Kühnen, U. (2004). Meta-cognition about biological sex and gender-stereotypic physical appearance: Consequences for the assessment of leadership competence. *Personality and
Social Psychology Bulletin, 30*, 13–21. doi:10.1177/0146167203258831

Shinar, E. H. (1975). Sexual stereotypes of occupations. *Journal of Vocational Behavior, 7*, 99–111.
doi:10.1016/0001-8791(75)90037-8

Smith, R. A. (2002). Race, gender, and authority in the workplace: Theory and research. *Annual
Review of Sociology, 28*, 509–542. doi:10.1146/annurev.soc.28.110601.141048

Timberlake, S. (2005). Social capital and gender in the workplace. *Journal of Management
Development, 24*, 34–44. doi:10.1108/02621710510572335

Towers, I., Duxbury, L., Higgins, C., & Thomas, J. (2006). Time thieves and space invaders:
Technology, work and the organization. *Journal of Organizational Change Management, 19*,
593–618. doi:10.1108/09534810610686076

UNIFEM. (2010). *Progress of the world's women 2008–2009: Who answers to women? Gender and
accountability*. Retrieved from http://www.unifem.org/progress/2008/media/POWW08_
Report_Full_Text.pdf

United Nations Development Programme. (2011). *Human development report 2011* (Table 4).
Retrieved from http://hdr.undp.org/en/media/HDR_2010_EN_Table4_reprint.pdf

U.S. Bureau of Labor Statistics. (2010a). *News: American time-use survey—2009 results*. Retrieved
from http: http://www.bls.gov/news.release/atus.nr0.htm

U.S. Bureau of Labor Statistics. (2010b). *Women in the labor force: A databook (2010 edition)*.
Retrieved from http://www.bls.gov/cps/wlf-databook2010.htm

U.S. Bureau of Labor Statistics. (2011). *Current population survey: Household data, annual aver-
ages* (Table 11). Retrieved from http://www.bls.gov/cps/cpsaat11.pdf

U.S. Office of Personnel Management. (2010). *Senior executive service: Facts and figure, demo-
graphics*. Retrieved from http://www.opm.gov/ses/facts_and_figures/demographics.asp

van Engen, M. L., & Willemsen, T. M. (2004). Sex and leadership styles: A meta-analysis of research published in the 1990s. *Psychological Reports, 94*, 3–18. doi:10.2466/pr0.94.1.3-18

von Hippel, W., Sekaquaptewa, D., & Vargas, P. (1995). On the role of encoding processes in stereotype maintenance. In M. Zanna (Ed.), *Advances in experimental social psychology* (Vol. 27, pp. 177–254). San Diego, CA: Academic Press.

Williams, C. L. (1995). *Still a man's world: Men who do "women's" work*. Berkeley, CA: University of California Press.

Williams, J. (2000). *Unbending gender: Why family and work conflict and what to do about it*. New York, NY: Oxford University Press.

Williams, J. E., & Best, D. L. (1990). *Measuring sex stereotypes: A multination study*. Newbury Park, CA: Sage.

Wolff, H. G., & Moser, K. (2009). Effects of networking on career success: A longitudinal study. *Journal of Applied Psychology, 94*, 196–206. doi:10.1037/a0013350

Worldcrunch. (2011, March 1). *Quotas for women on corporate boards, why not?* Retrieved from http://www.worldcrunch.com/quotas-women-corporate-boards-why-not/2596

5

Linking Personal and Social Histories With Collective Identity Narratives

Nicola Curtin and Abigail J. Stewart

Individuals identify themselves in many ways. They see themselves as belonging to families, places, historical generations, organizations, religions, occupations, and political parties, among other things. Some identify with additional groups that social scientists think of as *social categories* (gender, race, ethnicity, social class). People tend to recognize any one of these identifications only intermittently and to attach greater or lesser importance to different ones at different times. Which identity or identities matter a lot or hardly at all is a matter of individual differences and changes across the life span, as is whether and how they are related to each other and integrated into a whole personality. Because of this complexity, psychological theory and research can make collective identifications seem disconnected and lifeless. In this chapter, we bring them to life with two case studies. We illustrate how both a multidimensional model of collective identity that attempts to integrate various theoretical traditions and carefully considers social context (Ashmore, Deaux, & McLaughlin-Volpe, 2004) and a developmental model of personality (Stewart & Healy, 1986, 1989) can be applied to life narratives that include discussions of key politicized social identities (in these two instances, we focus specifically on politicized feminist identity).

After a brief overview of the two theoretical models and an introduction to the two women whose life narratives we analyzed, we consider each of the elements of the collective identity framework, providing examples of how they occur in these two women's narratives. Comparing the ways in which each element illuminates important aspects of both activists' collective identity as feminists, we illustrate the overall framework's utility for comparative and qualitative examinations of collective identification. We conclude with a discussion of the value of such examinations for developing understanding of political identity.

Theoretical Frameworks

In their 2004 article "An Organizing Framework for Collective Identity: Articulation and Significance of Multidimensionality," Ashmore et al. offered psychologists a seven-part framework for conceptualizing and studying collective identity. The seven elements are: (a) self-categorization, (b) evaluation, (c) importance, (d) attachment and sense of interdependence, (e) social embeddedness,

(f) behavioral involvement, and (g) content and meaning. Although the authors focused on how this framework can be used to situate and compare different theories of collective identity, we use their notion of collective identity stories to examine how the framework can be used to trace the development of collective identification within the life narrative of specific individuals. Additionally, the framework provides a means of understanding specific behavioral outcomes of collective identification (in this case, feminist activism). To fully capture the social and developmental context we found in the narratives, we also drew on Stewart and Healy's (1986, 1989) life-stage model of personality development to more adequately contextualize and understand each woman's narrative of collective identification.

The Stewart and Healy (1986, 1989) model links individual development and social changes. The model assumes that sociocultural events influence personality development differently, depending on the life stage in which they are encountered. Stewart and Healy argued that understanding individual differences requires contextualization in terms of the life stages during which important collective identifications develop, deepen, and shift. Significant events that occur during childhood and early adolescence should shape people's fundamental values and how they perceive and understand the world, whereas events that occur during early adulthood affect the kinds of conscious identifications described by Ashmore et al. (2004). Significant events experienced during middle adulthood can have important effects on behavior without necessarily influencing values or identities, although those during later adulthood may result in identity revisions, or only in the perception of new opportunities for change.

In this chapter, we bring these two theoretical perspectives together to examine two life narratives, or *identity stories*. According to Ashmore et al. (2004), one of the ways in which people articulate their collective identities to themselves and others is by developing a collective identity story. These stories are

> the individual's mentally represented narrative of self as a member of a particular social category. . . . A collective identity story includes thoughts, feelings, and images about the past (the person's past as a member of the group), the present (where the person is now and the role that social category membership plays in that current reality), and the future. (p. 96)

We drew our two case examples of collective identity from the Global Feminisms Project, an archive of life narratives produced by feminist scholar–activists. We examined the two accounts in terms of the collective identity framework and Stewart and Healy's (1986, 1989) developmental model.

Global Feminisms Project

The Global Feminisms Project began as an interdisciplinary collaboration among feminist scholars at four sites: China, India, Poland, and the United States (see Lal, McGuire, Stewart, Zaborowska, & Pas, in press; and Stewart,

Lal, & McGuire, in press, for overviews of the project). It is currently an archive of life narratives from 42 feminist activist–scholars. The project aimed to ground international knowledge in specific locations and histories to avoid homogenization or universalization of women, cultures, and feminism and women's movement activism. Each of the four sites independently decided how they would select 10 women who fit their definition of feminist activist–scholars, as well as the content of the life-narrative interviews they conducted. Here we focus on two women who are rough contemporaries from different sites: Loretta Ross from the United States and Lata P. M[1] from India. Although we focus on the ways in which the collective identity framework sheds light on each woman's collective identity, we recognize the complications inherent in using Western-based models to analyze the narrative of Lata P. M.

The women whose narratives we explore were born in the same decade, but in different countries, and they live and work in different political and social contexts. The original transcripts of the interviews cited here and supplemental contextual materials are available online on the project website maintained by the University of Michigan and include extensive footnotes explaining events and terminology (University of Michigan, n.d.).

Loretta Ross

Ross is an African American activist. She was born in 1953 in Temple, Texas, into a politically conservative military family. Her father was an immigrant from Jamaica, her mother a native Texan. Ross began her activism in college, when she was involved with both student activism and local women's rights organizations; she was one of the first African American women to direct a rape crisis center. Ross has worked on social justice issues such as human rights and reproductive choice, as well as monitoring hate groups and right-wing organizations in the United States. She is the founder and national coordinator of SisterSong Women of Color Reproductive Health Collective, a network of over 70 grassroots organizations.

Lata Pratibha Madhukar (Lata P. M.)

Lata P. M. is an Indian activist and poet who was born in 1955 in Nagpur (the largest city in central India). Her parents came from different castes, her father belonging to what is called a *scheduled* caste, that is, a caste that has access to affirmative action "reservations" in India, such as reserved places in universities and civil service positions. Scheduled castes have been historically marginalized. Lata began her feminist activism during the 1975 "emergency" period (when Prime Minister Indira Gandhi ruled by decree, suspending elections and

---

[1]Indian naming practices differ from those in the United States and may be unfamiliar to some readers. *Lata P. M.* is the name of our example from the Indian site, and referring to her as *Lata* is comparable not to a U. S. first name, but to a surname. Thus, *Lata* and *Ross* are comparable terms and are used to refer to the two women.

civil liberties). Lata worked as a lecturer and later as a radio journalist. After her marriage, she worked as a research assistant in the Research Centre for Women's Studies at SNDT (Shreemati Nathibai Damodar Thackersey) Women's University in Mumbai. Later she joined the Women's Centre (Nari Kendra) in Mumbai, and was with the Centre for 7 years, a time she was active in the women's rights movement. She has also been active in the environmental movement in India and has been the national convener for the National Alliance of People's Movements.

Methodological Approach

Our purposes in this chapter are exploratory and illustrative. We aim to simultaneously assess the utility of the collective identity framework for studying the narratives of feminist activists in the Global Feminisms Project and assess the degree to which those narratives might illuminate the collective identity framework. In pursuit of those two aims, we began by reading the two interview transcripts carefully and identifying places in the text where each woman mentioned feminist identity or life experiences related to feminism. During this phase of our project we did not focus at all on the collective identity framework. In the next phase we each carefully read the Ashmore et al. (2004) article and discussed in detail each of the different elements to ensure we had a shared understanding of all of them. Returning to the interview transcripts, we reread them in light of the collective identity framework elements, paying particular attention to those portions of the text we had already identified as being "about" feminist identity. We noted places where the interview text appeared to fit with the collective identity framework elements, as well as places where it seemed not to fit. We were then ready to link the narrative text to the elements within each interview and to compare the text associated with each element in the two interviews. The account that follows is the result of that process.

Applying the Framework

Self-Categorization

Self-categorization is the first and most basic element of collective identification. It involves placing oneself in a particular social category. In terms of understanding the development of collective identification, self-categorization might begin as the moment when a person first claims an identity. In the case of our two activists, these moments happened at somewhat different times in their lives. Further, both women's narratives illustrate how individual processes of self-categorization depend on social context and life stage. For Ross, the term *feminist* was initially fraught with larger meanings that conflicted with her racial identity; the term only made sense to her when she defined it in relation to her identity as an African American and her work in communities of color. For Lata, feminism was an early place of liberation and protection in a social context that devalued her based on both her gender and caste.

Interestingly, Ross did not use the term *feminist*, nor did she explicitly discuss feminism when she spoke about her childhood. In fact, she claimed that she did not use the term *feminist* to describe herself until many years after she started doing feminist work.

> I started doing feminist work in like 1972, '73. But it wasn't until 1985 that I actually chose the word "feminist" for myself. Because I used to say, 'I'm not a feminist, but . . .' yeah [laughs] 'I'm not a feminist, but this is wrong, you know. Violence against Black women in the Black community is wrong. But I'm not a feminist. . . . And that was my mantra . . . when I took the job at NOW [National Organization for Women], the question was called. Because a lot of people thought that I had sold out my Black credentials . . . when it was time to mobilize for the first march I had the job of going around to all these women of color organizations and talk about abortion rights. And a couple of them kept asking me, "Well, are you a feminist?" and at that point, "I'm not a feminist, but . . ." wasn't making sense anymore. How can I organize women to participate in a movement I'm afraid of claiming?

For Ross, for about 12 or 13 years when she was working on behalf of women's rights, claiming the collective identity of feminist was complicated by racial politics, and she felt it was in conflict with her identification as a politicized Black woman. Eventually however, Ross began to feel that her refusal to call herself a feminist was hypocritical.

Although Ross might not have openly claimed the term *feminist* until 1985, she was exposed to feminist ideas and writing in college. Her college years coincided with the rise of the Black Power movement in the early 1970s. As she described it,

> It was the time of Kent State, Jackson State. We were protesting the Vietnam War, but we were also protesting racism, and it certainly was my first encounter with anything called radical politics. Because I'd come from a solidly conservative Black family. And I remember my freshman year in college, people put . . . *The Black Woman* . . . in my hand, and it was like a universe had opened up for me. And I quickly decided that I was a Black feminist, even though I probably couldn't spell the word at the time. . . . Actually, we used to call it Black Pan-Africanist Feminism.

Ross's statement here (that she "quickly decided" that she was a Black feminist) could be said to contradict her later assertion that she did not "choose" the word *feminist* for herself until much later. Instead, we suspect her account shows that tentative self-categorizations do not necessarily steadily accumulate weight; they can be set aside, and then (as in this case) reclaimed in a different context. Ross was immersed in a context of large-scale social unrest and change during her college years. She characterized her first year of college as an opening up of new intellectual and behavioral possibilities different from her "solidly conservative" family background. During this time, she "quickly" claimed a *Black* feminist identity for herself, but publicly describing herself as a feminist was a gradual process, in tension with her involvement with the Black Nationalist movement.

It was not until she was deeply involved in mainstream feminist activism that Ross claimed the identity. It is interesting to note that this particular chain of events (becoming active, then developing a collective identity) is a reversal of the causal direction that most social movement and social identity theorists posit (i.e., the identity precedes engagement). This raises the following question: Under what circumstances are some people drawn to activism because of shared beliefs and only later willing to claim the particular social identity associated with that activism? In Ross's case, during the period she worked on behalf of Black women she found the label *feminist* irrelevant; however, it is clear that she had many shared beliefs with feminists, and when it felt necessary to claim the label she did.

Ultimately Ross articulated a specifically intersectional feminist collective identity. The conflict between Ross's collective race and gender identities came into sharp focus when she was invited to join NOW and in light of her work with the Black Nationalist movement.

> I was a bad fit for them [NOW] . . . [they] didn't trust me because I wasn't, quote, "feminist enough." I mean, I was paying attention to the anti-apartheid movement and to Black politics . . . and yet I was in the Black Nationalist movement raising all these embarrassing gender questions.

She realized, "I was into gender, felt I was a good gender advocate. But gender at the intersection of race, class, nationalism and all those other things. Not just gender in and of itself." Ross reconciled the perceived misfit of her racial and gender identities; she is a feminist, but one who sees gender at the intersection of other collective identities. This reconciliation allowed Ross to call herself a "flaming feminist" who "gladly use[s] the F [that is, 'feminist'] word, and proclaim[s] [it] in pretty loud letters." Through the negotiation of her initial perception of lack of fit, Ross became proud and certain of her collective feminist identity. Perhaps precisely because she had to fight so hard to find a place for herself as both Black and feminist, her collective identity was strongly articulated.

One reason that Ross's commitment to feminism during her young adulthood resulted in such a strong feminist identity may have been the timing of her negotiation of the tension between her work on gender and race. Stewart and Healy (1986, 1989) argued that major life events experienced during late adolescence and early adulthood are likely to most significantly affect a person's identity. Ross spent her college years and 20s trying to negotiate a space for herself as a feminist committed to racial equality. This developmental context may explain why her initially conflicted identity became so central and is often expressed explicitly in her descriptions of herself and her work throughout her interview.

In contrast to Ross, Lata linked the birth of her feminist identity very closely to a story she heard as a child about her family. She described learning about her grandmother's death from domestic violence at the hands of her grandfather. Even though this happened long before Lata was born (her father was 11 at the time), she said, "I feel this was the beginning of feminist thought in me and the basis of the strong feelings I had on domestic violence against women." Just as Ross's narrative explored her feminist identity in the context of her racial identity, Lata also described a layered and intersectional experience of her feminist identity that complicated her collective identity narrative. In particular, she described the ways in which her academic success was in tension with people's expectations of her based on both her caste and her sex. Here, in a different way, we can see the importance of a sense of fit in helping shape collective identity.

> I always heard them talking about me as an ideal, in my neighborhood. I had one or two friends who always got less marks. . . . Their parents would tell them that even though I was from a lower caste, I was doing so much which they could not although they were from upper caste. . . . They were not taking into account my caliber even though it was very much there. This was very difficult for me. And boys were told that even though I was a girl I could do it, which they couldn't despite being boys. I would think about all this comparison from both sides. The good thing was that I understood this, because otherwise I would have never been able to become a feminist fighting against casteism, communalism [in India, *communalism* usually refers to prejudice, discrimination, and conflict between different communities, e.g., religions or caste groupings] and even gender bias. . . . I could not have become a feminist.

Lata illustrated how both her lack of fit with caste and gender stereotypes sharpened her sense of injustice and shaped her feminist identity. However, although Ross initially struggled with her feminist identity because of tension between feminist and Black communities, for Lata the tension between her own success and others' inability to understand it because of prejudice served to strengthen her certainty that she was a feminist.

Additionally, because Lata's feminist identification developed early in her childhood, one can see how she linked it to her beliefs about the world and how it should be. In contrast to Ross, Lata less often used the term *feminist* to describe herself or her work. It was clear that she identified as a feminist and considered her work feminist. However feminist was not an identity that she explicitly "proclaims loudly." The story of her grandmother's death left a deep impression on Lata and underscored the ways in which gender inequality harmed women. Her experiences as a schoolgirl and later in college, as someone who was both the "wrong" gender and caste to be successful further strengthened Lata's feminist worldview, one that rejected caste and gender inequality. Consistent with Stewart and Healy's argument, Lata's infrequent overt invocation of her feminist identity may result from the fact that her sense of herself as a feminist developed during childhood; as a result, she experiences feminism less as an identity category and more as a worldview.

A notable similarity between the two women is that they both claimed an intersectional feminist collective identity. Both women articulated a collective feminist identity that was inseparable from other collective identities and concerns such as race, caste, and class. These particular self-categorizations underscore the ways in which collective identities operate in the context of other group identities a person may be born into or adopt. Ross's and Lata's accounts of how they came to identify as feminist also highlight the next component of the collective identity framework we discuss—how both the internal and external perceptions of social categories shape identity.

Evaluation

Evaluation is the individual's feelings (positive or negative) toward her group, including the judgments that group members have of their group (*private regard*) and their evaluation of how their group is perceived in the larger social context (*public regard*). Ross described the ways in which public regard—widely held beliefs about feminists—shaped her ability to claim a feminist identity. When she first started working at NOW, for example, she experienced negative reactions from both her Black community and her feminist community, based on perceptions each group had of the other. "They [her peers in the Black Nationalist movement] thought I'd sold out to the White women, and the White women thought I hadn't sold out enough." External perceptions of who was a feminist (e.g., White, middle-class women who were only—or primarily—concerned about gender inequality) and what it meant to be a feminist posed real challenges to Ross in claiming such an identity; these external perceptions had psychological and logistical consequences for her collective identification. At the time of her interview, however, Ross had a strong sense of private regard for herself as a feminist: "I'm a feminist and kind of proud of it."

Lata also had to contend with external ideas and expectations about her commitment to feminism. In her case, much of this external regard came from her extended family, in particular, her husband's immediate family. These expectations stemmed from beliefs about the proper role of a woman as wife (and later, mother), which were in conflict with the feminist ideals that Lata and her husband strove for in their marriage. For example, she described one of her first meetings with her in-laws after she and Ravi were married:

> I was not wearing a *mangalsutra* [a neck ornament indicating that a woman is married]—actually Ravi didn't put a mangalsutra on me. . . . We had decided that there will be no marriage symbols for both of us. My sister-in-law told me to wear the mangalsutra because I was going to my in-laws and if I wanted to compromise with my mother-in-law then I would have to wear it. . . . Only then I could go there.

In this case, Lata bowed to her in-laws' expectations of her as a wife, but these interactions only highlighted for her the fact that there was gender injustice that she was determined to fight:

> The night I went to my in-laws a journey began for me. It is only then I realized that getting married was not a very easy thing. . . . I didn't know that this was the beginning. . . . The onus of changing the atmosphere of the house was entirely on me.

In Lata's case, it was not that there seemed to be external ideas of who a feminist was, but that the only options open to her were to be a particular kind of woman. Yet, this still affected her sense of herself as a feminist. The expectations of womanhood set by her family contradicted Lata's own feminist ideals and there-fore helped strengthen her identity.

In terms of Lata's sense of internal pride, only glimpses of it spontaneously emerged during her interview. For example, she mentioned how during a speech she made later in her career as an activist, she "came across as a woman who was a witness, a participant, and a leader in the struggle." This was one of the few moments when the depth of Lata's private regard for herself as a femi-nist and as a feminist leader emerged. Comparing her with Ross in this sense is interesting and potentially illustrative—Do we get less of a sense of Lata's private regard simply because she is less expressive in this way, or is it perhaps because the interviewer did not ask the kinds of questions needed to elicit more explicit expressions of internal pride?

Importance

Importance is the degree to which a social category or identity is felt as a central part of the person; a defining element of who they are. Here we are deliberately interested in feminist identities that we expect to be important to both women, but it would be equally useful to examine feminist identities among women who differ in the importance of this identity to them.

One means of assessing the importance a social identity has to a person is the amount of time devoted to activities related to that particular identity. In Ross's case, most of her adult life has been devoted to feminism. She began doing feminist work when she was 19 years old, and she is still working on fem-inist issues today. In Ross's account of her adult life, the importance and cen-trality of her feminist identity were always present, but it intersected with her racial identity and her sense of being a woman of color: "I left NOW in 1989 to go work for the National Black Women's Health Project because I had worked within White feminist organizations so I wanted to go see what Black feminists were . . . and enjoyed that." In fact, we cannot understand the importance of Ross's feminist identity without understanding the importance of her racial identity. It is her commitment specifically to Black women, and more broadly to women of color, that directs Ross's activism, as well as how she understands social problems. If her feminist and racial identities were not both important to her, we might expect to see her undertake different activist projects or to understand social problems in a different way. As it is, Ross's feminist identity is shaped by an intersectional approach to social justice (e.g., Crenshaw, 1991), one that takes into account gender, race, and class in working for social change.

This intersectional analysis was clearly illustrated in Ross's mid-life found-ing of SisterSong, a coalition of organizations that focus on "reproductive justice":

> We use the phrase *reproductive justice* as reproductive rights married to social justice as . . . as what we mean. . . .We tend to see it as the full achieve-ment and protection of women's human rights. So that the labor, the repro-duction, the sexuality of women and girls can no longer be exploited . . . and the end of reproductive oppression. We've got a lot of discussion papers about it. And in a way, we're like doing cutting edge analyses, because we're looking at all the old theories of intersectionality. . . . And so that's why

> SisterSong is kind of like . . . it's not only exciting to us as women of color, but it's exciting to White women who are looking for a radical home. You know, and so that's what we've kind of become.

Although this passage does not directly articulate the importance of her feminist identity, it illustrates Ross's belief that an intersectional focus allows feminist activists to broadly frame the abortion debate in terms of the much larger issue of women's rights as human rights. Thus, her organization is a means of creating change and a home for many different feminists to work together. SisterSong is a concrete extension of the importance of Ross's own feminist identity, an identity that grounds gender in experiences of racial and class oppression and privilege.

Lata's narrative illustrates the ways in which the importance of a particular social category can be both liberating and a source of conflict in relation to other life commitments or social expectations. Throughout Lata's narrative, she described how her commitment to her feminist identity and the importance it had to her sense of self were often in conflict with roles that others expected her to fulfill. Much of this tension centered on her relationship with her in-laws. For example, she described some of her early involvement with the women's movement:

> Manu [Lata's daughter] was 6 months old and a 7-year-old girl was raped in Goregaon. I was upset with this case and I felt that I must go to the *morcha* [protest] and express my solidarity and *for me it was like a need to breathe* [emphasis added]. I felt that if I didn't, I won't be able to live. I went for that *morcha,* when I came back my mother-in-law's blood pressure had gone up. My husband and my sister-in-law were sitting near her. Even my sister-in-law had come along with me to the morcha but she was not talking to me. Nobody was talking to me and I was totally boycotted. Everybody told me I need not have gone right then. . . . I felt that it was very important for me to get out or else I would feel suffocated and would also feel suppressed from within.

Lata's need to show solidarity with her feminist peers was so deep that it felt "like a need to breathe." She risked her family's disapproval to attend the protest and placed her need to be a feminist above her other roles, at least temporarily. The above passage is of particular interest as it shows not only how deeply committed Lata is to the women's movement but also how she links her personal well-being to her feminist work. It is an example not only of importance but also of attachment and interdependence. Lata was so attached to this particular identity and to her colleagues who were protesting gender injustice that activism felt like a precondition for life itself, and she was willing to risk her family's censure in order to show solidarity with other feminists.

Attachment and Sense of Interdependence (Common Fate)

Attachment and *sense of interdependence* refer both to the depth of one's emotional involvement with a particular group and to degree to which one feels one's personal fate is tied to the fate of the group (*common fate*). In examining the attachment and sense of interdependence in both Ross and Lata, we can see how the content of one's feminist identity shapes the ways in which attachment is expressed. Ross experienced joy and pride in her feminist identity, even as she also described experiences of alienation from some feminists. Lata expressed a somewhat less joyful, though no less intense, attachment to her identity. Both women, however, also highlighted how attachment and interdependence do not necessarily fall along singular identity lines. That is, in both narratives we see that their feminist identities engender not only a sense of attachment to other women or to feminists but also to other social identity categories and the social movements associated with them.

Ross, as described previously, expressed feeling both attached to and alienated from other feminists. She described herself as a "flaming" feminist, and she used the term *feminist* "gladly" to describe herself. Ross also articulated a clear commitment to feminism and a feminist identity, "if you're going to get the benefits, then you have the responsibility of fighting the baggage." However, she also described a sense of frustration and alienation from mainstream White feminism both in her early career, as above, and in helping to organize the 2004 March for Women's Lives:

> And so at our 2003 national conference, the four organizations who decided to do the March . . . sent representatives to SisterSong's conference asking for our endorsement. . . . And when they first asked for our endorsement, I was the first one to say, "Hell, no" . . . the last thing I want to do is drop everything we're doing yet again for White women and their agenda. . . . They didn't even all have women of color to send to represent them at our conference. And that was just so unacceptable for me. . . . Here it is in 2003, you don't even have women of color in senior management?

Ross might have gladly proclaimed herself as feminist, but she also had a critical analysis of ways in which some feminists have failed to address the needs of women of color or create inclusive movements for social change. This critique resulted in frustration and alienation; she was not attached to, nor did she feel a sense of common fate with, all feminists. However, as it turned out, SisterSong did end up participating in the march, and their participation shifted and reshaped the way in which women's reproductive freedom was framed at the event.

> The March for Freedom of Choice was not a big enough thing for what we're talking about. Because I'd talked about "abortion or not to abort" that is not how women of color organize . . . reproductive rights means a whole lot more than to abort or not to abort as far as we're concerned. So, the March for Freedom of Choice wasn't working as a title. . . . And much to my amazement they changed the name of the March. And then they started reorganizing the March using our reproductive justice language that SisterSong had pioneered. . . . And it brought in a lot of new voices that historically that had not supported a women's rights march. . . . The NAACP [National Association for the Advancement of Colored People] endorsed the women's rights march. It had never done so. . . . The immigrant rights movement, the antiwar movement, the antiglobalization movement, all coming together to support a women's rights march.

Ross captured here how her intersectional and inclusive feminist identity created new possibilities for coalitional collaborations between different social movements. From an identity perspective, the passage also illustrates how Ross's feminist identity (an identity shared by her colleagues at SisterSong) allowed for (if not demanded) broad perspectives and cross-group attachments. Her march was not limited to "women" but included communities of color and antiwar and antiglobalization movements. Her attachments were not limited to other feminists. In fact, she described herself as distinctly separate from some specific feminists and their concerns, sharing common fate instead with communities of color, for example.

Although we noted that Lata was deeply "attached" to her feminist identity, there are fewer instances in her interview in which she explicitly referred to a sense of attachment to or alienation from her feminist peers. Of course, this may mean she simply decided not to talk about it, not necessarily that she did not have it. The passage cited above about the morcha is the clearest example of attachment to other feminists. Like Ross, Lata also made broad connections between her feminist activism and her activism in other domains. For example, she had been quite active in the antidevelopment and environmental movements in India. Much of this work had focused on international development and protesting the exploitation of people and natural resources. She saw this work as feminist and as deeply rooted in feminist ideals. Lata's sense of common fate was not limited to other feminists, but was more inclusive.

> Issue-based movements began which were not only talking about displacement and resettlement but also raised other questions. Like the movements for the right to information, right to work and the right to life. The right to life movement had three important demands. The rights on land, water, and environment. . . . The fight to save our natural resources began at various levels, like the Chipko movement [an organized nationwide resistance to the destruction of forests in India]. We consider the Chipko movement to be a part of women's movement but the movement in itself is quite a big thing.

What is of particular interest is that both women arrived at the same conclusion from very different experiences: Their feminist identities and commitment to gender justice cannot be separated from other social justice concerns or movements. Lata did not express the same sense of alienation from a mainstream feminist movement, nor did she describe experiences of exclusion from feminist organizations. She did not become active in the environmental movement because her concerns are not addressed by the feminist movement; rather, she saw the one as an extension of—or compatible with—the other. Ross similarly saw women's rights as embedded in a larger human rights framework, but also described her frustration with other feminist organizations that took a more singular, or decontextualized view of gender. Lata's articulation of her feminist attachments did not contain the same element of disappointment in other feminists.

The collective identity framework does not explicitly include the possibility of cross-category attachments, but it does not preclude it either. It is therefore incumbent on the researcher to pay close attention to the ways in which common fate may not necessarily be based on common, or primary, group membership. Both Ross and Lata have strongly articulated primary feminist identities. However, if we were only to ask about, or notice, their sense of common fate with other feminists, we might miss, for example, the fact that Ross illustrates how race and class can create divisions within feminism, disrupting feelings of common cause or common fate. Both women illustrate how an intersectional feminist identity makes it possible for them to feel attached to other social category groups, based on shared goals, or common cause. Although one could argue that this attachment to other groups is somehow separate from their social identity (and indeed there are instances where it likely is) these two women's personal feminist identities are deeply rooted in a sense that social justice concerns connect people across social category differences. This particular form of collective feminist identity informs the ways in which each woman makes social connections.

Social Embeddedness

Social embeddedness "refers to the degree to which an individual's collective identity is embedded in social networks and interpersonal relationships" (Ashmore et al., 2004, p. 92). Both Ross and Lata described everyday connections with many feminists over many years. One difference between their narratives is the degree to which they discussed their personal relationships. Ross's interview focused specifically on her activist work and less on her personal life. Lata, in contrast, discussed her personal life and its relationship to her activism in much more depth. Although in both cases feminist identity was deeply embedded in their social lives and ongoing social relationships, that embeddedness is much less visible in Ross's account. Moreover, Ross described multiple nonoverlapping social networks (associated with civil rights activism and women's movement activism) in her early life, although she created a more integrated network for herself later in her career. We did not find the same shift in Lata's account; instead, her narrative explicitly discussed the ways in which her personal and political lives overlapped. One possible explanation for this may be that Ross did not know the woman who interviewed her very well, whereas it is clear from several things that Lata said in the interview that she knew her interviewer. It may be that this dynamic led Lata to talk more about her social life. However, Ross certainly shared many personal details with her interviewer, such as her experiences with rape, incest, and abortion. It is difficult, therefore, to assess from the interviews alone whether these differences are due to the immediate context of the interviews themselves or true individual-level differences between the two women.

What we can assess from her interview, however, is that how Ross's feminist identity is embedded in her ongoing social relationships seems to have shifted somewhat across her adulthood. Ross described the tension between her racial identity and involvement in the Black Nationalist movement and her work with NOW during her early adulthood and feminist career. In one context, she was asking "embarrassing gender questions" and in the other, she was asked to prove she was "feminist" enough. Her Black feminist identity was embedded, and yet salient and subject to interrogation, in each context. In one context, her feminism was suspect, and in another, her Blackness.

Ross focused less on this tension when she described her contemporary activism and identity. She still experiences some frustration with mainstream feminists, but it seems that through the founding of SisterSong, Ross found a space that supported and reflected her feminist identity. In her words, "SisterSong now has evolved into that radical progressive home for anybody who has a critique of the liberal pro-choice movement." Because Ross's interview did not focus on personal relationships or friendships, it is difficult to assess the degree to which her feminist identity is embedded in those contexts. However, several statements she makes indicate that it likely is deeply embedded. For example, as discussed above, Ross repeatedly states that she is very openly and proudly feminist: "I gladly use the F [meaning feminist] word and proclaim in pretty loud letters which tends to scare off all the men I'm attracted to." However, although we might conclude that her activist work and her feminist identity affect her personal life, we are given little information as to what that looks like every day.

Lata's narrative more explicitly described the intersection of her personal and political lives. While Lata's feminist identity caused some tension within her family, it was also something that she and her husband, Ravi, shared. Here, she describes a campaign that they worked on together:

> The name was Forum Against Sex Determination and Pre-Selection and many of us were working in it. [Including] myself [and] Ravi . . . all of us took the lead. . . . We made beautiful posters sitting on the roads. . . . Sex determination was banned first in Maharashtra due to our campaign. . . . All the feminist women of Mumbai coming with their spouses and children and there was a big march of girls.

Lata's narrative illustrates the degree to which her feminist identity played a role in her marriage. Although she described instances in which Ravi was less than supportive (as above with her attendance at the morcha), it is also clear that feminism was a part of their daily lives together and that they shared feminist commitments. Lata also described the deep friendships that formed via her activism:

> It was a full time job at Women's Centre, it was a campaign group. . . . I met all of you in the Women's Centre, you all [meaning the women associated with the Indian site where the interview took place] were working there [lists names]. All of them became my friends. My experience in Women's Centre was very happy because there were a lot of creative activities there. Many women came with their own personal experiences. . . . Seven of us— actually twelve of us—were working on it. We raised twelve questions from seven cases. Twelve different questions on twelve issues related to Christian women, Muslim women, tribal women, educated women, housewives, working women and sexual harassment at workplace. Thus, we took up the cases that came to us and the ones we did counseling for, the ones we used to talk to and the ones we were fighting for in the courts.

Not only did Lata develop friendships with other feminists, but these friendships were generative for her. As a writer and poet, Lata's feminist social connections allowed her a means of expressing herself artistically. The connections to different women also allowed for the development of an intersectional perspective on women's lives, as evidenced by the 12 questions raised by the Women's Centre group. Lata's social circle is her activist network and includes women who are raising issues of religion, indigenous rights, and workplace harassment. Lata's identity is deeply embedded in her social circle, and that embeddedness engenders the development of a more complex feminist identity.

Behavioral Involvement

Behavioral involvement is the degree to which a person engages in behaviors or acts that result directly from a particular collective identity. Given that we chose to profile two feminist activists, it goes without saying that their behavior reflects their sense of collective identity. This becomes interesting not only because of the degree to which collective identity is implicated in behavior but also because of how behavior might also shape collective identity. In the case of Ross and Lata, having a life-span narrative available is a boon; we can examine the ways in which their activism might have affected their collective identity across time. In Ross's case we see how mid-life identity revision resulted from her activist organizing. Lata's narrative, meanwhile, underscores how role conflict with her initial forays into feminist activism served to strengthen and focus her feminist identification.

Ross's early feminist work shaped her commitment to an intersectional approach to understanding gender injustice; for example, how she used the framework of human rights to think more broadly about women's rights. However, Ross also underwent a later-life identity revision related to her feminist activism. During her years organizing women of color, Ross learned that there was little written history documenting women of color's reproductive experiences. So she began to piece together this history and write about it.

> If anything, I am certainly an accidental writer. I did not plan on being a writer. . . . But I'm slowly beginning to accept that I can, you know, at least do historical research and put it together in a narrative that convinces us that we have a history of organizing and stuff like that. I mean, I would never qualify I think as a legitimate historian, but I certainly can qualify as a, like you say, scholar–activist—emphasis on activist, less on the scholar. But I am in college getting a degree in women's studies trying to add some theory to my 35 years of practice. So eventually when I emerge from this process with a PhD in women's studies then I'll have more emphasis on the scholar than the activist part. . . .

Ross's feminist identity shifted somewhat in her later mid-life, so that now she put "more emphasis on the scholar than the activist part." This newly emergent feminist–scholar identity is consistent with Stewart and Healy's (1986, 1989) argument that changes in later adulthood may affect behavior in isolation (without affecting identity), but sometimes result in transformations of identity, as we saw in Ross's account.

Lata's narrative illustrates how behavioral involvement can serve to reinforce a person's commitment to a particular collective identity. As we have read, much of her activist work during the early years of her marriage put her at odds with her family. This conflict between her family roles and her own personal desires seems to have strengthened Lata's commitment to her feminist activism. For example, she described how she initially became involved with women's studies:

> Gradually I decided to attend the Friday meetings of Nari Atyachar Virodhi Manch [Forum Against Oppression of Women]. At that time Manu [Lata's daughter] was very young, she was just about a year old. . . . There was a women's studies conference. . . . Everyone was really worried about how I could leave her and attend the conference because I was not staying with my in-laws. Everyone said I can't leave her like that. . . . I was told about so many hurdles but I had decided to go to the conference.

Lata went on to describe how this decision then created new opportunities for her to be involved in feminism, which strengthened her feminist identity and eventually led her to leave academia and become a full-time activist. Although Lata's path to activism might have been the same had her family and others supported her decisions to be active, the conflict served as reinforcement of the centrality of feminism in her life. By having to constantly "choose" her feminist activism over other obligations, Lata developed a clear sense of how important feminism was to her and how directly she was willing to defy other people's expectations in order to maintain a sense of her own feminist identification. This kind of conflict between multiple roles and identities is one that is not often studied in the collective identity and collective action literature. Yet it may very well be important. One can imagine that for many people, such conflict would inhibit the development of a collective identification. Perhaps some nascent feminist activists are derailed by competing demands on their time. In the case of women's development of collective identifications this seems like a particularly relevant issue; many politicized identities, for example, may be viewed as conflicting with home and family roles.

Content and Meaning

The final component of the framework offered by Ashmore and colleagues (2004) includes several categories that are of interest to the current analysis, including self-attributed characteristics, ideology, and narrative (both the collective identity story and the group story). *Self-attributed characteristics* are the traits and dispositions that are associated with a social identity category and are used by the person to describe herself. *Ideology* includes beliefs about the social group's history, position in society, and experiences. *Narrative*, around which we have framed our current analysis, is the story that a person has developed about the self and the particular social category in question. Although this narrative is internally represented, it can also be shared, as in the Global Feminisms Project, via interview or storytelling. The narrative has two elements: a collective identity story, which is one's own narrative of one's self as a member of a particular social category, and a group story, which is one's narrative of the social category to which one belongs. For example, Ross and Lata both have stories about themselves as feminist individuals, as well as stories about feminist groups or organizations and the feminist movement.

We chose to use one aspect of this final element of the framework, narratives, as a way of understanding the preceding elements because, as Ashmore et al. (2004) wrote, "collective identity elements do, in fact, combine in various and sometimes unexpected ways to create unique profiles of collective identification" (p. 100). Such profiles can be found in life narratives. However, it is also worth looking at how content and meaning of collective identity can be understood in terms of self-attributed characteristics and self- and group narratives.

Ross's self-attributed characteristics are interesting because they reveal the ways in which she navigates larger social beliefs about feminists, as well as the expectations that some feminist communities may have of their members. We already discussed how she addressed tensions between her Black and feminist identities. Ross also stated, "I'm a feminist that likes macho men, so that's a whole 'nother contradiction." Ross was alluding here to the notion that feminists do not or should not like "macho" men. She was claiming a particular kind of feminist identity, one that conflicted with her understanding of what it means to like macho men. This comment illustrates how examining self-attributed characteristics can deepen our understanding of a particular person's collective identity. Ross gestured here to some negotiation that was necessary to reconcile her feminist identity with that of a woman who likes macho men. Her collective identity is in tension with norms that are considered appropriate to that particular social category. Self-attributions not only tell us about how a person thinks about herself, but also about her relationship to a larger social category.

Both women have a well-articulated ideology that accompanies both their feminist identity and their activism. In many ways, we see how the particular ideology each woman has developed shapes aspects of other elements in the framework. For example, both women's ideological expression of their feminist identity is intersectional; the boundaries between particular social categories (e.g., gender and race or caste) do not always seem as clear-cut for either Ross or Lata as they may be for other people.

Ross articulated this intersectional approach multiple times during her interview, when she talked about "gender at the intersection of race, class, nationalism" and later when she argued that movements for social change must be inclusive

> because we're not going to make this revolution by ourselves. Just like Black folks could not end racism without the participation of White folks. You know, we've got to. . . . And so I think we've got to go beyond identity politics and really focus on our commonality as human beings. But not as a little namby-pamby, color-blind way.

This ideology means that she must find ways to work with mainstream White feminists, as she did during the 2004 march. However, it is also this ideology that led her to reject mainstream feminism as too singular in its focus on gender to the exclusion of other social categories. It may be, in fact, that this ideology is the culmination of Ross's own struggles to develop a feminist identity that makes sense for her particular context.

Similarly, Lata's ideological approach to feminism is an intersectional one, as she stated, "the women's movement has never been only issue-based. But different issues have come up at different times . . . [it] included women from all caste and class [sic]." However, unlike Ross, Lata's experience of the women's movement in India was that it reflected her own intersectional and collective approach to feminism:

> There was collective leadership, the most important aspect of the movement was that it didn't belong to any one group. When we talk about the movement we have to take everybody's names. Not just of one individual or any single leadership. Secondly, women from different religions came to the movement. Questions relating to being women and women from a particular religion, both were handled by the movement.

In both cases, the contents of these women's feminist ideology and identity affected other elements of their collective identity. For example, both Ross's and Lata's feelings of common fate are shaped by their identities. However, the social context in which they expressed this particular intersectional ideology mattered, as did the larger feminist movements they had access to. Ross experienced a kind of alienation and exclusion that Lata did not; yet both women experienced feelings of common fate across differences such as race, caste, and gender. For both Ross and Lata their individual and group narratives are deeply affected by the ideological content of their feminist identity, yet the experiences themselves look quite different.

Conclusion

One purpose of this chapter has been to illustrate the ways in which individual life narratives can be used to deepen our understanding of theory. Ross's and Lata's narratives allow us to examine in depth each of the individual elements of the collective identity framework. Examining life narratives allows us to translate potentially abstract and decontextualized concepts (e.g., *self-categorization*) into the ways different people actually experience them across the life course. This may help clarify for students what elements of a theory "look like" in real life, including in the lives of people very different from them. It also allows researchers and theorists to clarify some implications of exactly what we mean when we invoke particular elements. For example, in the two narratives here, self-categorization might be understood as the degree to which both women apply the term *feminist* to themselves. However, it could also be understood as the moment in their lives in which the identity became personally meaningful and self-descriptive, or when it somehow changed in meaning. Articulating the precise meaning of self-categorization within an individual's life may both clarify terminology and allow us to consider how best to measure the concept we have in mind, within a particular context. Knowing that both Ross and Lata see their collective feminist identity as intersectional in different ways raises the question of whether or not some feminist collective identities are more or less intersectional than others, as well as whether that difference matters. Some research suggests that there are race (King, 2003) and individual-level differences (Greenwood, 2008; Greenwood & Christian, 2008) in the degree to which feminist collective identifications are indeed intersectional in their focus (e.g., some women's feminist identifications include awareness of other important identities that affect social relations). Measures that are sensitive to such differences allow us not only to detect them in the first place but also to understand how (or whether) they affect outcomes of interest.

Comparative analyses such as this one highlight both similarities and differences within a particular social identity category. Similarities suggest common features of a specific collective identity (in our case, feminists, activists, or feminists–activists from a particular generation). In contrast, differences point us towards individual, family-level, cohort, national, or cultural contexts or experiences. Part of our task is to develop measures that will identify commonalities between people, as well as ways in which differences emerge through particular life experiences, historical contexts, or social locations.

Using the examples of Ross and Lata, we might hypothesize that self-categorization often involves negotiation between different social identities or expectations. In the case of Ross, there are competing factors such as race to consider; Lata must find a way to reconcile her feminism with her roles as daughter, wife, and mother. As noted, both women also develop intersectional analyses of gender; do we understand these viewpoints as defining feminists of their particular generation? Given Ross's critique of her feminist peers in the United States, perhaps this is an unlikely attribute of the entire generation. At the same time, both women have multiple subordinate statuses within their culture (Ross as a Black woman and Lata as a female member of a protected caste), so perhaps social location plays a role in the development of intersectional feminist collective identity. The point is that through our examination of life narratives, we can develop empirical questions about collective identity.

Differences between the two women also raise theoretical and methodological questions. For example, Ross articulates a sense of alienation from White feminists and mainstream feminist organizations; she has had to create a feminist space for herself and other women of color. Lata describes no such alienation (even along lines of caste, which may be—or may be thought to be—similar to race or class). Is this difference about national or cultural differences across feminist movements? Or would feelings of alienation emerge from different Indian women's narratives of their feminist identity and community, or not emerge from different narratives by U.S. women of color? It is possible, among other approaches, to examine this question using other narratives in the Global Feminisms Project archive.

We are not arguing for the development of new theory or research questions based solely on the analysis of these two life narratives; rather, we point to ways in which such comparisons can form the basis of more extensive qualitative analyses of multiple life narratives, or inform survey or experimental research. Most of all, we hope we have demonstrated both the richness of the Global Feminisms Project life narratives and the flexibility and value of the collective identity framework offered by Ashmore, Deaux, and McLaughlin-Volpe (2004). Their framework shed light on how these individual feminist activist–scholars understand themselves in similar and different ways, and how those similarities and differences matter in the work they do.

References

Ashmore, R. D., Deaux, K., & McLaughlin-Volpe, T. (2004). An organizing framework for collective identity: Articulation and significance of multidimensionality. *Psychological Bulletin, 130*, 80–114. doi:10.1037/0033-2909.130.1.80

Crenshaw, K. W. (1991). Mapping the margins: Intersectionality, identity politics, and violence against women of color. *Stanford Law Review, 43*, 1241–1299. doi:10.2307/1229039

Global Feminisms Project. (n.d.). Retrieved from http://www.umich.edu/~glblfem/

Greenwood, R. (2008). Intersectional political consciousness: Appreciation for intragroup differences and solidarity in diverse groups. *Psychology of Women Quarterly, 32*(1), 36–47. doi:10.1111/j.1471-6402.2007.00405.x

Greenwood, R., & Christian, A. (2008). What happens when we unpack the invisible knapsack? Intersectional political consciousness and intergroup appraisals. *Sex Roles, 59*(5–6), 404–417. doi:10.1007/s11199-008-9439-x

King, K. R. (2003). Do you see what I see? Effects of group consciousness on African American women's attributions to prejudice. *Psychology of Women Quarterly, 27*(1), 17–30. doi:10.1111/1471-6402.t01-2-00003

Lal, J., McGuire, K. M., Stewart, A. J., Zaborowska, M., & Pas, J. (in press). Recasting global feminisms: Toward a comparative historical approach to women's activism and feminist scholarship. *Feminist Studies.*

Stewart, A., & Healy, J. (1986). The role of personality development and experience in shaping political commitment: An illustrative case. *Journal of Social Issues, 42*, 11–31. http://www.wiley.com/bw/journal.asp?ref50022-4537&site51 doi:10.1111/j.1540-4560.1986.tb00222.x

Stewart, A., & Healy, J. (1989). Linking individual development and social changes. *American Psychologist, 44*, 30–42. doi:10.1037/0003-066X.44.1.30

Stewart, A. J., Lal, J., & McGuire, K. (in press). Global feminisms' multiple histories: Learning from comparative case studies of women's activism and scholarship. *Signs: Journal of Women in Culture and Society.*

University of Michigan. (n.d.) *Welcome to the Global Feminisms Project!* Available: http://www.umich.edu/~glblfem/

6

Standing at the Crossroads of Identity: An Intersectional Approach to Women's Social Identities and Political Consciousness

Ronni Michelle Greenwood

In 2006, Jack Straw, British MP (Member of Parliament) and Home Secretary at the time, infamously proclaimed that a veil is "a visible statement of separation and difference" and began requiring Muslim women to remove their veils when they visit his office ("Jack Straw on the Veil," 2006). That same year, Aishah Azmi was fired when she refused to remove her veil while teaching students to read ("School Sacks Woman After Veil Row," 2006). Muslim women's experiences in British society vividly demonstrate the way in which women's experiences cannot be fully explained in terms of their gender identity. Rather, to understand the social psychological processes that shape gendered expressions and experiences, attention must be paid to the ways in which social category intersections create qualitatively different expressions of womanhood, qualitatively different experiences of gender discrimination, and qualitatively different, often conflicting, political and social agendas.

Although the multiplicity and complexity of gender as a social identity have been widely acknowledged in social psychology (e.g., Ashmore, Deaux, & McLaughlin-Volpe, 2004; Cole & Sabik, 2009; Deaux, 1992, 1993; Deaux & Major, 1987; Deaux & Martin, 2003; Deaux, Reid, Mizrahi, & Ethier, 1995; Skevington & Baker, 1989), until recently the study of gender within the social identity approach tended toward a singular and universal understanding of what it means to identify as a woman or a man.

Increasingly, however, social psychologists are becoming sensitive not only to social identity complexity (Roccas & Brewer, 2002) but also to the intersectional nature of social identities (e.g., Cole, 2009; Cole & Sabik, 2009; Greenwood, 2008; Shields, 2008; Stewart & McDermott, 2004). These researchers begin from assumptions drawn from the theory of *intersectionality* (Collins, 1990; Crenshaw, 1993), which explains how social identities are mutually constitutive:

I would like to thank Sarah Jay and Elaine Reynolds for their assistance preparing this manuscript. Thanks also to the editors and to Nick Hopkins, Leah Warner, Stephanie Shields, and Brett Stoudt for their insightful comments on an earlier version of this chapter.

They simultaneously shape the meaning, experiences, and expressions of one another in an inextricably interlocking and irreducible fashion.

Given that the overarching purpose of the social identity tradition is to explain how people's definitions of themselves in terms of social categories shape and are shaped by relations between social groups (e.g., Tajfel & Turner, 1979; Turner, 1999; Turner, Hogg, Oakes, Reicher, & Wetherell, 1987), the relevance of this tradition to understanding gender-related phenomena is clear. Accordingly, the utility of the social identity approach for understanding women's social identity has been extensively examined in other places (e.g., Deaux, 1992, 1993; Gurin & Markus, 1989; Gurin & Townsend, 1986; Kelly & Breinlinger, 1995a, 1995b; Skevington & Baker, 1989). Until now, however, there has been no systematic attempt to evaluate research in the social identity approach through an intersectional lens.

In this chapter, I argue that intersectionality is fundamentally about recognizing and foregrounding the context of women's lives in social psychological analyses of gender-related phenomena, and as such there is a natural affinity between the social identity and intersectional approaches. As Reicher (2004) wrote, "Above all else, the social identity tradition is based on an insistence that human social action needs to be understood in its social context" (p. 921). Unfortunately, important aspects of context are lost in much research on gender conducted in the social identity tradition because of researchers' tendencies to approach social identities as universal, singular, and additive.

Singular approaches are those in which the researcher focuses solely on a single strand of identity arising from a single social category—gender, race, or social class, for example—while statistically or conceptually holding all other social categories constant. An *additive* approach assumes that individuals experience their social identities in a summative way; that is, for example, the experiences of racism and sexism can be added together as though there is a linear increase in the quantity of discrimination a person experiences as a function of the number of devalued social categories to which she belongs (Almquist, 1975; Purdie-Vaughns & Eibach, 2008). Another assumption of the additive approach is that measures of commitment to and experiences of social categories can be subtracted from one another and analyzed separately in quantitative research.

In this chapter, I demonstrate how the intersectional approach is a valuable tool for those of us whose work lies within the social identity tradition and who wish to remain true to this tradition's mission to understand human social action in its social context. Throughout the chapter, research on political consciousness is used to illustrate these claims. I begin with a consideration of the ways in which the single-identity legacy of the minimal group experiments and the methodological preferences of social psychologists to study single strands of identity while holding all others constant have inadvertently led to the erasure of context from the study of gender as a social identity (Condor, 1989; Griffin, 1989; Greenwood, 2008). The literature on women's political consciousness (Gurin & Markus, 1989; Gurin, Miller, & Gurin, 1980; Gurin & Townsend, 1986; Miller, Gurin, Gurin, & Malanchuk, 1981) illustrates the ways additive approaches have obscured the ways in which social context produces importance of differences among women in their experiences and expressions of their identities as *women*.

More recent research illustrates how intersectional approaches to women's political consciousness reveal and explain these differences.

I then shift to a consideration of *system justification* theory (e.g., Jost & Banaji, 1994) to demonstrate the importance of an intersectional approach to understanding the political consciousness of women who belong to multiple subordinate social groups and how the intersectional approach can contribute to the recent debates about subordinate group members' outgroup favoritism and system justification (Jost, Banaji, & Nosek, 2004; Reicher, 2004; Rubin & Hewstone, 2004). The chapter closes with a consideration of ideas that social psychologists might usefully borrow from other disciplines (Aptheker, 1989; Caraway, 1991; Collins, 1990; hooks, 1984) as a means for advancing our understanding of human social action within its social and historical context (Reicher & Hopkins, 2001) and an example of research that does just this (Hopkins, Kahani-Hopkins, & Reicher, 2006). Before moving to these considerations, however, it is useful to review the basic principles of the intersectional approach.

Intersectionality, Gendered Expressions, and Gendered Experiences

According to the theory of intersectionality, macrolevel systems of domination and subordination based in sex, race, class, nationality, sexual orientation, and others interact with one another and systematically produce qualitatively distinct experiences of social inequality. Accordingly, to assume that women's social identities *as women* are shaped uniquely and only by their sex categorization is to overlook the pervasive differences among women that arise from their membership in different dominant and subordinate social groups (Crenshaw, 1993).

Crenshaw (1993) outlined the pitfalls of conceptualizing gender as a singular social identity in her groundbreaking article on intersectionality in which she argued that the identity politics of race and gender often erase the particular experiences of people at the intersections of subordinate social categories. Using the context of violence against women of color—intimate partner battering and rape—Crenshaw illustrated that although all women share vulnerability to gendered violence, their experiences are fundamentally shaped by their membership in other dominant and subordinate social categories such as class, race, sexual orientation, and religion. These differences are observed on three dimensions: (a) qualitative and quantitative differences in the actual experience of violence (racialized sexual violence); (b) differences in women's own interpretations of the causes of, solutions to, and legitimacy of the violence; and (c) differences in observers' responses to the woman and her abuser.

Differences in women's actual experience of sexual violence are shaped by observers' perceptions and beliefs that arise from intersecting social identities. For example, Black female rape survivors are believed less often and their accusations are taken less seriously; juries convict men tried for raping Black women at lower rates and sentence them to shorter prison terms than they do men tried for raping White women (Crenshaw, 1993). Perceptions of domestic abuse are also influenced by the race of the woman and her abuser. Esqueda and Harrison

(2005) found that domestic violence survivors' race influenced White participants' evaluations of the evidence of a domestic violence event. For example,
Black women were perceived to be more culpable than White women, especially
when the victim was portrayed as provoking the man prior to the violent inci-
dent. These examples illustrate that we must account for the ways in which
identity intersections create qualitative differences in experiences and expressions of gender, not only in the domain of violence against women but in all of
the gendered aspects of women's lives.

The failure to account for intersections in which actual intragroup differences are conflated or ignored can lead to false conclusions about the extent of
ingroup homogeneity (Purdie-Vaughns & Eibach, 2008). For example, Crenshaw
(1993) illustrated how racism is defined in terms of Black men and feminism in
terms of White women, although gendered experiences and expressions (desires,
fears, and ambitions) of those who fall at the intersections (Black women) are
rendered invisible and consequently excluded from both antiracist and feminist
ideology and action. Recent research has demonstrated that Black women's experiences are not only rendered invisible but they also are often quite literally left
out of perceivers' awareness through a cognitive conflation of Blackness and
masculinity (Goff, Thomas, & Jackson, 2008). The invisibility of these intersections occurs not only in everyday life but it is also reflected in and reproduced by
an overreliance on group-based similarity, shared experience, and common
oppression as explanations of important phenomena such as social categorization, collective action, cohesiveness, and group consciousness. Next, I turn to a
brief review of the basic principles that underpin social identity theory
(e.g., Tajfel, 1978; Tajfel & Turner, 1979) and review some of the historical decisions that have led researchers to rely on single-identity assumptions and practices in their research on social identity and political consciousness.

Legacy of Singular Identity Assumptions in
the Social Identity Approach

Research on the *minimal group paradigm* (Billig & Tajfel, 1973; Tajfel, Billig,
Bundy, & Flament, 1971; Turner, 1975, 1981) yielded the core insight of social
identity theory that mere categorization into *us* and *them* is sufficient to elicit
ingroup bias and intergroup competition (the *mere categorization effect*; Turner,
1999, p. 8). The minimal group paradigm strips away social context and creates
a situation in which two groups coexist with no past, no future, and no meaning
given to the ingroup–outgroup categorization. The minimal group paradigm can
be considered "maximal" because the situation is stripped of all group-based
cues (Leyens, Yzerbyt, & Schadron, 1994; Reicher, 2004). Because there are two
and only two available and relevant group memberships—you are either one or
the other—there can be no intersecting identities. In essence, the minimal
group paradigm is fundamentally a model of single-identity processes and
as a consequence, subsequent research on real-world, broad-based social
categories—such as gender—is infused with singular, unitary assumptions
about the nature of social identities (Billig & Tajfel, 1973; Tajfel et al., 1971;
Turner, 1975, 1981).

Tajfel's research on the mere categorization effect led to his social identity model of social change (Tajfel, 1978; Tajfel & Turner, 1979; Turner, 1999). According to this model, social categorization into "us" and "them" arises from an underlying motive to create, preserve, or enhance positive ingroup distinctiveness through group-based beliefs and actions that accentuate intergroup differentiation. Intergroup behavior such as ingroup favoritism or outgroup derogation can be viewed as the last link in a chain of social psychological phenomena that arises from the process of social categorization and a motivation for positive ingroup distinctiveness.

Social identity, "that part of an individual's self-concept that derives from his or her knowledge of membership in a social group together with the value and emotional significance attached to that membership" (Tajfel, 1978, p. 63), is an outcome of social categorization. Individuals use social categorization to order their environment, enable causal explanations, and generate guides for action. Social categorization usually occurs simultaneously with a value judgment about the dimensions that define and delineate the category features. This value judgement is arrived at through social comparison processes (Onorato & Turner, 2004).

Because social identity is an important component of an individual's self-concept, she or he is invested in evaluations of the group's standing compared with other groups in the social system (Tajfel, 1978). When an individual woman compares women with relevant others (men) and is satisfied with women's position, she will be unlikely to engage in any type of intergroup competition and will wish to maintain status quo relations of women with men because this positive relative comparison is a basis for positive social identity. However, if her social comparison comes up short for women, she may take actions intended to achieve a more positive social identity. For example, she may disidentify with other women and attempt to join in with men to improve her individual status relative to men, preserving the status quo for other women (social mobility); she may shift to a dimension of comparison for which women are consensually perceived to be superior to men, such as intuition or compassion (social creativity); or she may elect to engage in collective action (social change) to improve the status of one or more groups of women, relative to men.

Social mobility, to leave a lower status group for another of higher status either literally or psychologically, is the method people use by default to improve an unsatisfactory social identity (Tajfel, 1978). However, there are several sociostructural and social psychological factors that restrict social mobility. For example, an individual may be unable to leave her or his group. Conflicts of values and social sanctions against movement to another group are additional factors that make social mobility difficult. If the boundaries between the groups are perceived to be impermeable, the criteria for categorization judged to be illegitimate, or the lower status group begins to conceive of alternatives to the current status relations, group members' engagement in one or more social change actions may intensify. However, for women the intimacy shared with men as brothers, fathers, and intimate partners makes it more difficult to sustain a gendered categorization, thereby rendering social mobility strategies more likely than social change strategies (Henderson-King & Stewart, 1994).

Social change is "change in the nature of the relations between large-scale social groups, such as socioeconomic, national, religious, racial, or ethnic categories" (Tajfel, 1978, p. 46). When individuals interact primarily on the basis of their group memberships, their attitudes and behaviors toward relevant outgroups become more uniform. Ingroup members' attributions about outgroup members become more stereotyped, value judgments of relevant traits increase, and the emotional significance of belonging to a group increases (Tajfel & Turner, 1979). In addition, beliefs about the ingroup become consensualized; that is, they become more representative of and similar to the beliefs endorsed by fellow ingroup members (Turner et al., 1987).

Group commitment, perhaps better known as *strength of group identification*, is the intensity of emotional significance and connection expressed for the group and is an important predictor of social change behaviors (Ellemers, Barreto, & Spears, 1999; Ellemers, Spears, & Doosje, 1997, 2002; Spears, Jetten, & Doosje, 2001). When an individual's commitment to a group is strong, attitudes and behaviors will become more consensualized, or stereotypical, for the group as a whole (Doosje, Spears, & Ellemers, 2002). Also, individuals who are strongly committed to the group will be more likely to stick with the group and work to improve the group's status than will individuals who are weakly identified. Weakly identified individuals are more likely to leave the group when group membership no longer contributes to positive social identity (Doosje et al., 2002; Spears et al., 2001).

To summarize, a sequence of social psychological phenomena leads to intergroup behavior. These phenomena are social categorization, social comparison, and identification. When the result of intergroup comparison is unsatisfactory, group members may engage in behavior intended to restore or increase positive social identity. Permeability, legitimacy, and stability are sociostructural conditions that affect whether group members will respond to low status with social mobility or social change strategies. Collective efforts to improve the group's social status become more likely when a group's low status is perceived to be illegitimate, when boundaries between the groups are perceived to be impermeable, and when status relations between the groups are perceived to be unstable, so that cognitive alternatives to the status quo become possible (Ellemers, 1993; Kelly & Breinlinger, 1996; Tajfel, 1978; Tajfel & Turner, 1979; Turner & Brown, 1978; Turner et al., 1987).

Is it really possible to understand these social identity processes as arising from a singular, unitary social identity such as *woman*? Although research on these processes is typically conducted with minimal or quasi-experimental groups, much of the writing about the principles of social identity and self-categorization theories presents gender as the example and asks the reader to imagine a situation in which women engage in intergroup comparisons with men (e.g., Hogg & Turner, 1987; Onorato & Turner, 2004; Turner, 1999; Turner et al., 1987). But as Elizabeth Spelman (1988) asked,

> What is it to think of a woman "as a woman"? Is it really possible for us to think of a woman's "womanness" in abstraction from the fact that she is a particular woman, whether she is a middle-class Black woman living in North America in the twentieth century or a poor White woman living in France in the seventeenth century? (p. 13)

If the distillation of gender from all other sources of identity yields an empty abstraction, can it really tell us something about the reality of women's lives? Some have argued that neutral and universal abstractions of gender identity are not merely empty, they are impossible, and that attempts to study gender along a single dimension of identity actually result in ethnocentric universalization of gender as it is experienced and expressed by women who belong to the dominant racial, class, and sexual orientation categories (e.g., Cole & Sabik, 2009; Greenwood, 2008; Purdie-Vaughns & Eibach, 2008).

Despite the legacy of the single identity approach to researching gender as a social identity, internal differentiations among women long have been acknowledged by social psychologists working in the social identity tradition (e.g., Deaux 1992, 1993; Deaux & Martin, 2003; Deaux et al., 1995; Skevington & Baker, 1989). Gurin and Markus (1989) acknowledged that group identity is "rarely a simple matter of identifying with a whole category" and that "individuals may identify with members who share similar social origins, experiences, roles or lifestyles, but will not identify with others whose lives are different in these ways" (p. 158).

Unfortunately, even when internal differentiation is acknowledged the approaches and methods typically used to investigate women's political consciousness assume the standpoint of a universal woman and then define that standpoint from the perspective of women whose ideologies, needs, and experiences are reflective of those who are White, middle class, and heterosexual. Exceptions to this rule exist, as in Griffin's research (1989), but the possibilities raised by this early qualitative research on gender as a social identity were often eclipsed by the dominant force of more traditional experimental approaches to investigating gender consciousness.

The Singular Approach to Women's Political Consciousness

Gurin and colleagues built a program of research on women's political consciousness based on the principles of the social identity model of social change (Gurin, 1985; Gurin & Markus, 1989; Gurin et al., 1980; Kalmuss, Gurin, & Townsend, 1981). The resulting body of literature can truly be viewed as the foundational source for social psychological research on political consciousness (e.g., Duncan, 1999; Duncan & Stewart, 2000; Greenwood, 2008; Greenwood & Christian, 2008; Griffin, 1989; Henderson-King & Stewart, 1994, 1999; Stewart & Gold-Steinberg, 1990). As Aida Hurtado (2008) wrote in another context, the importance of early insights into gendered processes and experiences should not be diminished or dismissed in light of the theoretical and methodological innovations that followed. Indeed, Gurin's research on political consciousness is the platform from which current and future generations of researchers can and do advance our knowledge and understanding of the social psychological antecedents and consequences of political consciousness. It is in this spirit that Gurin's research on political consciousness is presented as a key example of the assumptions and consequences of a singular approach to social psychological research on gender as a social identity.

That said, Gurin and colleagues' research on political consciousness is a quintessential example of the way in which social identity researchers have approached broad-based social categories as singular, universal, and additive phenomena. As such, it is a useful demonstration of how approaches to gender as a single, unitary category conceal important differences among women and restrict our understanding of women's political consciousness to that of the White middle class. It is also useful as an historical contrast to more recent research that has used the tools of intersectionality—tools unavailable at the time of Gurin's research—to investigate women's political consciousness.

According to Gurin et al. (1980), political consciousness is a prerequisite to collective action and is defined as "a set of political beliefs and action orientations arising out of awareness of similarity" (p. 30) with others who belong to a single social stratum, such as race, sex, age, or social class. Three dimensions are typically identified as constituting political consciousness: collective discontent, which is dissatisfaction with the social influence of one's group relative to a relevant outgroup; perceived illegitimacy of the relations between the ingroup and outgroup; and collective action orientation, which is support for collective efforts toward improvement of the ingroup's status in relation to the relevant outgroup (Gurin & Markus, 1989; Gurin & Townsend, 1986; Kalmuss et al., 1981). In a typical study, the associations among identity, consciousness, and behavioral intentions are assessed.

Within this paradigm, political consciousness is studied as a single dimension of identity, such as gender, with all other social identities, such as race and class, held constant (Gurin, 1985; Gurin & Markus, 1989; Gurin et al., 1980; Gurin & Townsend, 1986; Kalmuss et al., 1981; Miller et al., 1981). These deliberate identity elisions (i.e., omissions) were the result of a series of methodological decisions intended to eliminate confounds (Gurin et al., 1980, p. 30). First among these was the decision to ask participants to choose the social stratum with which they identified "most" (Gurin et al., 1980, p. 31). Average levels of group consciousness were calculated, but only for participants who identified the most with a given social stratum. As a consequence, the participants in this research are described, for example, as "workingmen" [sic] who have no gender or as women or older people who have no ethnicity (race). The ways in which these decisions elide important identity intersections, for example, the intersection of race and gender for Black women, as described by Crenshaw (1993), Purdie-Vaughns & Eibach (2008) and Goff et al. (2008), should be apparent.

The first identity elision arises from asking women to choose which identity, gender or race, is "most important" to them. This method is common to approaches to social identity research that conceptualize identities as additive rather than intersecting. The assumption is that identities can be summed and also subtracted so accurate measures of the contribution of each identity to marginalization, prejudice, and discrimination may be independently assessed. A corollary, as Bowleg (2008) pointed out, is the assumption that social identities can be ranked in terms of importance. In her critique of the additive approach to identity complexity, Bowleg quoted Audre Lorde's (1984) description of "constantly being encouraged to pluck out some aspect of myself and present this as the meaningful whole, eclipsing and denying the other parts of the self" (p. 120, cited in Bowleg, 2008, p. 312). In essence, to ask women to rank their social identities, especially women who belong to two or more subordinate social groups, is to ask them to do something that does not necessarily authentically reflect the complexity of their lived experiences.

The second identity elision results from the assumption that it is possible to craft items whose content taps a universal experience of gender that will hold similar meaning for women from different social groups. In Gurin and Townsend's (1986) work on gender consciousness, this assumption rendered some identity intersections invisible and others universal. For example, items designed to measure perceived illegitimacy of status relations between women and men falsely universalized the experiences of nonworking-class White women, in that they narrowly measured women's agreement with the liberal feminist belief that entry and integration into the paid labor force will lead to equality between women and men (Gurin, 1985; Gurin & Townsend, 1986). This approach to measuring gender consciousness fails to recognize that poor and working-class White women and women of color have always been in the labor market, albeit marginalized within low-paying, low-skilled, and insecure jobs and that this marginalization is not only a consequence of their gender but also their social class and ethnicity (e.g., Dill, 2009; hooks, 1984).

The measurement of collective discontent, which is calculated from social influence judgments, is similarly limited. Respondents were asked to rate the social influence of the large-scale social categories "men," "women," and "Blacks," leaving the reader to wonder *which* men and *which* women are actually represented in respondents' scores (e.g., Gurin et al., 1980; Gurin & Townsend, 1986). Does a given respondent mentally calculate an average social influence score across several ethnic groups for all women? Does her own ethnic ingroup serve as the target of her evaluation? Or does the dominant ethnic group serve as her reference group for all men and all women?

In more recent research on collective discontent when women participants who were mostly White, heterosexual, middle class, and college educated were presented with a series of single and intersecting identities, the pattern of scores indicated that participants' ratings of "women" and "men" were more similar to their ratings of "White women" and "White men" than they were to their ratings of ethnic minority men and women. Rather than estimating an abstract average for all members of these groups, participants actually tended to equate "women" and "men" with the dominant and ethnic groups, rendering invisible their perceptions of the social influence of women and men from ethnic minorities (Greenwood & Christian, 2010). These findings suggest that identity intersections must be explicitly specified in research on political consciousness, and that social influence measures of broad social categories such as "men" and "women" are implicitly intersectional in nature. That is, in actuality they represent the social influence of the intersectional identities of White women and men rather than a universal abstraction of either one.

Foundational research on political consciousness that takes a singular approach to social identity starts from the questionable assumption that single strands of identity can be added, subtracted, ranked, and measured. However, as these examples demonstrate, the methods, findings, and interpretations of this research are not universal. Rather, they are infused with the ideology of individualism that characterized the dominant discourse within the second wave of the women's movement (Gurin, 1985; Gurin & Townsend, 1986).

Much subsequent research built on Gurin and colleagues' model of political consciousness and approached gender as a singular, unitary identity and as a consequence this research also reflects and universalizes the experiences of White middle-class women, rendering invisible the distinctiveness of gender consciousness as it is experienced by women from subordinate groups. Examples of later research that adopted the additive perspective include research on collective action and gender consciousness (Cole, Zucker, & Ostrove, 1998; Duncan, 1999; Kelly & Breilinger, 1995a, 1995b, 1996), Henderson-King and Stewart's (1994, 1999) investigation of the developmental aspects of women's political consciousness and collective action, and Zucker's (2004) research on self-labeling and feminist identification. Taken together, this research demonstrates that among White women, strong group identification and White liberal feminist consciousness predicts collective action. White women whose gender or feminist identity is weak are less likely to support, intend to (or actually) participate in collective action on behalf of their group. However, this research tells us very little about the gendered political consciousness of women from minority groups.

In sum, the experiences of minority women are rendered invisible, elided quite literally through the selection of samples that are predominantly White, well-educated, and heterosexual. Minority women are also rendered invisible through researchers' adoption of a singular and additive approach to studying gender identity, political participation, and gender consciousness. Item content reflects singular assumptions and reduction of the perceived illegitimacy dimension of women's political consciousness to a liberal feminist analysis of women's social status relative to men. As a consequence, a great deal of the most widely read and cited research on the social identity of women and women's political consciousness falsely universalizes White North American women's experiences, obscures the experiences of women from marginalized groups, and limits our ability to conceive of differences among women as forming an important component of women's political consciousness.

Some have suggested that because of the salience of racial discrimination for Black women and the tensions, described above, between racial justice and feminism, Black women's race consciousness inhibits gender consciousness (Torrey, 1979). The research by Gurin and colleagues reviewed here suggested that Black women's racial consciousness was stronger than their gender consciousness (Gurin et al., 1980). But as Bowleg (2008) pointed out, if you ask an additive question, you will get an additive answer. Standing in contrast to Gurin's research are studies of political consciousness that center the experiences of Black women. In their literature review, Gay and Tate (1998) cited several studies that found Black women's gendered political consciousness to be as strong if not stronger than White women's gendered political consciousness (e.g., Baxter & Lansing, 1983; Klein, 1984; Mansbridge & Tate, 1992), and that race consciousness and feminist consciousness are positively correlated amongst Black women (e.g., Baxter & Lansing, 1983; Wilcox, 1990).

Intersectional Approaches to Women's Political Consciousness

In contrast to the additive approach, an intersectional approach to gender consciousness takes differences among women seriously and foregrounds them in both theory and research. The idea that identification as *women* is best conceptualized in terms of multiple identities instead of a single identity has been a thread running through the literature for quite some time (Ashmore et al., 2004; Condor, 1989; Deaux, 1992, 1993; Deaux et al., 1995; Skevington & Baker, 1989). Indeed, some of the main themes of Skevington and Baker's (1989) edited volume on the social identity of women are multiplicity, complexity, and difference.

Of course, although these scholars emphasized identity complexity, they could not apply the intersectional lens that was later developed in sociology and critical race theory to explain the ways in which people from oppressed groups develop consciousnesses that are different in content from that of dominant groups. For example, Collins (1989, 1990) explained how Black women's membership in intersecting subordinate social categories shapes a psychological response to material conditions that is qualitatively different from the responses of White women, whose material conditions are shaped by the advantages conferred by membership, along with White men, in the dominant racial group.

Collins (1989, 1990) and Dill (2009, p. 32) reminded us that women's social stratification into different dominant and subordinate groups results not only in differences on economic, ideological, and experiential dimensions but also in differences in political and ideological standpoints. Again, consider the example of women's experiences in the paid labor force. In the United States, on average, women experience greater workplace discrimination than do men, who have historically enjoyed greater access to education and paid labor than women. However, Black women and White women experience workplace discrimination in qualitatively different ways. As bell hooks (1984) wrote, "While it does not in any way diminish the importance of women resisting sexist oppression by entering into the labor force, work has not been a liberating force for masses of American women" (p. 146). If social mobility into the paid labor force is not perceived to be a path to social change for Black women, then it will be reflected as low political consciousness scores on scales that measure women's political consciousness narrowly along this dimension of gender discrimination.

The working conditions of poor women, a living wage, access to training and education, adequate child care, as well as the right *not* to work, to be the primary caretaker of their *own* children, are challenges that disproportionately affect women of color. As a result, the gender consciousness of women from subordinate groups is shaped by their struggle for racial and economic emancipation as well as gender emancipation (Dill, 2009; Settles, 2006). As Dill explained, Black women's consciousness is deeply informed and shaped by their experiences of racism, including racism expressed by their feminist "sisters," and their commitment to improving the lives of Black women *and* men. This entails an analysis of class exploitation and racial discrimination that differs from that of White women's political consciousness, which historically focused on marriage and family, educational and professional discrimination.

Perspectives on Black feminist consciousness that include awareness of the intersections of class and race with gender have been increasingly integrated into social psychological research on women's political consciousness. This research is fundamentally important to advancing a fuller understanding of women's experiences and expressions of gender. For example, Henley and colleagues (Henley, Meng, O'Brien, McCarthy, & Sockloskie, 1998; Henley, Spalding, & Kosta, 2000) criticized the dominant measures of gender consciousness for including only the dimension of liberal feminism. They developed a measure of feminist perspectives that includes six dimensions: conservative, liberal, radical, socialist, cultural, and womanist.

The *womanist* dimension (labelled *womanist* to distinguish it from mainstream feminist consciousness, but sometimes called *Black*, *Chicana*, or *Asian* feminism) incorporates both gender and race consciousness. King (2003) defined womanist as

> the empowerment of all women, men and children; the struggles against sexism, racism, and classism, and the importance of recognizing their interactive effects, particularly in the lives of women of color; and, the conviction that a woman should not have to choose among different aspects of her identity. (p. 20)

Research on Black women's gender identities and consciousnesses has demonstrated how the intersection of ethnic and gender identity is more important to understanding responses to stereotyping and prejudice than singular gender and ethnic identities measured in isolation (King, 2003; Settles, 2006). In her examination of the relationship of three different dimensions of gender consciousness to Black women's attributions for prejudice, King (2003) found that participants' womanist and ethnic consciousness were stronger predictors of the personal relevance of an ambiguous experience as a target of discrimination based on their race and gender. Among these women, ethnic consciousness predicted perceptions of ethnic-based prejudice, and womanist consciousness was related to perceiving *ethgender prejudice* (defined as prejudice arising from the women's unique intersection of Black ethnicity and female gender; Jeffries & Ransford, 1980) as well as gender-based prejudice. In contrast, the measure of White liberal feminist consciousness was unrelated to both perceptions of sexism and attributions of prejudice. If only White liberal feminist consciousness had been measured, King could have wrongly concluded that gender consciousness is unrelated to Black women's responses to prejudice. Instead, by taking seriously the intersecting nature of Black women's identities, the author was able to demonstrate both the relatively greater importance of a womanist consciousness to Black women's subjective experiences and how the universalization of White women's experiences distorts and misrepresents Black women's responses to prejudice. The importance of this observation will be revisited in the following section on false consciousness and system justification.

In my own research on women's gender consciousness and solidarity I have drawn on Black (Collins, 1990; Crenshaw, 1993; Dill, 2009; hooks, 1984) and White (Alperin, 1990; McIntosh, 1990; Minnich, 2005; Pence, 1982; Pheterson, 1990) feminists' critiques of White liberal feminism to incorporate an intersectional dimension into the measurement of women's political consciousness (Greenwood, 2008). In this approach, I conceptualize gender consciousness as consisting of a singular dimension, which captures appreciation of similarity among women from different backgrounds in terms of shared vulnerability to gender discrimination, and an intersectional dimension, which captures appreciation for the different forms gendered expressions and experiences of discrimination may take as a consequence of women's varied memberships in other dominant and subordinate social groups. Findings from this research demonstrated that expressions of solidarity in heterogeneous groups are higher when the intersectional component is the dominant aspect of women's gender consciousness (Greenwood, 2008). When politically progressive White women's gender consciousness contained an intersectional element, appraisals of women from different groups were most positive and accepting (Greenwood & Christian, 2008).

In ways that an additive approach cannot, an intersectional approach to women's political consciousness illuminates the varied ways in which women's intersecting identities produce qualitative differences in their gendered experiences and expressions. These differences arise from the mutually constitutive influences of broad social categories. Our understanding of women's social identities and their relationship to political consciousness are thus best understood when viewed through an intersectional lens. Additive approaches, which rest on the assumptions that individuals can rank and separate the importance and impact their varied social identities—and that researchers can subtract and isolate identities in their statistical analyses—leave us with a distorted and biased understanding of women's political consciousness.

Cole and Sabik (2009) reminded us of Carolyn Sherif's (1998) warning that focusing our understanding of social psychological phenomena on the experiences of the powerful will systematically bias knowledge and, perhaps inadvertently, contribute to the perpetuation of inequality. An intersectional approach to political consciousness may reduce bias in and distortion of our understanding of women's political consciousness because an intersectional approach intentionally centers the standpoints of subordinate groups in assumptions, theories, and methods. Approaches to social identity research that do not take account of identity intersections may unintentionally reproduce and contribute to the development and perpetuation of social psychological theories that "claim that subordinate groups identify with the powerful and have no valid independent interpretation of their own oppression" (Collins, 1989, p. 746). In contrast, an appreciation for intersections is essential for a fuller and more accurate understanding of subordinate group members' political consciousness, resistance, and collective action. As an illustration of this point, in the following section I present an intersectional response to the system justification approach to understanding disadvantaged group's political consciousness.

Social Identity, Justification, and Resistance: Lessons From Intersectional Approaches to Black Feminist Consciousness

An intersectional approach to gender consciousness has the potential to make important contributions to the recent debate about system justification by centering the standpoint of women whose identities arise from the intersection of multiple subordinate social categories. In the following section, I give a brief overview of system justification theory (e.g., Jost et al., 2004; Jost, Burgess, & Mosso, 2001) and the common criticisms levelled against it by those who work within the social identity tradition (Huddy, 2004; Reicher, 2004; Rubin & Hewstone, 2004; Spears et al., 2001). I then present an intersectional response to system justification theory and lift up the points of convergence between the social identity and intersectional approaches to subordinate group consciousness.

False consciousness is a concept commonly attributed to Karl Marx, although some question the validity of this attribution (e.g., McCarney, 2005). False consciousness is commonly conceptualized as a belief system that leads disadvantaged group members to identify with their oppressors and prevents them from accurately apprehending the conditions and causes of their own oppression. The notion of false consciousness, which has a long history of contentious debate, was introduced into social psychology in the form of *system justification theory* (Jost & Banaji, 1994). System justification theory is a social–cognitive explanation for subordinate group members' internalization of system legitimating beliefs about their own low status and inferiority relative to other dominant social groups (Jost & Banaji, 1994; Jost et al., 2001, 2004, 2007; Jost, Kruglanski, Glaser, & Sulloway, 2003a, 2003b).

The controversy surrounding system justification theory within the discipline of social psychology centers on explanations for subordinate group members' outgroup favoring responses to discrimination and inequality. Whereas the system justification approach contends that individuals are motivated to justify the social system and that outgroup favoritism is an outcome of system justifying beliefs (Jost & Banaji, 1994; Rubin & Hewstone, 2004), *social identity theory* contends that outgroup favoritism is an outcome of group members' social comparison processes, moderated by particular sociostructural factors, namely, stability and legitimacy.

According to system justification theory, individuals have a fundamental motivation to justify the social system so that they can maintain belief in it as fair and legitimate (Jost & Banaji, 1994; Jost et al., 2001, 2003a, 2003b). This poses no problem for advantaged groups. Disadvantaged groups, however, are hypothetically faced with "conflicts or crises" among the self-protective and enhancing motives to view the self, the ingroup, and the system in a positive light (Jost et al, 2001, p. 364).

The motive to justify the system leads to self- or group-blame for ingroup disadvantage:

> Someone who is disadvantaged might well feel that if the system is legitimate, then his or her own state of disadvantage must be blamed on the shortcomings of the self or the ingroup. Conversely, if one holds the self or the group in high esteem, then the system must be illegitimate to deprive such a deserving party. (Jost et al., 2001, p. 364)

This motive to justify the system is used to explain attitudes and behaviors that contradict ingroup interests, such as when women accept unequal access to promotion (i.e., the *mommy track*) and use ideologies of individualism and meritocracy to explain away men's greater career success—explanations that certainly appear to work against women's own interests.

The social identity critique of system justification has been incisively articulated in other places (Huddy, 2004; Reicher, 2004; Rubin & Hewstone, 2004; Spears et al., 2001), so I will not repeat those arguments here in detail. However, there are key points that warrant mention in relation to the current consideration of social psychological research on women's political consciousness. According to social identity principles, when relations between dominant and subordinate groups are consensually perceived to be stable and legitimate, outgroup superiority is likely to be ceded only on the relevant dimension of comparison (e.g., Spears, Greenwood, de Lemus, & Sweetman, 2010; Spears et al., 2001). However, group members do not necessarily internalize ingroup inferiority; they need only to perceive that members of the majority are unlikely to accept their alternate interpretation of reality as credible in order to be motivated to strategically manage the expression of ingroup and outgroup favoritism (Spears et al., 2001).

As Jost et al. (2001) noted, "social systems impose themselves on groups and individuals with a normative force that is difficult to resist" (p. 363). Yet, normative force at the level of the system should not be reduced to a universal psychological process of internalization of ingroup inferiority (Spears et al., 2001). Beliefs about meritocracy and individual mobility are characteristic features of system level categories such as the nation. Self-categorization at lower (subgroup, e.g., female) and higher (superordinate, e.g., nation) levels of inclusiveness is flexible, fluid, and context dependent. The meaning, attitudes, beliefs, and behaviors experienced and expressed at the level of the ingroup may not be consistent with the norms, beliefs, and ideologies that are expressed at the level of the system (Spears et al., 2001, p. 354). For example, an individual woman may strongly identify with the group *American* and endorse the ideologies of meritocracy and individualism at the system level. As a consequence of her self-categorization as a member of the group *American* she may not perceive herself to be unfairly discriminated against as a woman but need not have internalized negative beliefs about women's inferiority in comparison with men.

Black feminist critiques of false consciousness remind us that it is simplistic—and wrong—to ask, "Are they resisting or giving into hegemony?" Resistance is almost always partial, negotiated, and shaped by social context, including audience. The importance of understanding the flexible and strategic aspects of the expression of subordinate group consciousness and resistance cannot be overstated. Collins's (1990) image of the "matrix of domination" (p. 203), in which she illustrated how most people belong to both dominant and subordinate groups, not solely to either, is useful for understanding the fluidity of resistance. A woman might try to maintain dominant status in one domain by derogating one subordinate social identity in the service of a dominant social identity. For example, a heterosexual woman may seek to maintain her hetero-sexual privilege by playing into gender stereotypes that function to reinforce heterosexual privilege. Thus, what looks like system justification and outgroup favoritism is more aptly understood as a strategy to maintain heterosexual ingroup advantage.

In addition, when subordinate groups do construct cognitive alternatives that challenge the status quo, the dominant group's power over ideological resources simply may be too powerful to overcome. Dominant groups have the power to define the norms and beliefs associated with superordinate categories (Mummendey & Wenzel, 1999). Hegemonic control over ideological resources makes it extremely difficult and sometimes dangerous for subordinate groups to express ingroup bias and alternative visions of the status quo. Even when cognitive alternatives to the status quo exist, it takes special circumstances for minority perspectives to gain credibility and even more so to capture and hold the hearts and minds of the majority. As long as the majority perceives the authority to be legitimate and stable, the minority has little chance for social change, no matter the extent and elaboration of ingroup cognitive alternatives to the status quo (Subasic, Reynolds, & Turner, 2008). But bleak outlooks for minority influence do not equate to internalization of inferiority.

One of the most important objections to the system justification approach to false consciousness is the distinction between internalization and strategic self-presentation. Spears and colleagues (2001) quoted Jost and Banaji's (1994) reference to Scott's (1985) critique of false consciousness: "what looks like false consciousness . . . is really a public display that differs considerably from the political resistance that disadvantaged groups and individuals express privately." Not only may the dominant group hold power over ideological resources, but they also hold the threat of use of force to contain and suppress alternative versions of reality and visions for social change (Spears et al., 2001).

The social identity approach reminds us that attitudes and behaviors that appear to be outgroup-favoring at the level of the system may be, in actuality, strategies for ingroup preservation. Although communication at the level of the superordinate group may be system-legitimating, ingroup communication may be far less so. Writings by women of color explain the importance of home spaces to the development and expression of womanist consciousness. Home spaces are places in which disadvantaged group members come together and collectively work out what Crenshaw (1993) called *alternative forms of reality* and what social identity theory calls *cognitive alternatives to the status quo* (e.g., Tajfel & Turner, 1979). The civil rights movement, in which many Black women assumed both leadership and supportive roles, emerged from home spaces, most notably the Black church. These home spaces functioned as protected sites of ingroup resistance that co-occurred with group-protecting system level public displays of outgroup favoritism in the context of hostile and intergroup behavior, of which lynchings and bombings are the most vivid but not the only deadly examples.

Reagon (1983) wrote about home spaces as places where Black women "come together to see what you can do about shouldering up all of your energies so that you and your kind can survive" (p. 358). These home spaces are

> nurturing space[s] where you sift out what people are saying about you and decide who you really are. And you take the time to try to construct within yourself and within your community who you would be if you were running society . . . you act out community. (p. 358)

Home spaces, or sites of resistance, are where minority group members collectively rehearse alternative visions of reality until the time is ripe and sociostructural conditions allow for collective efforts for social change (Subasic et al., 2008; Tajfel & Turner, 1979). Home spaces are fundamentally ingroup audiences and previous research has demonstrated the important moderating effects of ingroup versus outgroup audience on the expression of ingroup favoring attitudes and cognitive alternatives to the status quo (e.g., Reicher, Spears, & Postmes, 1995; Spears & Lea, 1994).

Neglect of audience is only one source of misrepresentation and distortion of subordinate group consciousness. As long as researchers begin their understanding of subordinate group consciousness from the vantage point of dominant groups, they will continue to misrepresent political consciousness from the vantage point of subordinate groups. When our theories and methods effectively render invisible the distinctive political consciousness of marginalized groups and then attribute the absence of critical consciousness to distorted cognitive processes, we shift blame for inequality from the dominant to the subordinate group and perpetuate the status quo. As Collins (1989) would probably assert, system justification theory is yet another explanation of subordinate group consciousness that attributes blame for oppression to the flawed consciousnesses of subordinate groups rather than to the forces that maintain and reproduce domination and subordination. In a very real sense, then, system justification is itself a system justifying ideology.

In Collins's (1989) penetrating analysis of Black feminist consciousness, she addressed the issue of false consciousness among marginalized groups and criticized the "view that subordinate groups identify with the powerful and have no valid independent interpretation of their own oppression" (p. 746). Drawing on scholarship on subordinate resistance (e.g., Fox-Genovese, 1986; Terborg-Penn, 1986; Scott, 1985), Crenshaw (1993) argued that Black women are "neither passive victims of nor unwilling accomplices to their own domination" (p. 747). As described earlier, she argued that Black women develop a distinctive group consciousness unlike that of groups that are not Black *and* female.

According to this analysis, it is not that Black women do not develop a critical consciousness about social inequality; rather, the dominant social and political forces have the power to effectively silence alternative consciousnesses and to protect and legitimize the status quo. Collins (1989) quoted Hanna Nelson, who stated, "I have grown to womanhood in a world where the saner you are, the madder you are made to appear" (p. 749). Collins went on to say,

> Nelson realizes that those who control the schools, the media, and other cultural institutions are generally skilled in establishing their view of reality as superior to alternative interpretations. While an oppressed group's experiences may put them in a position to see things differently, their lack of control over the apparatuses of society that sustain ideological hegemony makes the articulation of their self-defined standpoint difficult. Groups unequal in power are correspondingly unequal in their access to the resources necessary to implement their perspectives outside their particular group. (p. 749)

In essence, Collins's (1989) analysis of Black feminist consciousness contains elements that are similar to the basic principles of the social identity model of social change (e.g., Tajfel & Turner, 1979). The political consciousness of Black women is a minority challenge to the status quo as defined by Tajfel and Turner (1979). Because Black feminist consciousness challenges the status quo, its expression signals the emergence of the classic struggle between minority and majority groups in which a minority's resistance to the status quo is squelched by the majority's relatively greater power over the social, cultural, and symbolic resources needed to legitimate and support collective resistance.

Both social identity theory and Black feminist thought contain the recognition that subordinate groups interpret reality in ways that differ from those of the dominant group, who are motivated to suppress alternative interpretations in order to maintain the status quo. Both social identity theorists and Black feminist theorists criticize the notion of false consciousness and system justifying explanations of the apparent absence of critical consciousness on the part of marginalized groups. Unfortunately, singular approaches to conceptualizing and measuring political consciousness have limited our abilities to apprehend the intersectional nature of gender consciousness and the unique standpoints brought to the table by Black women and other subordinate groups.

Taken together, these two domains of political consciousness research—the structure and content of women's political consciousness (e.g., Duncan, 1999; Gurin & Townsend, 1986; Kelly & Breinlinger, 1995a, 1995b) and system justification (Jost & Banaji, 1994)—are intimately tied together. Both areas of research stand to benefit from the application of an intersectional lens. Each is partial and distorted by the absence of the standpoints of those whose identities result from the intersections of multiple subordinate group memberships. The inclusion of these standpoints and perspectives in our assumptions, theories, and methods would contribute to a fuller and more valid understanding of political consciousness, resistance, and social change.

To illustrate this point, it is useful to return to King's (2003) study of the relationship of different contents of group consciousness to Black women's perceptions of and attributions for prejudice. This research demonstrates profoundly how our knowledge of a minority group's political consciousness is at risk of being distorted and misrepresented when we fail to account for identity intersections. If (as is characteristic of much research on group consciousness) King had only measured liberal feminist consciousness, she and her readers may have falsely concluded that Black women "have" little gender consciousness and are therefore unlikely to make the system-level attributions to sex prejudice that are prerequisites for resistance to the status quo and collective action on behalf of the ingroup. Further, if King's (2003) nonsignificant findings in regard to liberal feminist consciousness were then combined with other research that compared Black and White women's levels of gender consciousness, readers could and likely would conclude that Black women are "lower" on gender consciousness than are White women. Readers may even be moved to conclude that Black women have "internalized" system justifying beliefs about their lower status position relative to White men. Instead, King's results demonstrate the importance of recognizing that the content of Black women's gender consciousness is shaped by their membership in various other dominant and subordinate groups and that these different contents of consciousness have consequences for responses to inequality that vary in important and meaningful ways.

The study of political consciousness benefits from centering the intersections of women from multiple subordinate groups. One example of how to value the experiences of women whose experiences have been rendered invisible by additive approaches to understanding political consciousness is bell hooks's (1984) notion of theorizing from the margins. Hooks reminded us that

> as a group, Black women are in an unusual position in this society, for not only are we collectively at the bottom of the occupational ladder, but our overall social status is lower than that of any other group. Occupying such a position, we bear the brunt of sexist, racist, and classist oppression. At the same time, we are the group that has not been socialized to assume the role of exploiter/oppressor in that we are allowed no institutionalized "other" that we can exploit or oppress. (p. 14)

However, as Caraway (1991) suggested, there are dangers in theorizing from the margins; she cautioned that "exclusionary tendencies and cultural insensitivities can operate 'in the margin' as well as in White mainstream feminisms" (p. 184). Margins can exist within margins, she reminded us, referring to tensions within the group *women of color* among, for example, lesbian and straight women or lighter- and darker-skinned women. If margins can exist within margins, then hooks's notion of theorizing from the margins runs the risk of pitting different marginalized groups against one another, resulting in the unintended outcome of duelling oppressions. Caraway warned that "the recognition of difference within difference and margins within margins is a constant reminder as well that the only posture we can take to fight the power which infuses all human interaction is a vigilant, searching eye" (p. 186).

Instead of centering margins, Caraway suggested that we "pivot the center," an idea first introduced by Aptheker (1989) and then extended by Brown (1989), that one can learn to

> center in another's experience, validate it, and judge it by its own standards without need of comparison or need to adopt that framework as their own. Thus, one has no need to "decenter" anyone in order to center someone else, one has only to constantly, appropriately, 'pivot the center.' (p. 192)

Collins (1990) also reminded us that although we remain rooted in our own experiences and group histories, we must "at the same time realize that in order to engage in dialogue across multiple markers of difference, (we) must 'shift' from (our) own centers" (p. 245).

For social psychologists, shifting from our own centers means moving from the comfort zone of being rooted in our own experiences and the assumptions that arise from our own unique identity intersections. More important, it means moving away from both the comfort zone of parsimonious and familiar additive approaches to identity, as well as the theories and assumptions of human social action that are rooted in cognitive explanations that replace the social and historical with the cognitive and intrapsychic.

Doing Intersectional Research: An Intersectional Lens on Women's Political Consciousnesses

How does one "do" intersectional research in psychology? A number of recent publications have grappled incisively with this question (Berger & Guidroz, 2009; Cole, 2009; Shields, 2008; Warner, 2008); however, due to space limitations I will not review these authors' arguments in this chapter. Nonetheless, it is useful to give some attention to the challenges that face those of us who wish to bring an intersectional approach to the social identity tradition.

Some who take an intersectional approach have questioned the usefulness of quantitative methods for their research (e.g., see Bowleg, 2008; Cole, 2009; Guidroz & Berger, 2009; and Warner, 2008, for more elaborate discussions of these issues). There are important ideological reasons for skepticism about the usefulness of quantitative methods, and many of them have to do with the role of power both in the intersectional approach and in traditional research methods. There are also methodological reasons. The notion of intersectionality brings to mind interactions in the sense of (quasi-)experimental design and statistical analysis, and quickly appears inconceivably complex when one begins to contemplate the sheer number of interactions necessary to comprehensively account for women's identity intersections.

However, I argue that as with all social psychological research, the decision to use qualitative or quantitative methods has more to do with the researcher's aims and questions than with whether the method itself is intrinsically intersectional. Indeed, all our research on women's social identities is inherently intersectional, whether or not the intersections are acknowledged. Unfortunately, the vast majority of research on gender within the social identity tradition contains an unacknowledged focus on the intersection of *woman* with *White*, *heterosexual*, *able-bodied*, *educated*, *youthful*, and *American*. One simple way to start doing intersectional research is to begin to acknowledge these intersections.

We begin to acknowledge the intersections when we stop assuming a common understanding of identity content. Researchers should be wary of imposing their definitions of identity onto others. To do so invites a distorted and biased understanding of identity and identity-related phenomena as arising from universal psychological processes rather than social and historical forces. When we acknowledge identity intersections, we begin to understand that identities are sites of contestation best understood within social context.

I agree with Bowleg (2008) that an appreciation of context is necessary for good intersectional work. The privileging of context is a place of convergence between the social identity and intersectional approaches. The spirit of the social identity tradition is one of contextual fluidity, flexibility, and change. Turner (1999) quoted Tajfel (1979, p. 185), who wrote, "The processes of social categorization, social identity and social comparison, as used in this theory, cannot be conceived to originate outside of their social contexts." Turner went on to conclude, "Acknowledging the causal role of social and psychological content is a way of facing the specific political, historical and ideological facts of society and moving to the interactionist social psychology which Tajfel advocated so powerfully" (p. 34). When we lose sight of, overlook, or otherwise fail to apprehend identity intersections in our research on gender identity, we then fail to attend to what I believe is perhaps the most fundamental aspect of the social and historical contexts of women's lives.

But there are further reasons to incorporate an intersectional approach into research in the social identity tradition. On the importance of context to social identity research, Reicher (2004) wrote,

> [social identity] is designed to explain how individuals can come to define themselves in terms of a construct that is irreducibly cultural, and to explain that this cultural content gives shape to all the processes that flow from our sense of who we are, how we relate to others, how we define and pursue our goals, what we see as possible, and what we want as desirable. (p. 928)

Reicher (2004) warned that by investigating social identities divorced from their context (which is what occurs in additive approaches to gender identity and gender consciousness), we run the risk not only of reifying fluid, flexible, and evolving social categories but of constructing a social psychology that legitimates the status quo. An intersectional approach to social identity reveals the ways in which collective identities are naturalized; in contrast, additive and social cognitive approaches conceal the naturalizing forces that reproduce social relations and maintain the status quo.

To illustrate the importance of history and context, let us return to where we began: to British Muslim women and an example that illustrates how, if we take women's identity intersections seriously, we might be surprised by what we observe. Hopkins and colleagues (2006) used the example of a Pakistani women's group called *Al Masoom* to illustrate the importance of contextualizing agency to the development of a political psychology that explains both resistance to and maintenance of the status quo and so does not blame the oppressed for "the limits to their political imagination and collective action" (Hopkins et al., 2006, p. 55).

In this example, Hopkins et al. (2006) demonstrated how a group of middle-class British Muslim women came into conflict with the local male Muslim leadership over their fundraising efforts for Palestine and Kashmir (see Werbner, 2000). Conflict between the women and the men ultimately led to the women's redefinition of what it means to be Muslim women in British society. It also opened avenues to empowerment, agency, and social change.

In response to opposition from local male community leaders, the women used their group meetings as home spaces (Reagon, 1983) where they could reflect on the mismatch between their own and the men's understandings of who they were, who they could be, and how they should act. Over time, through discussion and debate they came to redefine what it means to be a Muslim woman, to reject certain religious traditions and customs as "cultural backwardness," and to embrace the image of the Prophet Mohammad's wife, Ayesha, who is known for her "boldness and wisdom" (Hopkins et al., 2006, p. 56).

Although these women's identities would not be defined as feminist either from their own standpoint or from that of White liberal feminists, their identities and consciousness developed toward a particular understanding of themselves—an intersectional political consciousness—as "British" and "Muslim" and "women." Their redefined identity and group consciousness were both outcomes of their conflicts with the local male leadership and precursors to a sense of collective agency that led them to engage with the non-Muslim political establishment. This example demonstrates the importance of history and context to understanding women's political consciousness.

Imagine that the researchers had asked these women to complete a typical measure of women's political consciousness, the content of which was derived solely from ideologies of Western individualism. We could reasonably speculate that on average, their gender consciousness scores would have been quite low. And we might very well conclude on the basis of those scores that this group of Muslim women are passive receptacles for and transmitters of system-justifying beliefs supportive of Islamic practices that perpetuate status inequalities between Muslim women and men. As a consequence, we would thereby contribute to a body of knowledge that validates the system-justifying belief that Islam—but not Christianity—is oppressive to women, which in turn might (unintentionally perhaps) be used to legitimate and justify discrimination against Muslims and maintain power and status differences between Muslim and non-Muslim women living in Western societies.

Conclusion

When we attempt to understand gender as a singular social identity, we fall into the reification trap. Writing about the importance of situating social identities in context, Reicher and Hopkins (2001) stated,

> If you take a singular definition of self-categories for granted, or even suggest that we should be looking for such a singular definition, then you may be facilitating the removal of choice over the conditions under which people can live, and you may be impeding their capacity to imagine—and hence achieve—alternative worlds. A psychology that serves to facilitate and legitimate such presuppositions thereby also acts as a prop to the status quo. (p. 401)

Ultimately, when researchers approach gender as a singular identity they "project their categorization of the social world upon their subjects, and they include subjects in their analyses only to the extent that they accept those categories" (Reicher, 2004, p. 934). An intersectional approach is one important means of ensuring that the main thrust of the social identity tradition, which is to understand human social interaction in its social and historical context, is preserved (Reicher, 2004, p. 921).

As Shields (2008) argued, intersectionality is an urgent issue for psychology for several reasons, some of which I hope I illustrated in this chapter. First, focusing on gender alone elides, or erases, the experiences of women from marginalized groups (Bowleg, 2008; Collins, 1989; Crenshaw, 1993; Purdie-Vaughns & Eibach, 2008). Second, an intersectional perspective enables us to move beyond our own ethnocentric construals and attempt to understand the world from the standpoint of others (Aptheker, 1989; Caraway, 1991; Collins, 1989; hooks, 1984;

Hopkins et al., 2006; King, 2003; Yuval-Davis, 1997). Psychologists who adopt an intersectional approach can enhance experimental and quantitative research by shifting the focus from the researcher's subjectivity to the participant's subjectivity.

Third, I hope I also illustrated that the adoption of an intersectional perspective in research conducted in the social identity tradition is urgently needed if, like Reicher and Hopkins (2001), we want to grow a social psychology that contributes to a progressive agenda for social change. An intersectional approach not only keeps us alive to the importance of context in understanding group phenomena such as group consciousness and social change, it is a theoretical tool for centering the experiences of marginalized groups. It is a means for preserving our capacity for imagining alternative worlds (Reicher & Hopkins, 2001, p. 401). An intersectional approach is not only fundamentally compatible with the social identity tradition, it is a crucial means through which researchers active in this tradition can remain true to its spirit.

References

Almquist, E. M. (1975). Untangling the effects of race and sex: The disadvantaged status of Black women. *Social Science Quarterly, 56*, 129–142.

Alperin, D. J. (1990). Social diversity and the necessity of alliances: A developing feminist perspective. In L. Albrecht & R. M. Brewer (Eds.), *Bridges of power: Women's multicultural alliances* (pp. 22–33). Philadelphia, PA: New Society.

Aptheker, B. (1989). *Tapestries of life: women's work, women's consciousness and the meaning of daily experience*. Amherst, MA: University of Massachusetts Press.

Ashmore, R. D., Deaux, K., & McLaughlin-Volpe, T. (2004). An organizing framework for collective identity: Articulation and significance of multidimensionality. *Psychological Bulletin, 130*, 80–114. doi:10.1037/0033-2909.130.1.80

Baxter, S., & Lansing, M. (1983). *Women and politics: The visible majority* (Rev. ed.). Ann Arbor, MI: University of Michigan Press.

Berger, T. M., & Guidroz, K. (Eds.). (2009). Introduction. *The intersectional approach: Transforming the academy through race, class and gender* (pp. 1–24). Chapel Hill, NC: The University of North Carolina Press.

Billig, M., & Tajfel, H. (1973). Social categorization and similarity in intergroup behavior. *European Journal of Social Psychology, 3*, 27–52. doi:10.1002/ejsp.2420030103

Bowleg, L. (2008). When Black + lesbian + woman ≠ Black lesbian women: The methodological challenges of qualitative and quantitative intersectionality research. *Sex Roles, 59*, 312–325. doi:10.1007/s11199-008-9400-z

Brown, E. B. (1989). African-American women's quilting: A framework for conceptualizing and teaching African-American women's history. *Signs, 14*, 921–929. doi:10.1086/494553

Caraway, N. (1991). *Segregated sisterhood: Racism and the politics of American feminism*. Knoxville: The University of Tennessee Press.

Cole, E. R. (2009). Intersectionality and research in psychology. *American Psychologist, 64*, 170–180. doi:10.1037/a0014564

Cole, E. R., & Sabik, N. J. (2009). Repairing the broken mirror: Intersectional approaches to diverse women's perceptions of beauty and bodies. In M. T. Berger & K. Guidroz (Eds.), *The intersectional approach: Transforming the academy through race, class, & gender* (pp. 173–192). Chapel Hill: The University of North Carolina Press.

Cole, E. R., Zucker, A. N., & Ostrove, J. M. (1998). Political participation and feminist consciousness among women activists of the 1960s. *Political Psychology, 19*, 349–371. doi:10.1111/0162-895X.00108

Collins, P. H. (1989). The social construction of Black feminist thought. *Signs, 14*, 745–773. doi:10.1086/494543

Collins, P. H. (1990). Black feminist thought: Knowledge, consciousness, and the politics of empowerment. New York, NY: Routledge.

Condor, S. (1989). "Biting into the future": Social change and the social identity of women. In S. Skevington & D. Baker (Eds.), *The social identity of women* (pp. 15–39). London, England: Sage.

Crenshaw, K. W. (1993). Mapping the margins: Intersectionality, identity politics, and violence against women. In M. A. Fineman & R. Mykitiuk (Eds.), *The public nature of private violence* (pp. 93–120). New York, NY: Routledge.

Deaux, K. (1992). Personalizing identity and socializing self. In G. Breakwell (Ed.), *Social psychology of identity and the self-concept* (pp. 9–33). San Diego, CA: Academic Press.

Deaux, K. (1993). Reconstructing social identity. *Personality and Social Psychology Bulletin, 19*, 4–12. doi:10.1177/0146167293191001

Deaux, K., & Major, B. (1987). Putting gender into context: An interactive model of gender-related behavior. *Psychological Review, 94*, 369–389. doi:10.1037/0033-295X.94.3.369

Deaux, K., & Martin, D. (2003). Interpersonal networks and social categories: Specifying levels of context in identity processes. *Social Psychology Quarterly, 66*, 101–117. doi:10.2307/1519842

Deaux, K., Reid, A., Mizrahi, K., & Ethier, K. A. (1995). Parameters of social identity. *Journal of Personality and Social Psychology, 2*, 280–291. doi:10.1037/0022-3514.68.2.280

Dill, B. T. (2009). Race, class, and gender: Prospects for an all-inclusive sisterhood. In M. T. Berger & K. Guidroz (Eds.), *The intersectional approach: Transforming the academy through race, class, & gender* (pp. 25–43). Chapel Hill: The University of North Carolina Press.

Doosje, B., Spears, R., & Ellemers, N. (2002). Social identity cause and effect: The development of group identification in response to anticipated and actual changes in the intergroup status hierarchy. *British Journal of Social Psychology, 41*, 57–76. doi:10.1348/014466602165054

Duncan, L. E. (1999). Motivation for collective action: Group consciousness as mediator of personality, life experiences, and women's rights activism. *Political Psychology, 20*, 611–635. doi:10.1111/0162-895X.00159

Duncan, L. E. & Stewart, A. J. (2000). A generational analysis of women's rights activists. *Psychology of Women Quarterly, 24*, 297–308.

Ellemers, N. (1993). The influence of sociostructural variables on identity management strategies. In W. Stroebe & M. Hewstone (Eds.), *European review of social psychology* (Vol. 4, pp. 22–57). Oxford, England: Blackwell.

Ellemers, N., Barreto, M., & Spears, R. (1999). Commitment and strategic responses to social context. In N. Ellemers, R. Spears, & B. Doosje, (Eds.), *Social identity: Context, commitment, content* (pp. 127–146). Oxford, England: Blackwell.

Ellemers, N., Spears, R., & Doosje, B. (1997). Sticking together or falling apart: Ingroup identification as a psychological determinant of group commitment versus individual mobility. *Journal of Personality and Social Psychology, 72*, 617–626. doi:10.1037/0022-3514.72.3.617

Ellemers, N., Spears, R., & Doosje, B. (2002). Self and social identity. *Annual Review of Psychology, 53*, 161–186. doi:10.1146/annurev.psych.53.100901.135228

Esqueda, C. W., & Harrison, L. A. (2005). The influence of gender roles stereotypes, the woman's race, and the level of provocation and resistance on domestic violence culpability attributions. *Sex Roles, 53*, 821–834. doi:10.1007/11199s-005-8295-1

Fox-Genovese, E. (1986). Strategies and forms of resistance: Focus on slave women in the United States. In G. Y. Okihiro (Ed.), *In resistance: Studies in African, Caribbean and Afro-American History* (pp. 143–165). Amherst, MA: University of Massachusetts Press.

Gay, C., & Tate, K. (1998). Doubly bound: The impact of gender and race on the politics of Black women. *Political Psychology, 19*, 169–184. doi:10.1111/0162-895X.00098

Goff, P. A., Thomas, M. A., & Jackson, M. C. (2008). "Ain't I a woman?": Towards an intersectional approach to perception and group-based harms. *Sex Roles, 59*, 392–403. doi:10.1007/s11199-008-9505-4

Greenwood, R. M. (2008). Intersectional political consciousness: Appreciation for intergroup differences and solidarity in diverse groups. *Psychology of Women Quarterly, 32*, 36–47. doi:10.1111/j.1471-6402.2007.00405.x

Greenwood, R. M., & Christian, A. W. (2008). What happens when we unpack the invisible knapsack? Intersectional political consciousness and intergroup appraisals. *Sex Roles, 59*, 404–417. doi:10.1007/s11199-008-9439-x

Greenwood, R. M. & Christian, A. W. (2010, February). *What happens when we unpack the invisible knapsack? Intersectional consciousness and intergroup appraisals*. In S. Shields (Session Chair), Intersectionality of social identities: A gender perspective. Paper presented at the Annual Conference of the Association for Women in Psychology, Portland, OR.

Griffin, C. (1989). 'I'm not a Women's libber but . . . ': Feminism, consciousness, and identity. In S. Skevington & D. Baker (Eds.), *The social identity of women* (pp. 173–193). London, England: Sage.

Guidroz, K., & Berger, M. T. (2009). A conversation with founding scholars of intersectionality Kimberle Crenshaw, Nira Yuval-Davis, and Michelle Fine. In M. T. Berger & K. Guidroz (Eds.), *The intersectional approach: Transforming the academy through race, class, & gender* (pp. 61–78). Chapel Hill, NC: The University of North Carolina Press.

Gurin, P. (1985). Women's gender consciousness. *Public Opinion Quarterly*, *49*, 143–163. doi:10.1086/268911

Gurin, P., & Markus, H. (1989). Cognitive consequences of gender identity. In S. Skevington & D. Baker (Eds.), *The social identity of women* (pp. 152–173). London, England: Sage.

Gurin, P., Miller, A. H., & Gurin, G. (1980). Stratum identification and consciousness. *Social Psychology Quarterly*, *43*, 30–47. doi:10.2307/3033746

Gurin, T., & Townsend, A. (1986). Properties of gender identity and their implications for gender consciousness. *British Journal of Social Psychology*, *25*, 139–148. doi:10.1111/j.2044-8309. 1986.tb00712.x

Henderson-King, D., & Stewart, A. J. (1994). Women or feminist? Assessing women's group consciousness. *Sex Roles*, *31*, 505–516. doi:10.1007/BF01544276

Henderson-King, D., & Stewart, A. J. (1999). Educational experiences and shifts in group consciousness: studying women. *Personality and Social Psychology Bulletin*, *25*, 390–399. doi:10.1177/0146167299025003010

Henley, N. M., Meng, K., O'Brien, D., McCarthy, W. J., & Sockloskie, R. J. (1998). Developing a scale to measure the diversity of feminist attitudes. *Psychology of Women Quarterly*, *22*, 317–348. doi:10.1111/j.1471-6402.1998.tb00158.x

Henley, N. M., Spalding, L. R., & Kosta, A. (2000). Development of the short form of the feminist perspectives scale. *Psychology of Women Quarterly*, *24*, 254–256. doi:10.1111/j.1471-6402.2000. tb00207.x

Hogg, M. A., & Turner, J. C. (1987). Intergroup behavior, self-stereotyping, and the salience of social categories. *British Journal of Social Psychology*, *26*, 325–340. doi:10.1111/j.2044-8309.1987. tb00795.x

hooks, b. (1984). *Feminist theory from margin to center*. Boston, MA: Southend Press.

Hopkins, N., Kahani-Hopkins, V., & Reicher, S. (2006). Identity and social change: Contextualizing agency. *Feminism & Psychology*, *16*, 52–57. doi:10.1177/0959-353506060820

Huddy, L. (2004). Contrasting theoretical approaches to intergroup relations. *Political Psychology*, *25*, 947–967.

Hurtado, A. (2008). "Superserviceable feminism": Revisiting *Toward a new psychology of women*. *Feminism and Psychology, 18*, 341–346.

Jack Straw on the veil. (2006). Retrieved from http://news.bbc.co.uk/2/hi/uk_news/politics/5413470.stm

Jeffries, V., & Ransford, H. E. (1980). *Social stratification: A multiple hierarchy approach*. Boston, MA: Allyn & Bacon.

Jost, J. T., & Banaji, M. R. (1994). The role of stereotyping in system-justification and the production of false consciousness. *British Journal of Social Psychology, 33*, 1–27.

Jost, J. T., Banaji, M. R., & Nosek, B. A. (2004). A decade of system justification theory: Accumulated evidence of conscious and unconscious bolstering of the status quo. *Political Psychology, 25*, 881–919.

Jost, J. T., Burgess, D., & Mosso, C. (2001). Conflicts of legitimation among self, group, and system: The integrative potential of system justification theory. In J. T. Jost & B. Major (Eds.), *The psychology of legitimacy: Emerging perspectives on ideology, justice, and intergroup relations* (pp. 363–388). New York, NY: Cambridge University Press.

Jost, J. T., Kruglanski, A. W., Glaser, J., & Sulloway, F. J. (2003a). Political conservatism as motivated social cognition. *Psychological Bulletin, 129*, 339–375.

Jost, J. T., Kruglanski, A. W., Glaser, J., & Sulloway, F. J. (2003b). Exceptions that prove the rule: Using a theory of motivated cognition to account for ideological incongruities and political anomalies: Reply to Greenberg and Jonas (2003). *Psychological Bulletin, 129*, 383–393.

Jost, J. T., Napier, J. L., Thorisdottir, H., Gosling, S. D., Palfai, T. P., & Ostafin, B. (2007). Are needs to manage threat associated with political conservatism or ideological extremism? *Personality and Social Psychology Bulletin, 33,* 989.

Kalmuss, D., Gurin, P., & Townsend, A. L. (1981). Feminist and sympathetic feminist consciousness. *European Journal of Social Psychology, 11,* 131–147.

Kelly, C., & Breinlinger, S. (1995a). Attitudes, intentions, and behavior: A study of women's participation in collective action. *Journal of Applied Social Psychology, 25,* 1430–1445.

Kelly, C., & Breinlinger, S. (1995b). Identity and injustice: Exploring women's participation in collective action. *Journal of Community and Applied Social Psychology, 5,* 41–57.

Kelly, C., & Breinlinger, S. (1996). *The social psychology of collective action: Identity, injustice and gender.* London, England: Taylor & Francis.

King, K. R. (2003). Do you see what I see? Effects of group consciousness on African American women's attributions to prejudice. *Psychology of Women's Quarterly, 27,* 17–30.

Klein, E. (1984). *Gender politics.* Cambridge, MA: Harvard University Press.

Leyens, J. P., Yzerbyt, V., & Schadron, G. (1994). *Stereotypes and social cognition.* London, England: Sage.

Lorde, A. (1984). *Sister outsider: Essays & speeches.* Berkeley, CA: Crossing Press.

Mansbridge, J., & Tate, K. (1992). Race trumps gender: Black opinion on the Thomas nomination. *Political Science and Politics, 25,* 488–492.

McCarney, J. (2005). Marx myths and legends: Ideology and false consciousness. Retrieved from http://marxmyths.org/joseph-mccarney/article.htm

McIntosh, P. (1990). White privilege: Unpacking the invisible knapsack. *Independent School, 49,* 31–36.

Miller, A. H., Gurin, P., Gurin, G., & Malanchuk, O. (1981). Group consciousness and political participation. *American Journal of Political Science, 23,* 494–511.

Minnich, E. K. (2005). *Transforming knowledge* (2nd ed.). Philadelphia, PA: Temple University Press.

Mummendey, A., & Wenzel, M. (1999). Social discrimination and tolerance in intergroup relations: Reactions to intergroup difference. *Personality and Social Psychology Review, 3,* 158–174.

Onorato, R. S., & Turner, J. C. (2004). Fluidity in the self-concept: The shift from personal to social identity. *European Journal of Social Psychology, 34,* 257–278.

Pence, E. (1982). Racism—A White issue. In G. T. Hull, P. B. Scott, & B. Smith (Eds.), *All the women are White, all the Blacks are men, but some of us are brave* (pp. 45–47). New York, NY: Feminist Press.

Pheterson, G. (1990). Alliances between women: Overcoming internalized oppression and internalized domination. In L. Albrecht & R. M. Brewer (Eds.), *Bridges of power: Women's multicultural alliances* (pp. 34–48). Philadelphia, PA: New Society Publishers.

Purdie-Vaughns, V., & Eibach, R. P. (2008). Intersectional invisibility: The distinctive advantages and disadvantages of multiple subordinate group identities. *Sex Roles, 59,* 377–391.

Reagon, B. J. (1983). Coalition politics: Turning the century. In B. Smith (Ed.), *Home girls: A Black feminist anthology* (pp. 356–368), New York, NY: Kitchen Table Press.

Reicher, S. (2004). The context of social identity: Domination, resistance, and change. *Political Psychology, 25,* 921–945.

Reicher, S., & Hopkins, N. P. (2001). Psychology and the end of history: A critique and a proposal for the psychology of social categorization. *Political Psychology, 22,* 383–406.

Reicher, S., Spears, R., & Postmes, T. (1995). A social identity model of deindividuation phenomena. *European Review of Social Psychology, 6,* 161–198.

Roccas, S., & Brewer, M. B. (2002). Social identity complexity. *Personality and Social Psychology Review, 6,* 88–106.

Rubin, M., & Hewstone, M. (2004). Social identity, system justification, and social dominance: Commentary on Reicher, Jost et al., and Sidanius et al. *Political Psychology, 25,* 823–844.

School sacks woman after veil row. (2006, November 24). *BBC News.* Retrieved from http://news.bbc.co.uk/2/hi/uk_news/england/bradford/6179842.stm

Scott, J. C. (1985). Weapons of the weak: Everyday forms of peasant resistance. New Haven, CT: Yale University Press.

Settles, I. H. (2006). Use of an intersectional framework to understand Black women's racial and gender identities. *Sex Roles, 54,* 589–601.

Settles, I. H., Pratt-Hyatt, J. S., & Buchanan, N. T. (2008). Through the lens of race: Black and White women's perceptions of womanhood. *Psychology of Women Quarterly, 32,* 454–468.

Sherif, C. (1998). Bias in psychology. *Feminist Psychology*, 8, 58–75.

Shields, S. A. (2008). Gender: An intersectional perspective. *Sex Roles, 59*, 301–311.

Skevington, S., & Baker, D. (Eds.). (1989). *The social identity of women*. London, England: Sage.

Spears, R., Greenwood, R. M., de Lemus, S., & Sweetman, J. (2010). Legitimacy, social identity and power. In A. Guinote & T. K. Vescio (Eds.), *The social psychology of power* (pp. 251–283), New York, NY: Guilford Press.

Spears, R., Jetten, J., & Doosje, B. (2001). The (il)legitimacy of ingroup bias: From social reality to social resistance. In J. Jost & B. Major (Eds.), *The psychology of legitimacy: Emerging perspectives on ideology, justice inter-group relations* (pp. 332–362). New York, NY: Cambridge University Press.

Spears, R. & Lea, M. (1994). Panacea or panopticon: The hidden power in computer-mediated communication. *Communication Research, 21,* 427–459.

Spelman, E. V. (1988). *Inessential woman: Problems of exclusion in feminist thought*. London, England: Women's Press.

Stewart, A. J., & Gold-Steinberg, S. (1990). Midlife women's political consciousness. *Psychology of Women's Quarterly, 14,* 543–566.

Stewart, A. J., & McDermott, C. (2004). Gender in psychology. *Annual Review Psychology, 55,* 519–544.

Subasic, E., Reynolds, K. J., & Turner, J. C. (2008). The political solidarity model of social change: Dynamics of self-categorization in intergroup power relations. *Personality and Social Psychology Review, 12,* 330–352.

Tajfel, H. (1978). *Differentiation between social groups*. London, England: Academic Press.

Tajfel, H. (1979). Individuals and groups in social psychology. *British Journal of Social & Clinical Psychology, 18,* 183–190.

Tajfel, H. (1982). Social psychology of intergroup relations. *Annual Review of Psychology, 33,* 1–39.

Tajfel, H., Billig, M. G., Bundy, R. P., & Flament, C. (1971). Social categorization and intergroup behavior. *European Journal of Social Psychology, 1,* 149–178.

Tajfel, H., & Turner, J. C., (1979). An integrative theory of intergroup conflict. In W. G. Austin & S. Worchel (Eds.), *The social psychology of intergroup relations*, (pp. 33–48). Monterey, CA: Brooks/Cole.

Terborg-Penn, R. (1986). Black women in resistance: A cross-cultural perspective. In G. Y. Okihiro (Ed.), *In resistance: Studies in African, Caribbean and Afro-American History* (pp. 188–209). Amherst, MA: University of Massachusetts Press.

Torrey, J. (1979). Racism and feminism: Is women's liberation for whites only? *Psychology of Women Quarterly, 4,* 281–293.

Turner, J. C. (1975). Social comparison and social identity: Some prospects for intergroup behavior. *European Journal of Social Psychology, 5,* 5–34.

Turner, J. C. (1981). The experimental social psychology of intergroup behavior. In J. C. Turner & H. Giles (Eds.), *Intergroup behavior* (pp. 66–101). Oxford, UK: Blackwell.

Turner, J. C. (1999). Some current issues in research on social identity and self-categorization theories (pp. 6–34). In N. Ellemers, R. Spears, & B. Doosje (Eds.), *Social identity: Context, commitment, content*. Oxford, UK: Blackwell.

Turner, J. C., & Brown, R. (1978). Social status, cognitive alternatives, and intergroup relations. In H. Tajfel (Ed.), *Differentiation between social groups* (pp. 201–234). San Diego, CA: Academic Press.

Turner, J. C., Hogg, M. A., Oakes, P. J., Reicher, S. D., & Wetherell, M. (1987). *Rediscovering the social group: A self-categorization theory*. Oxford, England: Blackwell.

Warner, L. R. (2008). A best practices guide to intersectional approaches in psychological research. *Sex Roles, 59,* 454–463.

Werbner, P. (2000). Divided loyalties, empowered citizenship? Muslims in Britain. *Citizenship Studies, 4,* 307–24.

Wilcox, C. (1990). Black women and feminism. *Women and Politics, 10,* 65–84.

Yuval-Davis, N. (1997). *Gender and nation*. Thousand Oaks, CA: Sage.

Zucker, A. N. (2004). Disavowing social identities: What it means when women say "I'm not a Feminist but . . . ". *Psychology of Women Quarterly, 28,* 423–435.

Part III

Immigration

7

The Dehumanization of Refugees: Determinants and Consequences

Victoria M. Esses, Scott Veenvliet, and Stelian Medianu

In her 2006 volume, *To Be an Immigrant*, Kay Deaux persuasively argued that in analyzing the immigrant experience, social psychology perhaps has the most to offer at the mid-level of analysis—that is, at the intersection of macro forces and individual cognitions and feelings. Deaux's own work at this intersection has focused mainly on the experiences of immigrants and their perceptions of how they fit into American society. In this chapter, we provide a complementary focus and examine this intersection as it applies to how members of host societies view a particularly vulnerable category of immigrants—refugees. In particular, we focus on societal forces that can lead to the dehumanization of refugees and the processes and consequences of this dehumanization. The questions we address include: How do macro societal concerns become translated into individual attitudes and beliefs about refugees? What role do the media play in promoting particular representations of refugees and in the dehumanization of refugees? What function does this dehumanization serve and how does it affect attitudes toward refugees and support for relevant policies?

In discussing research that addresses these questions, we consider both the theoretical contributions of our work and its application to understanding and perhaps ameliorating the dire circumstances of the growing population of refugees worldwide. We argue that the simple process of categorizing a person as a *refugee*—a political term intended to convey a person's status with respect to home country and the country in which he or she is seeking refuge—has become imbued with meaning that goes well beyond political and legal definitions to include presumed motivations and characteristics. This extra baggage contributes to the social construction of the category *refugee* and the meaning we attach to it, influencing how we see and treat members of the group.

It is estimated that there are currently over 10 million refugees worldwide, with a substantial number seeking resettlement opportunities (United Nations High Commissioner for Refugees, 2010). The international community formalized its obligation to these individuals through the 1951 Geneva Refugee Convention and its 1967 Protocol. The 1951 Convention was put into place to protect European refugees after World War II, and the 1967 Protocol expanded

Preparation of this article was supported by a Social Sciences and Humanities Research Council of Canada grant to Victoria M. Esses.

the Convention's scope to apply to refugees from all locations and at any time. To date, there are 147 signatories to the Convention or its Protocol (United Nations High Commissioner for Refugees, 2010). Under the Convention and its Protocol, refugees are defined as

> individuals who, because of a well-founded fear of persecution for reasons of race, religion, nationality, membership in a particular social group, or political opinion, are outside their country of nationality or habitual residence, and are unable or unwilling by reason of that fear to return to that country. (Citizenship and Immigration Canada, 2008, p. 31)

Despite Western nations' stated commitment to the protection of refugees, however, individuals seeking entry into Western countries as refugees are often viewed with hostility and contempt and are perceived as not deserving of assistance (e.g., Human Rights Watch, 2009; Lusher & Haslam, 2007). Indeed, a central element of recent portrayals of refugees seems to be dehumanization—the perception that they are "less than human." For example, refugees have been described as uncivilized, lacking in morals, unhygienic, and as "cockroaches," "parasites," and "beasts" (e.g., Guterres, 2006; Henry & Tator, 2002). These attributions are then used to justify the inhumane treatment of refugees and restrictive refugee policies. By applying theoretical perspectives on dehumanization to these perceptions, we may gain insight into determinants of resistance to policies to allow refugees entry into Western countries and potential strategies for change.

At a theoretical level, there has been renewed interest in the dehumanization of outgroups (e.g., Haslam, 2006), and these recent perspectives can be rigorously tested and expanded by examining reactions to refugees. Thus, our research also makes important contributions to an understanding of dehumanization more generally, which can be applied to a variety of groups. In particular, it addresses conceptual and methodological issues surrounding the assessment of dehumanization, its determinants and potential functions, and its consequences.

Dehumanization: Conceptual and Measurement Issues

Dehumanization involves the denial of full humanness to others and their exclusion from the human species (e.g., Bar-Tal, 2000; Haslam, 2006). In an integrative review of dehumanization, Haslam (2006) suggested that an important way in which others may be denied full humanness is in an animalistic sense in which they are seen as not having risen above their animal origins. Further, Haslam suggested that this dehumanization is characterized by a perception that the dehumanized lack such characteristics as refinement, civility, morality, self-control, and cognitive sophistication. Similarly, O'Brien (2003a, 2003b) described the dehumanization of a variety of groups as involving animalization, such that group members are seen as having high procreation rates, being unable to live cultured lives, having a propensity for immoral and criminal behavior, being insensitive to pain, and being guided by instincts rather than rational thought.

Previous attempts to assess dehumanization focused on several of these specific dimensions. Leyens et al. (2000) focused on *infrahumanization*—the perception that outgroup members are less human than ingroup members—and suggested that one way of infrahumanizing outgroups is to deny that they experience complex, secondary emotions. That is, the infrahumanized may experience primary emotions (e.g., pleasure, fear) just as animals do, but they are less likely to experience secondary emotions generally attributed only to humans (e.g., hope, remorse). In a series of studies, Leyens and his colleagues (2000; see also Demoulin et al., 2004) demonstrated that both positive and negative secondary emotions are indeed more likely to be attributed to ingroup members than to outgroups, whereas primary emotions are equally attributed to both. In addition, they demonstrated that this effect is not attributable to familiarity with a group.

Another indication of dehumanization has been proposed by Schwartz and his colleagues. Schwartz and Struch (1989; see also Schwartz, Struch, & Bilsky, 1990) suggested that certain values, particularly prosocial values, are seen as hallmarks of the degree to which people have transcended their prehuman origins and developed moral sensibilities. To the extent that a group is seen as failing to uphold these values, and thus as immoral, the group is likely to be viewed as less than human. Thus, to assess dehumanization Schwartz and his colleagues used measures of the perceived values of a group (Schwartz et al., 1990; Struch & Schwartz, 1989).

In our research, we examine the dehumanization of refugees along this moral dimension in combination with several other aspects of dehumanization suggested by Haslam (2006) and O'Brien (2003a), including lack of refinement, civility, cognitive sophistication, and rational thought. In particular, in addition to assessing dehumanization using the value attributions suggested by Schwartz et al. (1990) we include an assessment of the barbarian/enemy image as proposed by Alexander, Brewer, and Herrmann (1999), which centrally includes perceptions of a group as crude, unsophisticated, and irrational, as well as immoral. We also developed a new measure to assess the extent to which a group is seen as trying to violate procedures and cheat the system. This perception of refugees is certainly prevalent in the media (e.g., Francis, 2001; see also Louis, Duck, Terry, Schuller, & Lalonde, 2007). The three measures are highly intercorrelated, suggesting that, as expected, they are tapping into an underlying dehumanization. Importantly, however, the latent variable underlying these measures has been demonstrated to be distinct from overall negative attitudes toward refugees (Esses, Veenvliet, Hodson, & Mihic, 2008), so that it is not merely tapping general negativity toward the group.

Determinants and Function of Dehumanization

An important issue our research seeks to address is why some individuals dehumanize members of other groups, particularly low-status, seemingly victimized groups such as refugees. That is, what functions might such dehumanization fulfill? We propose that the dehumanization of low-status groups in society may serve to justify the status quo and defend against threats to the ingroup position (Pratto, 1999; Sidanius & Pratto, 1999). By perceiving low-status group members as not completely part of the human ingroup, one can more easily believe that they deserve their negative outcomes and that members of more well-off groups do not have to work to increase social equality (Opotow, 1995; Schwartz & Struch, 1989). As a result, existing systems and the status quo are maintained and perpetuated (Jost & Hunyady, 2002).

Based on this reasoning, we hypothesized that *social dominance orientation* would be a strong predictor of the dehumanization of refugees. Individuals who are higher in social dominance orientation support group hierarchies and inequality in society, view the world as a competitive place in which only the toughest survive, and express a willingness to discriminate against other groups in order to attain or maintain group dominance (e.g., Duckitt, 2006; Sidanius & Pratto, 1999). These individuals are described as holding hierarchy-enhancing legitimizing beliefs that provide moral and intellectual justification for an unequal distribution of resources (e.g., Roccato & Ricolfi, 2005). Thus, higher social dominance–oriented individuals may dehumanize refugees in order to maintain group dominance and protect resources. By dehumanizing refugees, they legitimize their own entitlement to resources and justify the plight of refugees (Louis et al., 2007).

It may also be the case that in supporting the status quo, the media may promote the dehumanization of refugees (Leyens, Demoulin, Vaes, Gaunt, & Paladino, 2007). That is, media depictions of refugees that promote their dehumanization may serve as legitimizing myths for those who are members of dominant groups in society. Although there has been considerable discussion of the role of the media in promoting the dehumanization of refugees (e.g., Henry & Tator, 2002; Karim, 1988), to date research has neither experimentally evaluated this claim nor specifically addressed the function and consequences of this dehumanization. We suggest that by presenting portrayals of refugees that legitimize their plight, the message is provided that dominant group members may sit back and enjoy their resources without concern about taking remedial action to help those who are less fortunate. In doing so, existing systems and the status quo are maintained and perpetuated (Jost, Burgess, & Mosso, 2001; Wakslak, Jost, Tyler, & Chen, 2007).

To examine this issue, in our research we used a real editorial that appeared in a Canadian newspaper in 2001 and that (a) described Canada's costly refugee program and (b) promoted the dehumanization of refugees by depicting them as immoral cheaters who do not follow fair procedures (e.g., "Most are smuggled in or are queue-jumpers who lie their way into the country by pretending they cannot go home"; Francis, 2001). We hypothesized that this editorial would lead to the dehumanization of refugees and to the severe consequences of dehumanization to be discussed next.

Consequences of Dehumanization

The dehumanization of refugees may lead to specific negative emotional reactions to members of the group. In particular, as summarized by Haslam (2006), theorizing and prior research suggest that dehumanization may lead to contempt for a group. Similarly, research on the stereotype content model indicates that groups that are dehumanized through perceptions that they are low in competence and warmth elicit feelings of contempt (Fiske, Cuddy, Glick, & Xu, 2002; Harris & Fiske, 2006). It is also the case that just as anthropomorphism can turn nonhuman agents into moral agents who deserve respect and potentially admiration, dehumanization may strip humans of their moral agency and lead to lack of admiration and respect (Epley, Waytz, & Cacioppo, 2007). We expect, then, that to the extent refugees are dehumanized, they will elicit feelings of contempt and lack of admiration (see also Verkuyten, 2004).

A major goal of our research was to determine why the needs and rights of refugees are often denied, and why individuals often want to exclude refugees from their nation. Over the past decade there has been growing hostility and intolerance toward refugees in their countries of refuge (e.g., Frelick, 2010). Theorizing on dehumanization suggests that dehumanization may be a key determinant of the belief that members of a group are not worthy of fair, humane treatment, legitimizing their further victimization (e.g., Bar-Tal, 2000; Haslam, 2006; Opotow, 1995). Thus, in the current research, we hypothesized that the dehumanization of refugees would not only predict negative attitudes toward refugees but would also strongly predict support for restrictive refugee policies and lack of willingness to help refugees. In addition, based on previous research demonstrating the important role of emotions in determining attitudes (e.g., Esses, Haddock, & Zanna, 1993; Maio, Esses, Arnold, & Olson, 2004), we expected emotions to mediate the relation between dehumanization and negative attitudes toward refugees and toward current refugee policies in Canada.

Study One: Modeling Causes and Consequences of Dehumanization

Based on the previous discussion of potential determinants and consequences of dehumanization, the first study used structural equation modeling to test the model depicted in Figure 7.1 (Esses et al., 2008). We hypothesized that higher social dominance–oriented individuals would be especially likely to dehumanize refugees. This dehumanization was expected to then lead to contempt and lack of

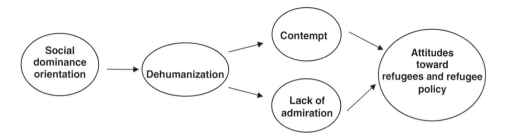

Figure 7.1. Proposed model of the role of dehumanization in leading to negative attitudes toward refugees and current refugee policy. From "Justice, Morality, and the Dehumanization of Refugees," by V. M. Esses, S. Veenvliet, G. Hodson, and L. Mihic, 2008, *Social Justice Research, 21,* p. 16. Copyright 2008 by Springer Science + Business Material, LLC. Adapted with permission.

admiration for refugees, resulting in negative attitudes toward refugees and lack of support for Canada's current refugee program, which is often described as quite open and nonrestrictive.

Participants were 132 undergraduates at the University of Western Ontario in Canada who volunteered to participate in a study of current events and social attitudes. All participants were Canadian residents, and the majority were Canadian citizens.

Participants completed a questionnaire containing measures of perceptions, emotions, and attitudes toward a variety of groups, including refugees. They also completed a variety of individual difference measures, including social dominance orientation, and provided demographic information about themselves.

Social Dominance Orientation

Social dominance orientation was assessed using the 16-item version of the scale (Pratto, Sidanius, Stallworth, & Malle, 1994), with ratings ranging from 1 (*do not agree at all*) to 7 (*strongly agree*). A sample item reads, "In getting what your group wants, it is sometimes necessary to use force against other groups." For purposes of the structural equation modeling, we used six indicators of social dominance orientation, with βs ranging from .42 to .78, $ps < 0.01$. This included four items on equality and two items on support for hierarchies.

Dehumanization

The dehumanization of refugees was assessed using three measures. First, we assessed the dehumanization of refugees through claims that they do not uphold moral values in comparison with Canadians (see Struch & Schwartz, 1989). In particular, participants rated the extent to which refugees uphold prosocial values and teach these values to their children, using three items (e.g., "Refugees raise their children to be humane"), with possible responses on each ranging from 0 (*strongly disagree*) to 4 (*strongly agree*). They also rated the extent to which Canadians uphold prosocial values and teach these values to their children using similar items. We then determined value dehumanization by calculating average scores for refugees (Cronbach's α = .81) and for Canadians (Cronbach's α = .74) and subtracting the average score for refugees from the average score for Canadians. Higher numbers thus indicate increasing dehumanization of refugees relative to the ingroup.

We also assessed enemy and barbarian images of refugees (see Alexander et al., 1999). Participants were asked to respond to a series of questions regarding their perceptions of refugees, including three items that assessed an enemy image (e.g., "Refugees would take advantage of any efforts on our part to cooperate, and they would even try to exploit us"), and three items that assessed a barbarian image (e.g., "Refugees are crude, unsophisticated, and willing to cheat to get their way") with possible responses on each ranging from 1 (*strongly disagree*) to 7 (*strongly agree*). Because factor analysis indicated that the enemy and barbarian images were not distinct, we calculated average scores across all six items (Cronbach's α = .87; see also Alexander et al., 2005). Higher scores indicate increasing dehumanization of refugees.

Finally, we included a measure of the extent to which potential refugees are seen as trying to violate procedures and cheat the system in claiming refugee status, which was developed specifically for the purpose of our research (Esses et al., 2008; based on Leventhal, 1980). In particular, participants responded to six items (e.g., "The problem with potential refugees to Canada is that they try to 'cheat the system'"), with possible responses on each ranging from −4 (strongly disagree) to +4 (strongly agree). Average scores across the six items were calculated (Cronbach's α = .82), with higher scores indicating increasing dehumanization of refugees.

For purposes of the structural equation modeling, we used the mean scores for value dehumanizing, enemy/barbarian images, and perceived procedural violation as indicators for dehumanization, with βs ranging from .54 to .85, ps < .001.

Emotions

Emotions toward refugees were assessed using a measure developed by Fiske et al. (2002). In particular, participants were asked to respond to a 15-item measure that asked them to rate the extent to which they felt a variety of emotions toward refugees, on 7-point scales ranging from 1 (not at all) to 7 (extremely). Contempt toward refugees was assessed using eight items (e.g., disgusted, angry, hateful, resentful). Lack of admiration for refugees was assessed using five items (e.g., admiring, fond, respectful—all reversed scored). For purposes of the structural equation modeling, the eight items used to assess contempt were used as indicators of contempt, with βs ranging from .52 to .80, ps < .001. Similarly, the five items used to assess lack of admiration were used as indicators of lack of admiration, with βs ranging from .64 to .80, ps < .001.

Attitudes Toward Refugees and Toward Canada's Refugee Policy

A five-item measure was used to assess attitudes toward refugees and toward Canada's refugee policy. Attitudes toward refugees were assessed first using a thermometer measure ranging from 0° (extremely unfavorable) to 100° (extremely favorable). This measure has been successfully used in past research in a variety of contexts and has been shown to be reliable and valid (e.g., Esses et al., 1993). To assess attitudes toward refugees, we also used two 9-point bipolar rating scales (−4 to +4), with one ranging from extremely unfavorable to extremely favorable and the other ranging from extremely negative to extremely positive. Attitudes toward Canada's current refugee policy were assessed using two 9-point rating scales −4 to +4), with one asking whether the number of refugees allowed into Canada should be decreased or increased and the other asking whether refugees to Canada should be discouraged or encouraged. Because attitudes toward refugees and toward Canada's refugee policy were so highly related, all five items were used as indicators of attitudes, with βs ranging from .69 to .95, ps < .001.

Findings

Structural equation modeling with latent variables was used to test the pre-dicted model. Using AMOS 5 software, we first tested whether the latent vari-ables were distinct by contrasting a series of models in which we included a single constraint between two constructs with a model in which the constructs were allowed to covary freely (i.e., no constraints). These analyses supported the utility of maintaining all the constructs in the model, including the impor-tant distinction between dehumanization and overall attitudes. Using the AMOS 5 software, we then tested the proposed model of dehumanization illustrated in Figure 7.1. The results of these analyses are shown in Figure 7.2. This model fit the data well, X^2 = 454.21, df = 312, p < .001; GFI-hat = .97; comparative fit index = .94; root mean square error of approximation = .059. As shown in Figure 7.2, each of the paths was highly significant, with social dominance orientation leading to the dehumanization of refugees, dehuman-ization resulting in contempt and lack of admiration for refugees, and these emotions leading to negative attitudes toward refugees and toward Canada's current refugee policy. We also tested models that included a variety of direct paths, but none of these paths improved the fit of the model significantly. Similarly, tests of alternative models and sequences resulted in poorer fits to the data.

The results of this study supported our predictions regarding the dehuman-ization of refugees. We found that individuals who were higher in social domi-nance orientation were especially likely to dehumanize refugees by perceiving them as less characterized by human qualities of morality (Alexander et al., 1999; Schwartz & Struch, 1989). As a result, they expressed more negative emotions toward refugees, which resulted in more negative attitudes toward refugees and toward Canada's current refugee policy. This highlights the crucial

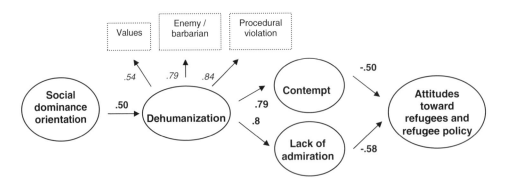

Figure 7.2. Structural equation model of the relations among social dominance orien-tation, dehumanization of refugees, contempt and lack of admiration for refugees, and attitudes toward refugees and refugee policy. Standardized beta weights are indicated on the figure paths. All beta weights are highly significantly at p < .001. From "Justice, Morality, and the Dehumanization of Refugees," by V. M. Esses, S. Veenvliet, G. Hodson, and L. Mihic, 2008, *Social Justice Research, 21*, p. 16. Copyright 2008 by Springer Science + Business Material, LLC. Reprinted with permission.

role of dehumanization in promoting contempt and lack of admiration for refugees, more negative attitudes toward refugees, and lack of support for current refugee policies. The strong relation with social dominance orientation suggests that dehumanization may be a legitimizing myth (Sidanius & Pratto, 1999) that provides moral justification for doing nothing to address refugees' dire plight. By dehumanizing refugees, high social dominance–oriented individuals can justify the status quo and defend against potential threats to their dominant position in society.

Study Two: The Role of the Media

Our second study approached the issue of dehumanization slightly differently, focusing on the role of the media in promoting dehumanization of refugees and the negative emotions and negative attitudes toward refugees and Canada's refugee policy that might result (Esses et al., 2008). This is an important issue to address because media depictions of refugees as immoral individuals who attempt to cheat the system are common (see Clarkson, 2000; Haslam & Pedersen, 2007; People Not Profit, 2005), and these depictions may serve to reinforce the dehumanization of refugees. Indeed, this point is reinforced by media attention to the arrival of a boatload of Tamil asylum-seekers off the coast of British Columbia, Canada, in August 2010. Depictions of the refugees as queue-jumpers who were attempting to abuse the system were extremely common (see Aulakh, 2010).

Thus, in the second study we randomly assigned participants to read one of two newspaper editorials on refugees to Canada and examined their reactions to the editorials and their subsequent perceptions of refugees and of Canada's refugee policy. In the experimental condition, participants read a real editorial that appeared in a Canadian newspaper in 2001 that described Canada's costly refugee program and dehumanized refugees by depicting them as immoral cheaters who do not follow fair procedures (e.g., "Most are smuggled in or are queue-jumpers who lie their way into the country by pretending they cannot go home"; Francis, 2001). In the control condition, we adapted this editorial so that it described Canada's costly refugee program but did not dehumanize refugees. We predicted that the editorial presented in the experimental condition (the *real* editorial) would promote dehumanization, leading to increased contempt and lack of admiration for refugees and more negative attitudes toward refugees and toward Canada's current refugee policy.

Participants were 38 undergraduates at the University of Western Ontario in Canada who volunteered to participate in a study of social attitudes. All were Canadian residents, and the majority were Canadian citizens.

Participants were asked to complete a number of measures relating to social attitudes, including those used for the study. Participants were told that we were interested in their perceptions of and reactions to newspaper articles about current affairs and that they would be asked to read an editorial about current affairs in Canada and to answer some questions about it. They were also asked to provide demographic information about themselves.

Editorials

Participants were randomly assigned to read one of two editorials about Canada's refugee policy. In both cases, the editorial described the high cost of Canada's current refugee policy. For example, the editorials stated, "'We send the federal government a bill every month for our portion [20%] of costs for refugees. We have done so for the past three years. Last year, our 20% totaled $1.5-million,' Hazel McCallion, Mayor of Mississauga, said."

The editorial used in the experimental condition went on to promote the dehumanization of refugees by describing them as immoral individuals who are trying to cheat the system. For example, it stated,

> Refugees are not people who have been displaced and are brought in for humanitarian reasons into Canada. Only a few are in that category. Most are smuggled in or are queue-jumpers who lie their way into the country by pretending they cannot go home and get all the entitlements they need immediately. . . . These people come here by plane, have passports when they board then flush them down the toilet and declare refugee status, even when they are from rich countries.

The editorial used in the control condition went on to provide a definition of refugees and then stated, "These people come here by plane, but have nowhere further to go once they arrive. They sign up for social assistance until they can get themselves settled and look for work."

Dehumanization

To determine whether the experimental editorial led to increased dehumanization of refugees, we included two of the same measures used in Study 1: perceived procedural violation (1–9 scale) and enemy/barbarian images (1–7 scale). Mean scores were calculated for each, and both were reliable (Cronbach's α: perceived procedural violation = .83; enemy/barbarian images = .87).

Emotions

Emotions toward refugees were assessed using the same 15-item measure used in the first study (1–7 scale). Contempt toward refugees was calculated as the mean of eight items (Cronbach's α = .88). Lack of admiration for refugees was calculated as the mean of five items (Cronbach's α = .87).

Attitudes Toward Refugees and Toward Canada's Refugee Policy

To assess attitudes toward refugees and toward Canada's refugee policy, we used the four ratings of attitudes toward refugees and Canada's refugee policy from Study 1 (−4 to +4 scale), with two assessing attitudes toward refugees and two assessing attitudes toward Canada's current refugee policy (Cronbach's α = .95).

Findings

As predicted, participants who read the experimental condition editorial were significantly more likely to dehumanize refugees than participants who read the control condition editorial; perceived procedural violation: $Ms = 5.33$ and 4.19, respectively, $t(36) = 2.63$, $p = .012$; enemy/barbarian image: $Ms = 3.05$ and 2.34, respectively, $t(36) = 2.27$, $p = .03$. Thus, the experimental condition editorial had the expected effect of dehumanizing refugees.

Because the editorial in the experimental condition led to the dehumanization of refugees, we expected that participants who read it would also be likely to express contempt and lack of admiration for refugees. The results fit this prediction. Participants who read the experimental condition editorial expressed more contempt toward refugees than did those who read the control condition editorial, $Ms = 2.57$ and 1.85, respectively, $t(36) = 2.13$, $p < .05$. Similarly, participants who read the experimental condition editorial expressed more lack of admiration for refugees than those who read the control condition editorial, $Ms = 4.52$ and 3.41, respectively, $t(36) = 2.84$, $p < .01$.

We also predicted that the editorial that promoted the dehumanization of refugees would cause participants to express more negative attitudes toward refugees and toward Canada's refugee policy. In support of this prediction, participants who read the experimental condition editorial expressed significantly more negative attitudes toward refugees and toward Canada's refugee policy than participants who read the control condition editorial, $Ms = 0.17$ and 1.88, respectively, $t(36) = 3.70$, $p < .001$.

Two separate mediational analyses were conducted to determine whether contempt and lack of admiration toward refugees mediated the effect of reading the experimental condition editorial on attitudes. As shown in Figure 7.3, lack of admiration significantly mediated the effect of condition on attitudes toward refugees and refugee policy, with the effect of condition reduced considerably. The Sobel test for the indirect effect of condition was significant, $z = -2.62$, $p < .01$. Contempt also partially mediated the effect of condition on attitudes toward refugees and refugee policy, with the effect of condition somewhat reduced. In this case, the Sobel test for the indirect effect of condition was marginally significant, $z = -1.86$, $p < .06$. These results suggest that the editorial that promoted the dehumanization of refugees led to negative attitudes toward refugees and refugee policy because it promoted a lack of admiration and contempt for refugees.

Overall, this study demonstrates that the media can indeed promote the dehumanization of refugees. In particular, the experimental condition editorial led participants to be especially likely to dehumanize refugees. What is noteworthy is that the editorial used in this condition was a real editorial that appeared in a Canadian newspaper. In contrast, the control condition editorial contained identical information about the high cost of Canada's refugee policy, but removed the suggestion that refugee claimants often lie and cheat to get ahead.

Of importance, we found that the editorial that specifically promoted the dehumanization of refugees led to more lack of admiration for refugees, more contempt, and less favorable attitudes toward refugees and Canada's current refugee policy. In addition, lack of admiration and contempt mediated the effect

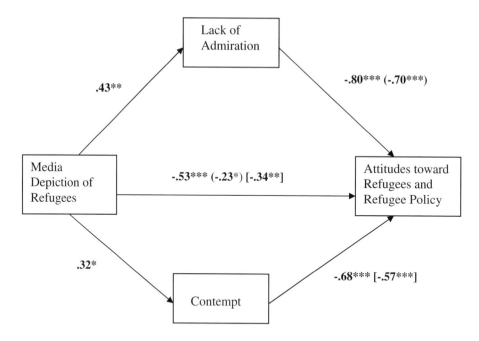

Figure 7.3. Lack of admiration and contempt as mediators of the effect of the editorials on attitudes toward refugees and refugee policy. Dummy coding of Editorial Condition (control = 0, experimental = 1). Numbers represent the standardized regression coefficients. Numbers in parentheses represent the standardized regression coefficients when editorial condition and lack of admiration are used together to predict attitudes. Numbers in square brackets represent the standardized regression coefficients when editorial condition and contempt are used together to predict attitudes. From "Justice, Morality, and the Dehumanization of Refugees," by V. M. Esses, S. Veenvliet, G. Hodson, and L. Mihic, 2008, *Social Justice Research, 21,* p. 16. Copyright 2008 by Springer Science + Business Material, LLC. Reprinted with permission. *$p < .05$, **$p < .01$, ***$p < .001$.

of the editorial on attitudes toward refugees and refugee policy. Thus, at a theoretical level, this research demonstrates the important role of emotions in promoting the negative effects of dehumanization. At a more applied level, it suggests that by promoting the dehumanization of a group such as refugees the media can strongly influence the public's overall attitudes toward the group as well as support for policies and procedures relevant to the group. Perhaps not surprisingly, the ability to elicit emotions is an important component of the effectiveness of these media portrayals.

Implications

This research has important implications for understanding attitudes toward refugees and current refugee policies and for theorizing regarding dehumanization more generally. In terms of attitudes toward refugees and refugee policy, the findings suggest that the widespread belief that many refugee claimants are fraudulent (e.g., Dasko, 2002) presents a strong obstacle to their fair treatment and acceptance. That is, when the dehumanization of refugees is promoted through claims that they are fraudulent, contempt and lack of admiration are likely to be elicited, resulting in prejudice toward group members and lack of support for policies and programs designed to improve their circumstances. Not only is this dehumanization likely to be supported by the very individuals who are most able to institute change (members of high-status groups, who are likely to be high in social dominance orientation; Sidanius & Pratto, 1999) but the media may also promote the dehumanization of refugees by highlighting stories of deceit and deception on the part of individual refugee claimants.

At a theoretical level, this research has implications for understanding the process of dehumanization more generally. As shown in the first study, individuals who are higher in social dominance orientation are especially likely to dehumanize refugees, and this may be part of a more general tendency to dehumanize groups who are at the bottom of the social hierarchy. That is, the effects demonstrated here for individuals who are higher in social dominance orientation may be evident toward a variety of other low status groups, with dehumanization acting as a legitimizing myth for higher social dominance oriented individuals (Pratto, 1999; Sidanius & Pratto, 1999). As shown in the second study, media depictions of a group as immoral may also promote the dehumanization of that group, suggesting that such depictions in the media may also serve as legitimizing myths for those who are members of dominant groups in society.

Thus, the dehumanization of low-status groups in society may serve to justify the status quo and defend against threats to the ingroup position (see also Pratto, 1999; Sidanius & Pratto, 1999). That is, by excluding low-status group members from the *human* ingroup, one can more easily believe that they deserve negative outcomes and as a result, that other members of society do not have to provide assistance (see also Opotow, 1995; Schwartz & Struch, 1989). As a result, the status quo is maintained and perpetuated (Jost & Banaji, 1994; Jost, Burgess, & Mosso, 2001). The pairing of dehumanizing messages with the information about Canada's costly refugee program that appeared in the actual editorial used in Study 2 (Francis, 2001) may be quite telling in this regard, with dehumanization making it easier to deny the need to invest in such a program. Dehumanization was also shown to lead to contempt and lack of admiration for refugees. In turn, these negative emotions promoted overall negative attitudes toward refugees and negative attitudes toward the country's current refugee policy. Thus, dehumanization seems to promote negative consequences for the group in question through the emotions that it engenders. Indeed, the real editorial used in the experimental condition of Study 2 was noteworthy for its emotional appeal. After negative emotions such as contempt and lack of admiration are elicited, it may be easier to openly express negative attitudes toward the group in question and deny the group access to required resources. This adds to the growing literature documenting the importance of emotions in determining relations among groups (e.g., Mackie & Smith, 2002). It also adds to our understanding of factors that may promote prejudice and discrimination toward low status groups in society.

Conclusion

Our research to date suggests a number of important issues worthy of further investigation. First, at an empirical level, we are currently examining the dehumanization of refugees using alternative measures of dehumanization in order to ensure that dehumanization per se is at the core of our findings (e.g., Esses, Medianu, & Lawson, 2010).

Second, we are examining additional factors that may promote the dehumanization of refugees and other low-status groups in society. One such factor may be the *belief in a just world theory* (Lerner & Miller, 1978). According to the belief in a just world theory (see Furnham, 2003), individuals feel the need to preserve their belief that the world is a just place in which people get what they deserve. As a result, when confronted with unjust situations, individuals may reorganize their beliefs to restore consistency between their perceptions of a group and the group's outcomes (Correia & Vala, 2003). Although much of the research on belief in a just world focused on the consequences for blaming innocent victims, it also seems possible that consistency may be restored by dehumanizing these victims. In particular, by dehumanizing low status, disadvantaged groups, a seemingly just world is maintained—subhuman groups live in subhuman conditions. These beliefs may also function to reassure individuals that they would never end up in the types of situations in which these others have found themselves. That is, individuals may find it easier to accept the subhuman living conditions in which low status group members are forced to live, which they could not endure (see Leyens et al., 2000).

Based on this reasoning, we would expect that individuals who are higher in belief in a just world, that is, individuals who are highly likely to endorse the belief that the world is just, would be especially likely to dehumanize refugees and other disadvantaged groups in society. These are individuals who are most likely to feel threatened by perceived injustice in the plight of refugees and to act to restore their belief that good things happen to good people (Furnham, 2003). In previous research, individuals who are higher in belief in a just world have been shown to be most likely to blame the needy for their situation, minimize their existing needs, and justify their own advantage (Reichle, Schneider, & Montada, 1998). Thus, these individuals may also be especially likely to dehumanize low-status groups in society, particularly those who are in dire circumstances, to preserve their belief in a just world.

Third, as mentioned earlier, it is important to understand more fully the consequences of dehumanization for the treatment of refugees and other disadvantaged groups in society, given the large number of individuals in dire circumstances worldwide. Thus, an important issue is whether dehumanization leads to willingness to neglect groups in need (e.g., unwillingness to provide medical supplies, food, and care), as well as willingness to act against them (e.g., detention and deportation, closed borders, aggression). Recent research from our laboratory suggests that dehumanization is indeed predictive of lack of willingness to empower refugees and of the perception that refugees must change themselves if they are to improve their situation, placing the responsibility for their poor situation on refugees themselves (Medianu & Esses, 2010).

Fourth, in investigating the process through which dehumanization may lead to neglect and even abuse of disadvantaged groups in society, an important issue is the role of perceived need and entitlement in promoting such outcomes. Theorizing on dehumanization suggests that dehumanization may be a key determinant of the belief that members of a group are not worthy of fair, humane treatment, legitimizing their further victimization (e.g., Bar-Tal, 2000; Haslam, 2006; Opotow, 1995). Thus, in future research, we plan to assess the consequences of the dehumanization of refugees and other disadvantaged groups for beliefs about the needs and rights of these groups and their entitlement to basic resources (e.g., health care, housing, education). We predict that dehumanization will lead to denial of the needs and rights of these groups and denial of their entitlement to basic resources. After all, if these groups are not completely human, do they really need the resources that we as humans enjoy and should they be entitled to share these resources with us? In turn, these beliefs may mediate the relation between dehumanization and behavior, providing clear justification for the poor treatment of those who are most in need.

Finally, by examining these processes of dehumanization, we hope to not only map out the mechanism involved but also contribute to interventions and solutions. For example, social marketing campaigns designed to improve attitudes toward refugees and other disadvantaged groups may be particularly effective if they humanize group members. One strategy for doing so might involve using the common ingroup identity model (Gaertner & Dovidio, 2000) to promote the perception of a common, more inclusive ingroup (e.g., "We are all part of the human race"), which may promote more humanizing perceptions of group members (see also Nickerson & Louis, 2008). Indeed, previous research demonstrated that interventions based on forming common identities can improve attitudes toward immigrants among higher social dominance–oriented individuals (Esses, Dovidio, Semenya, & Jackson, 2005). Similarly, campaigns that elicit admiration and respect for group members, perhaps by demonstrating the hardships that they have successfully overcome, may prevent negative attitudes and behavior toward these groups. Through such mechanisms, the social construction of the category *refugee* and the meaning attached to it may be altered so refugees are brought back into the human fold and their needs addressed.

In conclusion, following Kay Deaux's lead, we suggest that it is important to examine the intersection of macro forces and individual cognitions and feelings in determining how we react to refugees who come to our nation seeking a new life. By understanding the determinants and processes through which dehumanization operates, we may be able to reduce its pervasive effects. This is a particularly worthy goal. After all, an important indication of our own humanness is how we treat others.

References

Alexander, M. G., Brewer, M. B., & Herrmann, R. K. (1999). Images and affect: A functional analysis of outgroup stereotypes. *Journal of Personality and Social Psychology, 77,* 78–93. doi:10.1037/0022-3514.77.1.78

Aulakh, R. (2010, August 16). Tamil asylum-seekers spark Canadian vitriol, anger. *Toronto Star.* Retrieved from http://www.thestar.com/news/canada/article/848212—tamil-asylum-seekers-spark-canadian-vitriol-anger

Bar-Tal, D. (2000). *Shared beliefs in a society.* Thousand Oaks, CA: Sage.

Citizenship and Immigration Canada. (2008). *Annual report to parliament on immigration: 2008.* Ottawa, Canada: Minister of Public Works and Government Services Canada.

Clarkson, B. (2000). 600 is too many. *Ryerson Review of Journalism.* Retrieved from http://www.rrj.ca/issue/2000/spring/306/

Correia, I., & Vala, J. (2003). When will a victim be secondarily victimized? The effect of observer's belief in a just world, victim's innocence, and persistence of suffering. *Social Justice Research, 16,* 379–400. doi:10.1023/A:1026313716185

Dasko, D. (2002, January). Attitudes toward immigration. *Centre for Research and Information on Canada, Portraits of Canada 2001.* Retrieved from http://www.cric.ca/pdf/cahiers/cricpapers_dec2001.pdf

Deaux, K. (2006). *To be an immigrant.* New York, NY: Russell Sage Foundation.

Demoulin, S., Rodriguez-Torres, R., Rodriguez-Perez, A., Vaes, J., Paladino, M. P., Gaunt, R., . . . Leyens, J.-P. (2004). Emotional prejudice can lead to infrahumanization. In W. Stroebe & M. Hewstone (Eds.), *European review of social psychology* (Vol. 15, pp. 259–296). Hove, England: Psychology Press.

Duckitt, J. (2006). Differential effects of right wing authoritarianism and social dominance orientation on outgroup attitudes and their mediation by threat from and competitiveness to outgroups. *Personality and Social Psychology Bulletin, 32,* 684–696. doi:10.1177/0146167205284282

Epley, N., Waytz, A., & Cacioppo, J. T. (2007). On seeing human: A three-factor theory of anthropomorphism. *Psychological Review, 114,* 864–886. doi:10.1037/0033-295X.114.4.864

Esses, V. M., Dovidio, J. F., Semenya, A. H., & Jackson, L. M. (2005). Attitudes toward immigrants and immigration: The role of national and international identities. In D. Abrams, M. A. Hogg, & J. M. Marques (Eds.), *The social psychology of inclusion and exclusion* (pp. 317–337). Philadelphia, PA: Psychology Press.

Esses, V. M., Medianu, S., & Lawson, A. S. (2010, May). The dehumanization of immigrants and refugees. In M. Inzlicht (Chair), *Less than human: Dehumanization and lack of empathy hurt intergroup relations.* Symposium conducted at the annual meeting of the Association for Psychological Science, Boston, MA.

Esses, V. M., Haddock, G., & Zanna, M. P. (1993). Values, stereotypes, and emotions as determinants of intergroup attitudes. In D. M. Mackie & D. L. Hamilton (Eds.), *Affect, cognition, and stereotyping: Interactive processes in group perception* (pp. 137–166). New York, NY: Academic Press.

Esses, V. M., Veenvliet, S., Hodson, G., & Mihic, L. (2008). Justice, morality, and the dehumanization of refugees. *Social Justice Research, 21,* 4–25. doi:10.1007/s11211-007-0058-4

Fiske, S. T., Cuddy, A. J. C., Glick, P., & Xu, J. (2002). A model of (often mixed) stereotype content: Competence and warmth respectively follow from perceived status and competition. *Journal of Personality and Social Psychology, 82,* 878–902. doi:10.1037/0022-3514.82.6.878

Francis, D. (2001, May 15). Cities fight for fair refugee policies. *National Post.* Retrieved from http://www.dianefrancis.com/

Frelick, B. (2010). Refugees are not bargaining chips. *Human Rights Watch.* Retrieved from http://www.hrw.org/en/news/2010/01/06/refugees-are-not-bargaining-chips

Furnham, A. (2003). Belief in a just world: Research progress over the past decade. *Personality and Individual Differences, 34,* 795–817. doi:10.1016/S0191-8869(02)00072-7

Gaertner, S. L., & Dovidio, J. F. (2000). *Reducing intergroup bias: The Common Ingroup Identity Model.* Philadelphia, PA: Psychology Press.

Guterres, A. (2006). Abusers or abused? *Refugees Magazine, 142,* 3.

Harris, L. T., & Fiske, S. T. (2006). Dehumanizing the lowest of the low: Neuroimaging responses to extreme outgroups. *Psychological Science, 17,* 847–853. doi:10.1111/j.1467-9280.2006.01793.x

Haslam, N. (2006). Dehumanization: An integrative review. *Personality and Social Psychology Review, 10,* 252–264. doi:10.1207/s15327957pspr1003_4

Haslam, N., & Pedersen, A. (2007). Attitudes toward asylum seekers: The psychology of exclusion. In D. Lusher & N. Haslam (Eds.), *Yearning to breathe free: Seeking asylum in Australia* (pp. 208–218). Sydney, Australia: Federation Press.

Henry, F., & Tator, C. (2002). *Discourses of domination: Racial bias in the Canadian English-language press.* Toronto, Canada: University of Toronto Press.

Human Rights Watch. (2009). *Jailing refugees.* Retrieved from http://www.hrw.org/en/reports/2009/12/29/jailing-refugees-0

Jost, J. T., & Banaji, M. R. (1994). The role of stereotyping in system-justification and the production of false consciousness. *British Journal of Social Psychology, 33*(1), 1–27.

Jost, J. T., Burgess, D., & Mosso, C. O. (2001). Conflicts of legitimation among self, group, and system: The integrative potential of system justification theory. In J. T. Jost & B. Major (Eds.), *The psychology of legitimacy: Emerging perspectives on ideology, justice, and intergroup relations* (pp. 363–388). New York, NY: Cambridge University Press.

Jost, J. T., & Hunyady, O. (2002). The psychology of system justification and the palliative function of ideology. In W. Stroebe & M. Hewstone (Eds.), *European review of social psychology* (Vol. 13, pp. 111–153). Hove, England: Psychology Press.

Karim, K. H. (1988). Covering refugees with figures of speech. *Media Awareness Network.* Retrieved from http://www.media-awareness.ca/english/resources/articles/diversity/covering_refugees.cfm

Lerner, M. J., & Miller, D. T. (1978). Just world research and the attribution process: Looking back and ahead. *Psychological Bulletin, 85,* 1030–1051. doi:10.1037/0033-2909.85.5.1030

Leventhal, G. S. (1980). What should be done with equity theory? New approaches to the study of fairness in social relationships. In K. Gergen, M. Greenberg, & R. Willis (Eds.), *Social exchange: Advances in theory and research* (pp. 27–55). New York, NY: Plenum Press.

Leyens, J.-P., Demoulin, S., Vaes, J., Gaunt, R., & Paladino, M. P. (2007). Infrahumanization: The wall of group differences. *Social Issues and Policy Review, 1,* 139–172. doi:10.1111/j.1751-2409.2007.00006.x

Leyens, J.-P., Paladino, P. M., Rodriguez-Torres, R., Vaes, J., Demoulin, S., Rodriguez-Perez, A., & Gaunt, R. (2000). The emotional side of prejudice: The attribution of secondary emotions to ingroups and outgroups. *Personality and Social Psychology Review, 4,* 186–197. doi:10.1207/S15327957PSPR0402_06

Louis, W. R., Duck, J., Terry, D. J., Schuller, R., & Lalonde, R. (2007). Why do citizens want to keep refugees out? Threats, fairness, and hostile norms in the treatment of asylum seekers. *European Journal of Social Psychology, 37,* 53–73. doi:10.1002/ejsp.329

Lusher, D., & Haslam, N. (Eds.). (2007). *Yearning to breathe free: Seeking asylum in Australia.* Sydney, Australia: Federation Press.

Mackie, D. M., & Smith, E. R. (Eds.). (2002). *From prejudice to intergroup emotions: Differentiated reactions to social groups.* Philadelphia, PA: Psychology Press.

Maio, G. R., Esses, V. M., Arnold, K., & Olson, J. M. (2004). The function–structure model of attitudes: Incorporating the need for affect. In G. G. Haddock & G. R. Maio (Eds.), *Contemporary perspectives on the psychology of attitudes* (pp. 9–33). London, England: Psychology Press.

Medianu, S., & Esses, V. M. (2010, January). *The dehumanization of refugees.* Paper presented at the annual meeting of the Society for Personality and Social Psychology, Las Vegas, NV.

Nickerson, A. M., & Louis, W. R. (2008). Nationality versus humanity? Personality, identity, and norms in relation to attitudes toward asylum seekers. *Journal of Applied Social Psychology, 38,* 796–817. doi:10.1111/j.1559-1816.2007.00327.x

O'Brien, G. V. (2003a). Indigestible food, conquering hordes, and waste materials: Metaphors of immigrants and the early immigration restriction debate in the United States. *Metaphor and Symbol, 18,* 33–47. doi:10.1207/S15327868MS1801_3

O'Brien, G. V. (2003b). People with cognitive disabilities: The argument from marginal cases and social work ethics. *Social Work, 48,* 331–337.

Opotow, S. (1995). Drawing the line: Social categorization, moral exclusion, and the scope of justice. In B. B. Bunker & J. Z. Rubin (Eds.), *Conflict, cooperation, and justice: Essays inspired by the work of Morton Deutsch* (pp. 347–369). San Francisco, CA: Jossey-Bass.

People Not Profit. (2005). *Nailing press myths about refugees.* Retrieved from http://www.peoplenotprofit.co.uk/asylum_seekers_myths.htm

Pratto, F. (1999). The puzzle of continuing group inequality: Piecing together psychological, social, and cultural forces in social dominance theory. In M. P. Zanna (Ed.), *Advances in experimental social psychology* (Vol. 31, pp. 191–263). San Diego, CA: Academic Press.

Pratto, F., Sidanius, J., Stallworth, L. M., & Malle, B. F. (1994). Social dominance orientation: A personality variable predicting social and political attitudes. *Journal of Personality and Social Psychology, 67,* 741–763. doi:10.1037/0022-3514.67.4.741

Reichle, B., Schneider, A., & Montada, L. (1998). How do observers of victimization preserve their belief in a just world cognitively or actionally. In L. Montada & M. Lerner (Eds.), *Responses to victimizations and belief in the just world* (pp. 55–64). New York, NY: Plenum Press.

Roccato, M., & Ricolfi, L. (2005). On the correlation between right-wing authoritarianism and social dominance orientation. *Basic and Applied Social Psychology, 27*, 187–200. doi:10.1207/s15324834basp2703_1

Schwartz, S. H., & Struch, N. (1989). Values, stereotypes, and intergroup antagonism. In D. Bar-Tal, C. G. Grauman, A. W. Kruglanski, & W. Stroebe (Eds.), *Stereotypes and prejudice: Changing conceptions* (pp. 151–167). New York, NY: Springer-Verlag.

Schwartz, S. H., Struch, N., & Bilsky, W. (1990). Values and intergroup motives: A study of Israeli and German students. *Social Psychology Quarterly, 53*, 185–198. doi:10.2307/2786958

Sidanius, J., & Pratto, F. (1999). *Social dominance: An intergroup theory of social hierarchy and oppression*. New York, NY: Cambridge University Press.

Struch, N., & Schwartz, S. H. (1989). Intergroup aggression: Its predictors and distinctness from ingroup bias. *Journal of Personality and Social Psychology, 56*, 364–373. doi:10.1037/0022-3514.56.3.364

United Nations High Commissioner for Refugees. (2010). *Refugee figures*. Retrieved May 1, 2010, from http://www.unhcr.org/pages/49c3646c1d.html

Verkuyten, M. (2004). Emotional reactions to and support for immigrant policies: Attributed responsibilities to categories of asylum seekers. *Social Justice Research, 17*, 293–314. doi:10.1023/B:SORE.0000041295.83611.dc

Wakslak, C. J., Jost, J. T., Tyler, T. R., & Chen, E. S. (2007). Moral outrage mediates the dampening effect of system justification on support for redistributive social policies. *Psychological Science, 18*, 267–274. doi:10.1111/j.1467-9280.2007.01887.x

8

Xenophobia and How to Fight It: Immigrants as the Quintessential "Other"

Susan T. Fiske and Tiane L. Lee

Like other scientists, psychologists work on what captures their imagination. This synergy between the personal and the scientific provides the wellspring for creativity and passion. The topics that fascinate Kay Deaux, for example, clearly relate to her identity in her social context. Moving in mid-career to the City University of New York Graduate Center, a far richer multicultural venue than Purdue University in Indiana, she became one of the first social psychologists to study immigrants in the modern era. Culminating in her book, *To Be an Immigrant* (Deaux, 2006), her social insights and evidence drew on the side benefits of her move, which originally stemmed from both professional and personal goals.

Immigrants themselves also move most often to improve their lot or join their families. The move may accomplish these goals, but it also produces unintended side effects. Prominent among those accidental effects are encounters with xenophobia in their host country. As this chapter suggests, the nature of xenophobia itself is systematic and predictable from the social context in which it occurs. Immigrants are often the feared *other*. Anti-immigrant prejudice is particularly an apt laboratory for studying reactions to outgroups because although they all share the situation of being newcomers, each immigrant group differs critically in its particular structural context, resulting in distinct and systematic forms of xenophobia. According to our lab's recent research, many national and ethnic stereotypes are accidents of immigration circumstances and the historical contexts that motivated particular groups to leave at a particular time and to choose their new destination.

In the spirit of Kay Deaux's inspiring research, our work on this topic has valued description as a foundation to theory, has dared to try different methods, and (we hope) goes boldly where none have gone before. First, we describe the model that informs our research on xenophobia in general; second, we apply it to images of immigrants across cultures, with the United States as a focal case; third, we show why these images matter; and we close with ideas about how to challenge xenophobia.

Stereotype Content Model: A Framework for Understanding Immigrants' Place in Society

Fundamental Dimensions: Warmth and Competence

Immigrants join a society with its own prior structure. They fit, as all groups do, along two fundamental dimensions of social cognition (for a brief review, see Fiske, Cuddy, & Glick, 2007). When people encounter a new group—for example, immigrants from a novel origin—they first want to know whether these others are friend or foe; that is, are they with us or against us? Essentially, this is a question of intent: Do they intend us good or ill? If they are well-intentioned, they are trustworthy and friendly, seen as warm overall. Otherwise, not. People judge other people's individual trustworthiness in a split second, and this is likely the first thing societies want to know about a new influx of immigrants. Are they hostile exploiters and cold competitors or are they warm joiners and trustworthy cooperators?

After attributing the first dimension, warmth of intent, people want to know whether the group can enact those intentions. That is, can they produce outcomes that matter? If so, then the group is competent (capable, intelligent, skilled). Otherwise, not. After all, an incompetent, hostile other is easier to manage than a competent one. And an incompetent ally is not much use. These two dimensions, warmth and competence, appear in Figure 8.1, with examples from each combination (e.g., Fiske, Cuddy, Glick, & Xu, 2002).

The diagonal quadrants, low on both perceived warmth and competence, or high on both, exemplify straightforward us/them stereotypes. Traditionally, prejudice research has described such unambivalent ingroup favoritism: we and our close allies against outgroups with no redeeming features. This love-us/hate-them contrast makes sense if sheer evaluation is all that matters.

Four Clusters of Societal Groups

Granted, some groups seem all good or all bad. National ingroups, such as citizens, the middle class, and the dominant religion (Christianity in the

	Low competence	High competence
High warmth	older, disabled (physical, mental) *Pity*	ingroup, allies, reference groups *Pride*
Low warmth	poor, homeless, immigrants *Disgust*	rich, professionals, entrepreneurs *Envy*

Figure 8.1. Stereotype content model stereotype trait dimensions, example, and emotional prejudices.

United States), form societal reference groups, role models deemed warm and competent. These groups typically inspire pride and admiration, emotions that signal approach.

In contrast are the alleged dregs of society, groups simultaneously disliked as hostile and disrespected as useless. National rejects, such as homeless people or any kind of poor person, end up in this quadrant, as do generic immigrants, about whom a later section elaborates. Such low–low groups elicit disgust and contempt, emotions that signal avoidance.

More theoretically novel is the stereotype content model's (SCM) identification of two kinds of ambivalent prejudices toward outgroups that appear mixed on warmth and competence. Groups perceived as well-intentioned (warm) but incompetent seem pathetic and harmless. Older people and people with disabilities stereotypically fit this ambivalent case. Because they seem likeable but not worthy of respect, other people tend to express pity and sympathy, ambivalent emotions that communicate the other is inferior, though not responsible for being down.

The converse ambivalent combination is high competence but low warmth. Rich people, professionals, and entrepreneurs stereotypically evoke dislike at the same time as grudging respect, which add up to envy and jealousy. Envy implies that the other holds desirable resources but probably for unjust reasons. Envy too is ambivalent because, while it acknowledges competence, it resents the other's position as illegitimate.

Generalizability

These warmth and competence stereotypes—and the resulting emotional prejudices of pride, disgust, pity, and envy—appear across a wide range of populations. In American samples, everyone (regardless of own group memberships) can report how groups are seen in society (Cuddy, Fiske, & Glick, 2007). In surveys, people express consensus about the map of groups in society; they agree about mapping their society, rather than merely expressing sheer own-group favoritism. Even when rating their own immediate emotional reactions to photographs stereotypic of individuals from each quadrant, participants produce the hypothesized emotional prejudices regardless of group identity (Harris & Fiske, 2006).

Outside the United States, European and Asian samples demonstrate the same two dimensions for outgroups in their own societies: locating poor people in the disgust quadrant, rich people in the envy one, and older people in the pity one (counter to the image of respected elders in more traditional societies; Cuddy et al., 2009; Durante et al., 2011). Consistent with East Asian modesty norms, those samples moderate the Western high–high, societal reference-group-enhancing ratings, choosing more neutral locations for national prototypes. Nevertheless, the outgroups array across the two dimensions in the same way across American, European, and Asian samples.

Recent data suggest that the model similarly describes societal groups in Latino, Middle Eastern, and African settings (Durante et al., 2011), adding up to dozens of countries. Another emerging variation across countries is the predominance of ambivalent clusters. Almost all countries sampled so far show a majority of groups in the ambivalent clusters, but they vary on the relative prevalence. Societies with stable inequality (as indicated by the Gini coefficient of income inequality) appear to have a higher prevalence of ambivalent groups. Perhaps their stability rests on placating at least some of the disadvantaged groups with ambivalence and containing at least some of the advantaged groups by viewing them through another ambivalent lens. We next explore some of these social structural features.

Origins

If the Warmth × Competence dimensions are fundamental, where do they originate? Arguably, they answer universal human queries and originate from features of societal context that also are universal. All societies distinguish cooperators and competitors, those who facilitate the larger group's goals and those who hinder them, either by exploiting or freeloading. Across cultural samples, cooperative groups appear warm and trustworthy, whereas competitive or exploitative groups do not, with a reliable, medium effect size ($r \sim .30$; Cuddy, Fiske, & Glick, 2008). When competition comprises both economic threat and values threat, the effect of perceived competition on warmth shows a large effect size approaching .80 (Kervyn, Fiske, & Yzerbyt, 2011). All societies perceive groups to compete, more or less.

All human societies also have hierarchies, with some groups having higher status than others. Although the degree of verticality may differ, everyone distinguishes up and down. People reliably attribute a group's societal status to their personal competence to a much greater degree than we expected; the effect size is not only reliable but large ($r \sim .80$). At least in our samples, meritocracy (i.e., people get what they deserve) wins over sour grapes (i.e., the privileged cheated to get there, so who wants to pay that price to gain their position). What's more, not only are these cooperation–warmth and status–competence correlations reliable, they are not merely halo effects, because the divergent correlations (cooperation–competence and status–warmth) are essentially zero. Scenario studies show the predicted causal direction, from manipulations of perceived structure (groups' competition and status) to perceived stereotypes (respectively, warmth and competence; Caprariello, Cuddy, & Fiske, 2009). The stereotypes, in turn, predict emotional prejudices in a variety of settings (see Cuddy et al., 2008, for a review). This causal model, from perceived social structure to stereotypes and thence to emotions, appears as Figure 8.2's first three steps. (The final one is at the end of the chapter.)

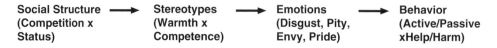

Figure 8.2. Hypothesized causality within the stereotype content model and BIAS map.

Historical Accidents Create Images of Immigrants

If societal context shapes images of social groups, then immigrants provide a natural experiment in how this happens. Different immigrant circumstances—due to particular combinations of history, politics, and economics—drive groups of different social status and different benign or hostile intent to seek new shores. Some arrive as refugees of modest means, whereas others arrive as accomplished experts; however, the entire ethnicity is often painted with the colors of the subset that happens to come. Thus, the social status of the few who immigrate determines the image of the majority who remain in their home country. Most Mexicans in their native country are not, naturally, migrant farmworkers. In the same way, some groups arrive in their host country as allies with shared goals and benign intent, whereas others arrive as outsiders determined to resist or even undermine their host society. The majority of Muslims do not hate Western society, yet the tiny minority who become terrorists taint the image of all the rest. The SCM provides a framework for understanding how the circumstances of those who happen to immigrate then determine stereotypes of that ethnicity as a whole.

Consider the following scenario used in some of our research (Caprariello et al., 2009):

> Due to political and economic circumstances, demographers predict waves of immigration in the next few years from an ethnic group outside our borders called *Wallonians*. In their home country, members of this group typically have low-status jobs and are uneducated and economically unsuccessful. However, they also take power and resources from members of other groups. When members of this ethnic group arrive here, [how] will people here be likely to view incoming group members? (p. 151)

Under this particular scenario, Wallonians would share with other generic immigrants the image of being low status and exploitative, locating them in the low-competence, low-warmth quadrant, along with homeless people and poor people. When people know nothing about an immigrant group, they assume the worst (low status and exploitative) because immigrants are the quintessential *other*, by definition outsiders to the societal system.

But in fact, Wallonians are French-speaking Belgians, were our World War II allies, now host the political home of the European Union, and as immigrants are economically successful professionals with resources to share. Other versions of the scenario portrayed them as low or high status, exploitative or cooperative, producing the predicted stereotypes (Caprariello et al., 2009). Consistent with the SCM, the social structures under which immigrants arrive then determine how they are welcomed. Chinese immigrants to the United States are a case in point. During the late 19th century, Chinese workers came to build the American transcontinental railroad. Regarded as peasant laborers, they were expelled when their low-status work was no longer needed. During that era, Chinese people suffered from disgusting stereotypes and severe discrimination. Fast-forward to the late 20th and early 21st centuries, and Chinese immigrant stereotypes now boast an image of technical expertise and educated skill, albeit still foreign. So, specific immigrant groups arrive under different circumstances, which then determine the prevailing stereotype of their entire ethnicity.

Immigrants in general—ethnicity unspecified—do not fare well, as the next section elaborates. Generically, immigrants to various countries are stereotyped as extreme outgroups, low on both warmth and competence (Cuddy et al., 2009; Durante et al., 2011; Eckes, 2002). This fits the idea that they are viewed in general as untrustworthy and exploitative, competing with the native born for jobs, or operating in a criminal underground economy. We decided to see how immigrants, general and specific, appear in the United States (Lee & Fiske, 2006).

Images of Immigrants

Xenophobia in the United States

As a focal case, the United States offers contradictions. Identified as a nation of immigrants, indeed the longest immigrant-receiving nation in the modern world, as well as attracting an unparalleled range of ethnicities and nationalities, the United States also periodically harbors severe nativist sentiments as in the current era, when irate localities are passing punitive and possibly unconstitutional laws to stop, search, incarcerate, and deport suspected "illegal aliens." The current immigration debates are the latest installment of a vicious cycle in U.S. politics.

To begin to get some descriptions of current immigrant images, we (Lee & Fiske, 2006) started by asking Princeton and Stanford undergraduates to name types of immigrants in American society; we then selected those mentioned by at least 13% of the sample to ensure recognition. Participants nominated a rich array of groups from across continents. We added some reliable anchors from the four corners of the SCM space (low–low homeless and poor; low-competence but high-warmth housewives and older people; high-competence but low-warmth rich and professionals; high–high students and Americans). We also added generic documented and undocumented immigrants because of their prominence in current political debates. Farmworkers and tech industry workers appear too because they would help indicate effects of socioeconomic status. We also added generic first-generation and third-generation immigrants to gauge the effects of time in the host country.

A second sample of undergraduates (U.S. residents for at least 5 years) rated the resulting 33 groups on warmth, competence, status (prestige of immigrants' jobs, their economic and educational success), and competition (anticipated impact on one's ingroup if immigrants received special breaks, had power, and received more resources). Five Warmth × Competence clusters emerged, one in each corner of the SCM space, plus one low on warmth but moderate on competence (see Figure 8.3).

The low–low cluster houses the primary targets of anti-immigrant political resentments: undocumented, farmworkers, Mexicans, South Americans, and generic Latinos. Generic African immigrants appear here, suggesting that the anti-immigrant prejudices focus on immigrants of color, or at least

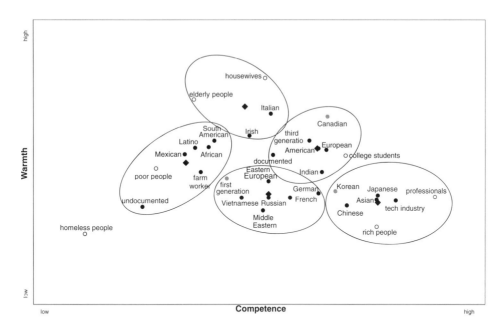

Figure 8.3.   Immigrants in the stereotype content model. Ovals indicate cluster analysis results. Dots indicate average rating of each group; diamonds indicate cluster centers. From "Not an Outgroup, but Not Yet an Ingroup: Immigrants in the Stereotype Content Model," by T. L. Lee and S. T. Fiske, 2006, *International Journal of Intercultural Relations, 30,* p. 759. Copyright 2006 from Elsevier Limited. Reprinted with permission.

Black and Brown ones. Unspecified first-generation immigrants appear here, as if the default immigrant must hail from one of these groups. The low–low cluster includes the SCM anchor case of poor people, and homeless people appear in the same quadrant (though even more extreme). The ethnic focus of this cell ignores the variability in the status of Latino and Black immigrants. And it ignores the status of undocumented immigrants, many of whom are Europeans or Asians who overstay a tourist visa, entering the underground economy.

In the high–high cluster are the anchor groups, Americans and students, as expected. Also, third-generation immigrants appear to be accepted as American. Joining them are nonspecific Europeans, generic documented immigrants, and Canadian immigrants, who appear superior to everyone else. Indian immigrants land at the corner of this space, apparently more accepted than other Asians, who appear nearby but distinctly lower on warmth.

Most Asians land in one ambivalent corner, the stereotypic competent-but-cold immigrants sharing a cluster with rich people, professionals, and tech-industry employees. All of them hail from East Asia—Japanese, Chinese, and Korean—or are unspecified "Asian." Pointedly, these groups are rated even more competent than the societal ingroup/allies/reference groups.

The contrasting ambivalent cluster holds harmless immigrants, stereotypically warm-but-incompetent Irish and Italians, who share this cluster with older and housewife anchors. Although the Irish and the Italians were viewed as not quite White a century ago, now students view them as nearly ingroup but patronize them as harmlessly amiable.

The anomaly in this data set is an unexpected cluster of moderately competent but definitely not warm immigrants: Eastern Europeans, Russians, French, Germans, Middle Eastern, and Vietnamese. These seem to be immigrant groups who are thought of "not us, not on our side" but otherwise lack a strong stereotype. If they were completely neutral, they would be in the middle of the space, not in the low-warmth/competitor part of the space, as they are. Several of these nationalities are former or current wartime foes. In past samples other ambiguous groups have landed here. For example, Arabs in general would probably include the lower status subtype of the Arab street- or front-line terrorists and the higher status subtypes of terrorist organizers and oil-rich nobility; in combination, they would all be seen as "not on our side" but ambiguous as to status.

As in other data sets, people strongly associate competence and status ($r = .96$), and negatively relate warmth and competition ($r = -.55$). At the group level, respectively, meritocracy prevails (immigrants get the status they deserve), as does societal loyalty (assimilative immigrants are "with us").

Overall, the pattern of data suggests that generic immigrants in the United States primarily evoke Mexicans and South Americans, farmworkers, and undocumented migrants. The current immigration debates seem to ignore all other types of immigrants, whether skilled or not, traditional or not, European or not. The intersection of ethnicity and immigrant status appears, as the ethnicity of Latino immigrants appears to dominate perceptions of generic immigrants, confounding several of the most negative stereotypes. The next study explores this possibility further.

Do Generations and Legality Matter?

Besides the apparent focus on Mexicans, the initial study highlighted the intersection of immigrant status with (lack of) documentation and (first) generational status. Both undocumented and generic first-generation immigrants are the lowest of the low, but generic documented and third-generation immigrants are among the highest of the high. What a difference a couple of generations make. Not to mention what a difference having papers makes. Hence, the next study systematically manipulated the documentation and generational-status factors for a subset of immigrant groups stereotyped at the corners of the societal map. Undergraduates rated Mexicans and farmworkers (both previously low–low), Canadians and Europeans (high–high), Asians and tech workers (competent but low-warmth), and Irish and Italians (warm but less competent). The resulting four clusters resemble the previous data (see Figure 8.4).

Documentation and generational status seem to matter less than ethnicity or socioeconomic status. Mexicans, regardless of legal status, are disliked and disrespected the most. Being in the third generation improves their status only slightly. More or less the same pattern appears for farmworkers, usually viewed as Mexican or Latin American. In contrast, Canadians land in the high–high cluster regardless of generation or legal status. Europeans do not vary much by

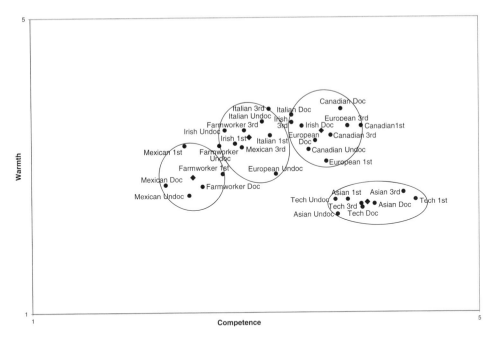

Figure 8.4.   Immigrant groups, specified by documented and generational status. Ovals indicate cluster analysis results. Dots indicate average rating of each group; diamonds indicate cluster centers. Data from T. L. Lee and S. T. Fiske, 2007.

generational status, although being undocumented moves them slightly out of the firmly ingroup cluster.

Moving to the two ambivalent cells, do the manipulations (documentation and generation) affect these more mixed stereotypes? Asians and tech workers do not budge from the competent-but-cold cluster, regardless of documentation or generation. Being an Asian or a tech-industry immigrant appears to be a sticky stereotype. On the other hand, Italians and Irish in this context readily move into the "us" cluster if documented and if third generation. The Irish especially polarize along these factors; the Italians less so.

For the ambivalently stereotyped immigrant groups, status/competence changes more easily than competition/warmth. Immigrants can more easily demonstrate objective circumstances (occupation, education, wealth) that would change perceived status and therefore perceived competence than do the equivalent for competition/warmth. However, recent data suggest that the perceived warmth of an immigrant can change by changing the perceiver's empathy for the person's circumstances or by priming a cooperative image of the immigrant's group (Sevillano & Fiske, 2010).

After rating warmth and competence, the participants responded to two additional questions, combined to measure the perceived Americanism of immigrant groups: "How much does this group's presence fit American values?" and "How American is this group?" In Lee and Fiske (2006), groups' locations in the SCM space were assumed to reflect their perceived degree of ingroup membership, with the high–high cluster perceived as most American. In this follow-up study, we included these two questions to inquire more explicitly.

As expected, documentation and generation both increase perceived Americanness. People believe documented immigrants are more American than undocumented immigrants and third-generation more than first-generation immigrants. The American ingroup cluster equals the Italians and Irish, but the ingroup cluster seems decidedly more American than the Asians and techies, as well as Mexicans and farmworkers. The intersections of ethnicity, occupation, generation, and documentation combine to form images of immigrants.

Does Time Matter?

Immigrant generation matters to the experience of immigrant identity (Deaux et al., 2007), and it should matter to images of immigrants as well. A historical perspective seems apt for our premise that immigrant stereotypes are accidents of history and national circumstances. Fortunately, we can compare Princeton students' perceptions of immigrant ethnic groups in 1932 and in 2001 to 2007 (Bergsieker, Leslie, Constantine, & Fiske, 2011). Katz and Braly's (1933) social psychology classic asked Princeton students to choose among 80 adjectives that might describe several ethnic and national groups salient in the period between the two World Wars. Using the heirs to those original respondents, 70 years later we asked what current Princeton students thought about the same groups.

Some groups remain in the same locations: Americans and English share the high–high location both times. Latinos were not a salient ethnic group in 1932, but the original study asked about Turks, so we repeated the query in 2001 and 2007; both times, they unaccountably land in the low–low part of the map. Americans appear to have little content for this stereotype, merely a consistent dislike and disrespect.

In the ambivalent quadrants, one cluster also remains the same among the immigrant groups discussed here: Japanese and Chinese were viewed as competent but cold, even in 1932. In the other ambivalent quadrant, Irish and Italians were rated as warm but not so competent in our 2001 to 2007 data, as in the other studies described here. But in 1932, they were not viewed as warm at all, yet they appeared more competent, especially the Irish. In the early 20th century, waves of Irish immigrants constituted, to some nativists, a threat parallel to the perceived threat of Mexican and Asian immigrants today. Germans, a growing menace in the 1930s, also appeared in the competent-but-cold threatening cluster in 1932 but among the European "us" by 2001.

Immigrants Across Cultures

Earlier, we described the SCM as applicable across a range of cultures, applied to their respective societal groups. Several samples have nominated immigrants, mostly from neighboring countries, as relevant groups and all denigrated them as incompetent and untrustworthy/cold (Cuddy et al., 2009;

Durante et al., 2011). Generic immigrants appear in the low–low cluster—or if not the lowest, at best low-to-moderate on warmth and competence, with the clear majority of other groups higher on both dimensions—Italians, Swiss Greeks, Spanish, Northern Irish, and those from the rest of the United Kingdom. Where they appear, Muslim immigrants are usually viewed even more negatively. Beyond Europe, generic immigrants also appear in the low–low cluster: those from Australia, New Zealand, Malaysia, Hong Kong, and South Korea. In Costa Rica, the Nicaraguans constitute the derogated immigrants; in Chile, it is the Peruvian immigrants. Many countries identify their particular immigrant populations as the lowest of the low.

Why the Images Matter

The stereotypes matter because of the emotions and behavior they inspire toward immigrants. Alone, the stereotypes are categories; however, combined with emotional prejudices, they become volatile catalysts of discrimination. According to the BIAS map (Cuddy et al., 2007), the warmth dimension, being primary, provokes active help and harm. The competence dimension, being secondary, provokes more passive help and harm.

This means that the low–low groups such as generic immigrants are targeted for active attack but also passive neglect. In the case of another such group, homeless people, other people tend to dehumanize them, not expecting to interact with them, having trouble imagining their minds, and even failing to activate the social cognition networks in the brain when they see them (Harris & Fiske, 2006, 2009). It's as though the low–low groups are less than human. Although these studies did not use immigrants as targets, a parallel dehumanization is likely whenever waves of anti-immigrant hysteria sweep a country. The immigrant others are seen as a dirty tide, a teeming horde, or a mass onslaught, all undifferentiated and subhuman.

Some specific immigrant groups, such as Asians in the United States, who are viewed as competent-but-cold, may be targeted for a volatile mix of emotional prejudices and behaviors. Envied outgroups receive grudging respect but simultaneous dislike, so people go along to get along, associating with them, using their expertise. But under societal breakdown, they may be targets of active attack, even mass violence. For example, riots target entrepreneurial outsiders (Asian shopkeepers, Jewish businesses). Data from social neuroscience suggest the potential for schadenfreude linked to the suffering of envied outgroups and harm directed toward them (Cikara, Botvinick, & Fiske, 2011; Cikara & Fiske, 2011).

Still other immigrant groups, the rarely pitied ones according to our data, would be helped but also neglected, ignored, and demeaned. Although this might seem contradictory, simultaneous help and neglect describe the institutionalization of older or disabled people. However, in our immigrant data few groups are pitied. Quite possibly, refugees would elicit pity if the cause of their displacement was due to external circumstances (natural disasters, war) and not somehow construed as their "fault" (unemployment). This remains a topic for future research.

How to Challenge Xenophobia

Anti-immigrant backlash is global, evidently, and it takes predictable forms. Fortunately, this research offers some suggestions that might help mitigate it. If indeed the causal sequence goes from perceived social structures—the accidents of history and immigration circumstances—to stereotypes, emotional prejudices, and discrimination (see Figure 8.2), then we know the place to start. The causal power of perceived social structure appears in both the cross-cultural reliability of the competition–warmth and status–competence correlations (Cuddy et al., 2008) and in its experimental simulations (Caprariello et al., 2009; Kervyn et al., 2011). Immigrants stereotyped as having low-status jobs, being uneducated, and being economically unsuccessful will be resented, demeaned, and attacked if they also appear to take power and resources from members of other groups. In short, if immigrants are framed as unskilled and exploitative, then they will fare poorly in societal debates over their fates.

Instead, if immigrants are framed as bringing needed skills, taking jobs that no one else wants, or even creating new jobs, then they will be seen as growing the economy. When present-day immigrants are framed as one of "us," as past generations of new Americans have been, and considered well-intentioned, hardworking, and generous, then xenophobia will decrease.

In the inspiration of Kay Deaux's research, first one must understand the problem, and in Lewin's (1951) oft-sided dictum, "there's nothing so practical as a good theory" (p. 169), to work on the psychological study of social issues. Consistent with Deaux's vision, the intersection of immigrant status with generation, documentation, and ethnicity determines immigrant images, and from them emotional prejudices and discrimination, but also paths toward remedies. Description allows work toward alleviation.

References

Bergsieker, H. B., Leslie, L. M., Constantine, V. S., & Fiske, S. T. (2011). *Stereotyping by omission: Eliminate the negative, accentuate the positive.* Manuscript submitted for publication.

Caprariello, P. A., Cuddy, A. J. C., & Fiske, S. T. (2009). Social structure shapes cultural stereotypes and emotions: A causal test of the stereotype content model. *Group Processes & Intergroup Relations, 12,* 147–155. doi:10.1177/1368430208101053

Cikara, M., Botvinick, M. M., & Fiske, S. T. (2011). Us versus them: Social identity shapes neural responses to intergroup competition and harm. *Psychological Science, 22,* 306–313. doi:10.1177/0956797610397667

Cikara, M., Eberhardt, J. L., & Fiske, S. T. (2010). From agents to objects: Sexist attitudes and neural responses to sexualized targets. *Journal of Cognitive Neuroscience, 23,* 540–551.

Cikara, M., & Fiske, S. T. (2011). *Stereotypes and Schadenfreude: Affective and physiological markers of pleasure at outgroup misfortunes.* Social Psychological & Personality Science. doi:10.1177/1948550611409245

Cuddy, A. J. C., Fiske, S. T., & Glick, P. (2007). The BIAS map: Behaviors from intergroup affect and stereotypes. *Journal of Personality and Social Psychology, 92,* 631–648. doi:10.1037/0022-3514.92.4.631

Cuddy, A. J. C., Fiske, S. T., & Glick, P. (2008). Competence and warmth as universal trait dimensions of interpersonal and intergroup perception: The Stereotype Content Model and the BIAS Map. In M. P. Zanna (Ed.), *Advances in experimental Social psychology* (Vol. 40, pp. 61–149). New York, NY: Academic Press.

Cuddy, A. J. C., Fiske, S. T., Kwan, V. S. Y., Glick, P., Demoulin, S., Leyens, J.-Ph., . . . Ziegler, R. (2009). Is the Stereotype Content Model culture-bound? A cross-cultural comparison reveals systematic similarities and differences. *British Journal of Social Psychology*, *48*, 1–33. doi:10.1348/014466608X314935

Deaux, K. (2006). *To be an immigrant*. New York, NY: Russell Sage Foundation.

Deaux, K., Bikmen, N., Gilkes, A., Ventuneac, A., Joseph, Y., Payne, Y. A., & Steele, C. M. (2007). Becoming American: Stereotype threat effects in Afro-Caribbean immigrant groups. *Social Psychology Quarterly*, *70*, 384–404. doi:10.1177/019027250707000408

Durante, F., Fiske, S. T., Cuddy, A. J. C., Kervyn, N., et al. (2011). *Nations' income inequality predicts ambivalence in stereotype content: How societies mind the gap*. Manuscript submitted for publication.

Eckes, T. (2002). Paternalistic and envious gender stereotypes: Testing predictions from the stereotype content model. *Sex Roles*, *47*, 99–114. doi:10.1023/A:1021020920715

Fiske, S. T., Cuddy, A. J. C., & Glick, P. (2007). Universal dimensions of social perception: Warmth and competence. *Trends in Cognitive Sciences*, *11*, 77–83. doi:10.1016/j.tics.2006.11.005

Fiske, S. T., Cuddy, A. J., Glick, P., & Xu, J. (2002). A model of (often mixed) stereotype content: Competence and warmth respectively follow from perceived status and competition. *Journal of Personality and Social Psychology*, *82*, 878–902. doi:10.1037/0022-3514.82.6.878

Harris, L. T., & Fiske, S. T. (2006). Dehumanizing the lowest of the low: Neuroimaging responses to extreme outgroups. *Psychological Science*, *17*, 847–853. doi:10.1111/j.1467-9280.2006.01793.x

Harris, L. T., & Fiske, S. T. (2009). Dehumanized perception: The social neuroscience of thinking (or not thinking) about disgusting people. In M. Hewstone & W. Stroebe (Eds.), *European review of social psychology* (Vol. 20, pp. 192–231). London, England: Wiley.

Katz, D., & Braly, K. (1933). Racial stereotypes of one hundred college students. *Journal of Abnormal and Social Psychology*, *28*, 280–290. doi:10.1037/h0074049

Kervyn, N., Fiske, S. T., & Yzerbyt, Y. (2011). *Why is the primary dimension of social cognition so hard to predict? Symbolic and realistic threats together predict warmth in the stereotype content model*. Manuscript submitted for publication.

Lee, T. L., & Fiske, S. T. (2006). Not an outgroup, but not yet an ingroup: Immigrants in the Stereotype Content Model. *International Journal of Intercultural Relations*, *30*, 751–768. doi:10.1016/j.ijintrel.2006.06.005

Lee, T. L., & Fiske, S. T. (2007). [Immigrant groups, specified by documented and generational status] Unpublished data.

Lewin, K. (1951). *Field theory in social science; selected theoretical papers*. New York, NY: Greenwood.

Sevillano, V., & Fiske, S. T. (2010). *Warming up stereotypes: Empathy warms up stereotype content but ignores perceived incompetence*. Unpublished raw data.

9

The Dynamics of Multicultural Identities

Ying-yi Hong

> How many times, since I left Lebanon in 1976 to live in France, have people asked me, with the best intentions in the world, whether I felt "more French" or "more Lebanese"? And I always give the same answer: "Both!" I say that not in the interests of fairness or balance, but because any other answer would be a lie. What makes me myself rather than anyone else is the very fact that I am poised between two countries, two or three languages and several cultural traditions. It is precisely this that defines my identity. Would I exist more authentically if I cut off a part of myself?
>
> —Amin Maalouf (2000, p.1)

Maalouf's experience may resonate with the experiences of some immigrants and sojourners around the world. People who have been extensively exposed to multiple cultures may feel that each culture has contributed to shaping the self and is an inalienable part of their identity. Moreover, many of them may have acquired skills of two or three languages and knowledge about several cultural traditions. These individuals are arguably privileged, such that they can use the language skills and knowledge of multiple cultures as resources to achieve the goals they wish to pursue. Professionals in anthropology, international business, and global innovation industries, among others, often benefit from such knowledge and skills, allowing them smooth navigation between multiple cultures. The movie director Ang Lee's impeccable mastery of Chinese and American cultures is a case in point. Ang Lee grew up in Taiwan and pursued higher education at the University of Illinois at Urbana–Champaign and New York University. He was famous for his detailed portrayal of Chinese cultural nuances in movies such as *Pushing Hands*, *The Wedding Banquet*, and *Crouching Tiger, Hidden Dragon*. Astonishingly, he can also portray equally well the nuances of Western cultures, as shown in his movies *Sense and Sensibility* and *Brokeback Mountain*. He exemplifies someone who has successfully reaped the benefits from multiple cultural exposures.

The preparation of this article was partially supported by a grant from the Academic Research Fund (Tier 1) of Singapore's Ministry of Education, awarded to Ying-yi Hong. The author thanks Carol Dweck, Jennifer Rosner, Shaun Wiley, and Gina Philogène for their invaluable comments on an earlier draft of this chapter.

165

If all immigrants and sojourners could smoothly navigate between multiple cultures, this would be an ideal world. In reality, exposure to multiple cultures gives rise to a wide range of experiences, many of which are more negative than positive, such as Park's (1928) notion of the marginal man: A person who is

> living and sharing intimately in the cultural life and traditions of two distinct peoples, never quite willing to break, even if he were permitted to do so, with his past and his traditions, and not quite accepted, because of racial prejudice, in the new society in which he now sought to find a place. (p. 892)

More than 7 decades have passed, and some immigrants still confront similar feelings:

> When I go to Chinatown in San Francisco, Chinese old people looked at my red, fire engine red hair and their eyes told me that they feel sorry for my mom. People thought that I was born in the United States. They are wrong. I was born in Hong Kong. I attended elementary school in Hong Kong. I feel that I am a Chinese and I am an American as well.
> (Narrative of an Asian American, National Public Radio, July 5, 2001)

The ambivalent feeling associated with being bicultural may stem from the fact that cultures come in a "package"—they are not only defined by shared beliefs, norms, and practices but are also demarcated by race, ethnicity, and social class. In most societies, unfortunately, there are still wide power differentials among racial and ethnic groups (Lott, in press); immigrants and their descendants, especially visible ethnic minorities, are often bestowed with less power than their ethnic majority host in the society (see Deaux, 2006). These power differentials may manifest in a tendency for the majority group to dominate over ethnic minority groups. To justify and legitimize their domination, the majority group could hold negative stereotypes against the ethnic minority groups, as well as display prejudice and discrimination toward them (social dominance theory; Sidanius & Pratto, 1999). Facing such unfavorable treatment, ethnic minority group members understandably feel unjustly treated, angry, and resentful, thereby making it hard for them to identify with the mainstream culture (Verkuyten & Yildiz, 2007). Under these circumstances, it is unlikely that these individuals would incorporate the mainstream culture as a part of their self-definition.

Likewise, if acting and thinking like a member of the host culture is not an option for these individuals, they are unlikely to reap the benefits from multicultural exposure. Some of them may even use extreme actions to undermine the host culture, causing harms to innocent others. For example, Sheikh Omar Saeed, a British-born militant of Pakistani descent, is infamous for his alleged masterminding of the 2002 kidnapping and murder of *Wall Street Journal* reporter Daniel Pearl. In his youth Sheikh attended Forest School, a prestigious school in northeast London and later attended the London School of Economics, where he studied applied mathematics and economics. Although Sheikh was undeniably steeped in Western culture, he did not seem to have embraced Western culture, nor had he built a secure identity around it.

An Analytical Framework

How does one understand these disparate responses to multicultural exposure? Previous research has focused mainly on acculturation strategies on the part of ethnic minorities, arguing that bicultural individuals have different strategies for managing their multiple identities, such as fusion, blending, and alternation (LaFromboise, Coleman, & Gerton, 1993; Phinney, 1996; as reviewed in handbook chapters such as Hong, Wan, No, & Chiu, 2007; Tadmor, Hong, Chiu, & No, in press). Although these different ways of managing identities each seem probable, could there be a unified psychological mechanism that underlies the dynamic interplay of the potentially beneficial and damaging outcomes of multi- or bicultural exposure? Based on my research over the past 10 years, I have come up with an analytic framework to understand the mixed outcomes, as shown in Figure 9.1. Mainly, the framework is composed of two reciprocal processes: One involves the *multicultural mind* in acquiring and applying multicultural knowledge, and the other involves the *multicultural self* in making inferences about the self from the multiple cultural encounters.

Also, whereas the multicultural mind involves the learning and deployment of learned knowledge without intense emotional reaction (analogous to the *cool* system espoused by Metcalfe & Mischel, 1999), the multicultural self involves relatively automatic, emotional responses (analogous to the *hot* system in Metcalfe & Mischel's, 1999, model). Importantly, when it involves the exposure to cultures of other racial or ethnic groups, the interplay of these two processes is moderated by individuals' lay theories (beliefs) about the nature of race. Specifically, we postulate two types of lay theories, each setting up a different framework within which its beholders view the racial–ethnic world and result in a harmonious versus discordant interplay between multicultural mind and multicultural self.

Because this model was built from my research on East Asian Americans (mainly Chinese Americans and Korean Americans), I focus the discussion that follows based on evidence from this particular group of bicultural individuals. (The participants were selected by the general criteria that they had resided in the United States for at least 3 years and were competent in their

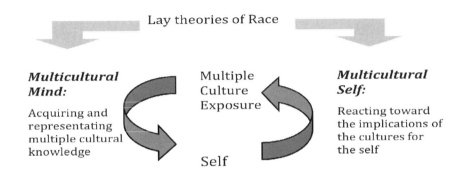

Figure 9.1.   An analytical framework.

native Asian language; as such, the participants were likely to have been exposed to both American and Asian cultures.) My focus on East Asian Americans was not an accident. The first reason is because I grew up in Hong Kong, was socialized in Chinese culture, and later studied in Japan; these experiences have given me ample knowledge about Chinese and other East Asian cultures.

The more important reason, however, is that thanks to the tireless efforts of many cross-cultural psychologists, there is copious empirical evidence regarding the differences between East Asians and Westerners in cognition (e.g., attribution and thinking style, Norenzayan, Choi, & Peng, 2007; categorization and reasoning, Medin, Unsworth, & Hirschfeld, 2007; subjective well-being, Tov & Diener, 2007; work-related behaviors, Sanchez-Burks & Lee, 2007; see definitive reviews in the *Handbook of Cultural Psychology*, edited by Kitayama & Cohen, 2007, and the *Oxford Handbook of Chinese Psychology*, edited by Bond, 2010). This rich body of research serves as the foundation upon which I have built my own lines of work to understand the process through which Asian Americans navigate between Asian and American cultures. In effect, the documented cross-cultural differences provide benchmarks for evaluating the consequences of cultural exposure (shifting toward more typically Asian culture vs. more typically Western culture). In the rest of this chapter, I delineate each of the three components of the model—multicultural mind, multicultural self, and lay theories of race—and reinforce the discussion with empirical evidence.

Multicultural Mind

There are many ways to define *culture* (Kroeber & Kluckhohn, 1963); to the extent that culture represents a collection of shared beliefs, norms, and practices among a group of people, it can be acquired through learning. That is, after a person has been submerged long enough in a culture, he or she will likely acquire the knowledge of the culture through explicit learning (e.g., attending language classes) or implicit learning (e.g., media exposure or interactions with the natives in the culture). Knowing the shared beliefs, norms, and practices, together with the culture's language, allows individuals to operate and function smoothly in their daily discourse with the local, native people of the culture. After substantial exposure, a point may be reached at which the bicultural individual can display culturally appropriate behavior spontaneously when the immediate context calls for it. For example, in Japan, people bow at different inclinations according to the relative seniority of the interacting partners and formality of the setting. After having been immersed in the Japanese culture long enough, expatriates and sojourners may automatically adjust the inclination of their bows accordingly.

To understand how bicultural individuals can adjust their thoughts, affect, and behaviors spontaneously and appropriately in different cultural contexts, my colleagues and I (Hong, Benet-Martinez, Chiu, & Morris, 2003; Hong, Chiu, & Kung, 1997; Hong, Morris, Chiu, & Benet-Martinez, 2000) have examined the social cognitive underpinnings of navigating between cultural frames, a process we term *cultural frame switching*. The following transcript, extracted from Hong, Roisman, and Chen's (2006) interview of a Taiwanese American, illustrates the phenomenology of cultural frame switching.

> Um . . . well, since I live in both places [Taiwan and the United States] and like every year I go back to Taiwan to visit, I find myself changing within the two cultures. It's like I go back to Taiwan they sometimes get scared of me because I'm too open and stuff. So I try to be more and more like, um, like fit into their definition, um, but when I come back I sometimes feel myself a little bit overwhelmed like, oh everybody's so open but then after like a month I get used to it. And then I go back to Taiwan again and then they're not used to me again so it's like a cycle kind of.

What is the mechanism underlying cultural frame switching? As cultural beliefs, norms, and practices are knowledge systems, they should operate according to the principles of knowledge activation (Higgins, 1996; Wyer & Srull, 1986): *availability, accessibility,* and *applicability.* First, people who have been exposed to multiple cultures acquire those knowledge systems and have them available in their cognitive repertoire. Given their availability, the associated cultural knowledge systems are activated and become temporarily accessible through priming (e.g., cuing the culture subtly through exposure to cultural icons). As a result of priming, participants can think, feel, or behave in ways that match the most accessible and applicable cultural knowledge system.

To test the validity of these ideas, we developed an experimental method called *cultural priming* (Hong et al., 1997, 2000). This method involves randomly assigning bicultural participants (e.g., Chinese American biculturals) to one of three experimental conditions: a Chinese culture priming condition, an American culture priming condition, and a control condition. In the Chinese culture priming condition, participants are exposed to pictures of Chinese cultural icons (e.g., Confucius, a Chinese opera, the Great Wall). In the American culture priming condition, participants are exposed to pictures of American cultural icons (e.g., Abraham Lincoln, a Western opera, the Statue of Liberty). Finally, in the control condition, participants are exposed to pictures of different shapes of clouds in the sky.

Following the slide show, participants are typically asked to perform a task in which we can gauge whether their responses were more Chinese- or American-like. In a series of experiments (Hong et al., 1997, 2000, 2003; Wong & Hong, 2005), we have shown that participants in the Chinese condition responded in ways typical of Chinese people, whereas participants in the American condition responded in ways typical of American people. For example, we conducted studies on the effect of cultural priming on attributions. After being exposed to Chinese, American, or neutral pictures, Chinese American biculturals (Hong Kong Chinese, Chinese Americans) were asked to interpret an ambiguous event (e.g., a picture of a fish swimming in front of a school of fish, a story about an obese boy eating a high-calorie cake while on a diet). The ambiguous event could have been explained in terms of the target actor's individual attributes (e.g., the fish in front is a leader, the obese boy lacks self-control) or in terms of the social group surrounding the actor (e.g., the fish is being

chased by the fish behind him, the obese boy is influenced by a friend's persua-
sion to eat the cake). Across several studies, we consistently found that participants in the Chinese priming condition made more group attributions (a
pattern typical of Chinese) and fewer individual attributions (a pattern typical
of Americans) than did their counterparts in the American priming condition.
Responses from participants in the control condition lie in between those of the
two cultural priming conditions.

Although the activation of cultural knowledge appears to be spontaneous,
it is important to note that activation is not a knee-jerk response to situational
cues. In accordance with the principles of knowledge activation (Higgins, 1996),
the evoked cultural frame will be appraised for its applicability to the immediate context before it is applied. That is, an accessible cultural idea will not have
any influence over an individual's judgments or behaviors unless it is applicable to the task at hand. For example, as noted, Chinese American biculturals
will be more likely to focus on the group (vs. the individual) to explain an event
when they are primed with Chinese cultural icons than when they are primed
with American cultural icons (Hong et al., 2000). However, this occurs only
when the group (versus the individual) causality perspective is applicable to
the context within which one need to make a judgment, such as when the intergroup dimension is salient (Hong et al., 2003).

Similarly, in the behavioral domain individuals might choose to compete or
cooperate with their partners in a Prisoner's Dilemma game. In Chinese cultural contexts, a cooperative (vs. competitive) script is applicable only when
interacting with friends but not when interacting with strangers. In an experiment (Wong & Hong, 2005), Chinese American bicultural participants were
primed with Chinese icons or American icons to activate the particular knowledge system before playing the Prisoner's Dilemma game with either friends or
strangers. After being primed with Chinese cultural icons, participants playing
with friends showed more cooperation than those who were primed with
American cultural icons; however, they did not show the cultural priming effect
toward strangers. This pattern of findings showed that accessibility of a cultural knowledge system only sets up a necessary but not sufficient condition for
the effects of cultural priming to occur. The applicability of the accessible cultural knowledge system on the immediate context is equally important.

Other researchers have used experimental procedures similar to ours and
found cultural priming effects on a multitude of dependent measures including
spontaneous self-construal (Ross, Xun, & Wilson, 2002), representations about
work and family (Verkuyten & Pouliasi, 2002), and managerial decisions
(Friedman, Liu, Chi, Hong, & Sung, in press). Importantly, these three studies
used different bicultural samples (Chinese Canadians, Dutch Greek bicultural,
managers from Taiwan who had studied or worked abroad, respectively) and a
variety of cultural primes (language, experimenter's cultural identity, and
environmental primes, such as decoration, music, and general room ambiance,
respectively). As a whole, the cultural priming effects are robust.

Some recent studies (Ng & Han, 2009; Ng & Lai, 2009; Sui, Hong, Liu,
Humphreys, & Han, 2011) have added to the list of cultural priming effects in
an important way—they suggest that cultural priming modulates neural sub-
strates of self-referencing. In one study, after activating participants' Chinese

versus Western cultural knowledge using the typical cultural priming procedures, Ng and Lai (2009) asked Hong Kong Chinese college students to judge
whether certain adjectives could be used to describe themselves (self-referencing), their mother (mother-referencing), or a person with whom they are familiar but do not identify (NIP-referencing). As a control, in some trials, the
participants were asked about the font type in which the adjectives were
printed. Later, participants were given a surprise recall and recognition test of
the adjectives they saw earlier. The participants in the Western priming condition remembered more of the adjectives that appeared in the self-referencing
questions than those in the other three question types, which suggests a relatively distinctive self-construal (typical of Western culture). By contrast, participants in the Chinese priming condition remembered the adjectives that
appeared in the mother- and NIP-referencing questions equally well as those in
the self-referencing questions, suggesting a relatively socially connected self-
construal (typical of Chinese culture). Importantly, because these two patterns
of recall have been linked with distinct neurological activation (Zhu, Zhang,
Fan, & Han, 2007), researchers suggest that cultural priming may have led to
the corresponding neurological activations. Indeed, Ng and Han (2009) presented preliminary evidence to support this argument.

The cultural frame switching and cultural priming results illustrate the
dynamic constructivist approach (espoused by Hong et al., 2000), which claims
that the retrieval of cultural knowledge among bicultural individuals is a
dynamic process contingent upon the individual's cultural experiences, the
unfolding cultural milieu, and how appropriate the knowledge is for the situation. We assert that culture does not rigidly determine human behaviors, nor
are individuals passive recipients of their cultural environment. Instead, individuals flexibly shift their responses and use culture as a cognitive resource for
grappling with their experiences. Although traditional cross-cultural psychology focuses on comparing the similarities and differences between groups of
individuals demarcated by race, ethnicity, or nationality, our new dynamic constructivist approach views cultural systems as open and ever changing.
Individuals are not limited by their racial, ethnic, or national identities in making their responses. Moreover, the cultural priming procedures we developed
make it possible to study the *causal* effects of culture, as we randomly assigned
participants into different cultural priming conditions, making it possible to
infer culture as a cause of the subsequent responses.

Multicultural Self

Aside from its impact on knowledge acquisition, coming into close contact with
another culture could also compel a person to reflect upon his or her own identity, leading to questions such as, Who am I? or Who are we? In this context, the
individual might evaluate the self (or the collective self) with reference to the
other culture. Am I qualified to be a member of this new cultural group? Will
the new cultural group question my membership? Can I meaningfully define
myself in terms of the new culture? Can I find comfort and a safe haven in the
new culture? A long tradition of acculturation literature has shown that it is

often challenging for immigrants and their descendants to build a "secure" identity within the host culture (e.g., the notion of cultural attachment; Hong et al., 2006; see also Ward, Bochner, & Furnham, 2001). Deaux (2006), in her seminal book *To Be an Immigrant*, elaborated beautifully on the complexity of identity negotiation. She used two examples: A Bangladeshi immigrant in New York City who experienced doubts about her identity after September 11th as she realized that her skin color and features bore resemblance to the terrorists; a young French man of African descent felt that other French people have never considered him as French. In both cases, the protagonists constantly negotiate and renegotiate their identities by

> deciding how to conceptualize ethnic and national identity, weighting possible combinations between the identity of origin and a newly claimed identity in the country to which they have moved; merging that newly formulated sense of identity with other important aspects of self; and doing all of this within a social context in which beliefs about immigrants and about one's ethnic and national group are held and conveyed. (Deaux, 2006, p. 91–92)

One crucial determinant of building a secure identity within the new culture could be the perceived inclusion versus exclusion by the host culture. For example, after having lived in the United States for over 11 years, from time to time I have been asked "Where do you come from?" by people whom I had just met. Sometimes I would answer, "I am from Champaign, a town located south of Chicago." But shortly after my response the questioner would often further press, "Where do you *really* come from?" I would never infer cruel intentions from the questioner, nor was I bothered by the question, since I do have a place where I *really* come from—Hong Kong. However, how would an Asian American born in the United States feel about such questions? Cheryan and Monin (2005) found that it is common for U.S.-born Asian Americans to encounter questions such as, "Where do you *really* come from?" These questions communicate to U.S.-born Asian Americans that they are not seen as full-fledged members of the United States, thereby threatening their American identity. When experimenters in Cheryan and Monin (2005) asked such questions of U.S.-born Asian Americans, the participants felt that their American identity was being denied, and they subsequently displayed responses to assert their American identity (e.g., through the demonstration of American cultural knowledge or claiming participation in American practices).

Identification with the mainstream American culture is arguably more challenging for non-White than for White immigrants and their descendants. Devos and Banaji (2005) showed that to be American is implicitly synonymous with being White. In their study, they used the Implicit Association Test and consistently found across five studies that both African and Asian Americans were perceived to be less associated with the "American" national category than were White Americans. This finding is astonishing because some of the White stimuli were well-known foreign White European celebrities (e.g., Hugh Grant) and some of the Asian stimuli were well-known Asian American celebrities (e.g., Connie Chung). Despite the presumed familiarity with these celebrities, there was still a tendency for participants to spontaneously associate the

White European celebrities more than the Asian American celebrities with being American. These findings may reflect a widely held spontaneous assumption that American = White. Given these findings it is challenging, if not daunting, for ethnic minorities to be accepted as full-fledged Americans.

When faced with these challenges, some ethnic minorities may remain resilient despite the occasional negative experience and remain hopeful that ethnic boundaries can be eventually crossed or even erased. By contrast, other ethnic minorities may avoid potentially negative experiences by shying away from interethnic encounters. These ethnic minorities often perceive ethnic boundaries to be rigid and impermeable, thereby justifying their lack of effort in attempting to cross over them. The responses of the former group may provide a basis for acquisition of new cultural knowledge to build a multicultural mind, whereas the responses of the latter group may evoke reactive, defensive processes that would disrupt the acquisition and application of new cultural knowledge. Importantly, we wonder as to the driver of these two response patterns. My research has suggested that the two kinds of responses may be systematically linked with the individual's understanding of the nature of race and racial boundaries. Specifically, it seems that people who remain resilient may be encouraged by the belief that racial boundaries are fluid and malleable, whereas those who responded defensively are fueled by the belief that racial boundaries are rigid and unalterable. In the following section, I discuss how these two types of understanding are rooted in two types of lay beliefs (implicit theories) regarding the nature of race: the essentialist theory of race versus the social constructionist theory of race.

Lay Theories of Race as a Moderator

In many societies around the globe, there are social disparities that are linked with groups of people with distinct outer physical characteristics (e.g., skin tone, hair texture, nose shape, body type), behavioral tendencies, performance, and personality traits. Lay theories of race are beliefs that individuals hold that allow them to make sense of how these outer differences in physical characteristics correspond to inner personal attributes such as abilities and personality traits. Our research (Chao, Chen, Roisman, & Hong, 2007; No et al., 2008; for a review, see Hong, Chao, & No, 2009) has focused on two opposing views of race often contested in social discourse and scientific debates (Celious & Oyserman, 2001; Gossett, 1997; Ossorio & Duster, 2005; Tate & Audette, 2001).

One theory contends that race is determined by some nonmalleable, deepseated essence, defined as something genetic or otherwise biological, or by other "essence placeholders" such as ancestry or normative cultural practices. According to this theory, termed the *essentialist theory of race*, racial essence gives rise to personality traits and abilities that are stable over time and across situations such that race is not only "real" and not only has a material basis but is also diagnostic of a multitude of human characteristics. The opposing theory discussed in our work, termed the *social constructionist theory of race*, denies the real existence of racial essence—in fact, scientists have not found genetic markers for race in the human genome (Bonham, Warshauer-Baker, & Collins, 2005). For some who endorse this theory, racial taxonomies are invented (often by members of the dominant group) to justify and rationalize existing inequalities between groups. For others who endorse this theory, racial taxonomies are just convenient labels people use in certain societies or cultures. As such, a person may be categorized differently depending on where he or she goes in the world (e.g., the United States vs. Brazil), and the meaning of the racial categories to which he or she belongs can be altered when social circumstances change (Fairchild, Yee, Wyatt, & Weizmann, 1995; Zuckerman, 1990).

In both cases race is a social construction that is arbitrarily created for social and political reasons in historical contexts. Because racial categorization is conceptualized as fluid, any differences observed among racial groups do not reflect deep-seated differences among the groups. To assess individuals' extent of endorsement of these two beliefs, we designed an eight-item questionnaire in which participants are asked to rate their degree of agreement with statements such as, "To a large extent, a person's race biologically determines his or her abilities and traits"; "What a person is like (e.g., his or her abilities, traits) is deeply ingrained in his or her race. It cannot be changed much"; "Races are just arbitrary categories and can be changed if necessary" (reverse item); see the full scale in No et al. (2008). Thus far, we have surveyed over 1,000 undergraduate students at the University of Illinois at Urbana–Champaign, a large state university located in the midwestern United States, and about the same proportion of students endorsed the essentialist theory as the social constructivist theory (the scores were largely normally distributed). This result has surprised some of my colleagues, as they thought that most college students would be progressive enough to endorse the social constructionist theory, and that those endorsing the essentialist theory would be hard to come by.

However, equally interesting, other colleagues disputed the lack of a genetic basis for racial differences and questioned whether those who deny the genetic basis for race are politically motivated. This criticism is understandable because race is a widely accepted concept, and it would be a daunting task to convince people that race is just a myth. To this end, Marshall Segall, an eminent cross-cultural psychologist and his associates have admirably designed an exhibition entitled "All of Us Are Related, Each of Us is Unique" that uses scientific findings to convincingly argue that racial categorization is just skin deep, with no inherent deep-seated differences between racial groups. (This exhibition has toured around the world in the past 10 years and can be viewed at http://allrelated.syr.edu/.)

The goal of our research is not to determine whether the essentialist theory or social constructionist theory holds more truth (although that could prove to be interesting). Rather, our goal is to understand whether holding the essentialist versus social constructionist theory of race leads to different consequences in interracial/intercultural settings. Regardless of what the objective evidence is, we did find that people are divided in their endorsement of the two theories. The next logical question to ask is whether the two theories set up different lenses through which individuals see the ethnic/cultural world.

Our approach follows Kelly's (1955) and Heider's (1958) argument that laypeople are naive scientists who generate and use theories about the social world, and Medin and colleagues' (Medin, 1989; Murphy & Medin, 1985) findings that, indeed, people's reasoning in a domain is guided by their lay theory of that domain. In our case, we argue that the lay theory of race creates a lens through which individuals understand racial differences and conceptualize racial reality, which in turn leads to particular ways of encoding, representing, and organizing information related to race. To illustrate how lay theories operate, take a look at Figure 9.2. Are the three big dots in the middle of the figure protruding out or caving in? Use your spontaneous impression to answer this question. I have shown this figure in my talks several times, and audiences usually see that the three dots are protruding out rather than caving in. Why? It is because most audiences assume that the light source comes from above, just as though we might experience it outdoors under the sun or inside a lit room. This background assumption then sets up a framework within which we infer a three-dimensional percept from a two-dimensional picture. Now, close your eyes and imagine that the light source is located at the bottom of the figure rather than from the top. Then, open your eyes and look at Figure 9.2 again. The three dots should now appear to cave in, rather than protrude out.

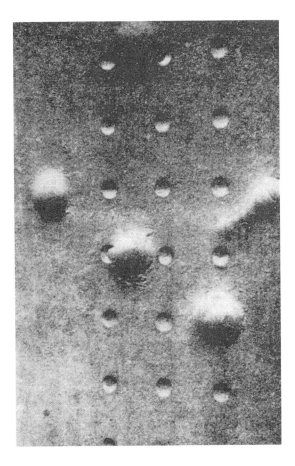

Figure 9.2.   Are the three dots in the middle protruding out or caving in?

The two lay theories of race are analogous to the two background assumptions about the location of the light source. They provide two frameworks through which the same information can be interpreted in totally opposite ways.

The two lay theories of race are reminiscent of the implicit theories that Dweck and her associates have identified for human attributes (Dweck, Chiu, & Hong, 1995; Hong et al., 2004; Hong, Levy, & Chiu, 2001). A myriad of research (see reviews by Dweck, 1999; Dweck et al., 1995) has shown that some people are prone to view human attributes as reflecting deep-seated dispositions that cannot be changed (i.e., an entity theory), whereas other people are prone to view human attributes as dynamically affected by the psychological states of the person in a given context, and hence malleable (i.e., an incremental theory). These two theories were found to coexist within a single person's mind, but were also shown to differ in their relative chronic accessibility. Thus, when asked directly participants were able to indicate their relative endorsement of the entity or incremental theory. Importantly, individuals' relative endorsement of one theory over the other has been found to predict their social judgments and intergroup perceptions such that stronger endorsement of the entity theory (vs. the incremental theory) was associated with more stereotyping and prejudice (Hong et al., 2004; Levy, Stroessner, & Dweck, 1998; cf. Keller, 2005).

The lay theories of race are also related to psychological essentialism. Research has shown that people tend to infer a core defining essence underlying observed physical differences among groups (Gelman & Hirschfeld, 1999; Gil-White, 2001; Haslam, Rothschild, & Ernst, 2000, 2002; Medin & Ortony, 1989; Prentice & Miller, 2006). According to Rothbart and Taylor (1992), the imputation of an *essence* rests on whether a particular social category is believed to possess inductive potential and unalterability. *Inductive potential* refers to whether group membership is telling of individual members' characteristics (e.g., traits, abilities, behaviors), whereas *unalterability* refers to whether group membership is fixed for a relatively long duration. Extending these earlier analyses of essentialism, Haslam and colleagues (2000, 2002) differentiated between two dimensions of psychological essentialism: *the natural kind* and *entitativity*. The idea of the natural kind is associated with discreteness and a biological basis, whereas the idea of entitativity is akin to the perception of members in a social category as a coherent, unified, and meaningful unit.

The essentialist theory of race maps onto the natural kind component of psychological essentialism, which emphasizes the discreteness of racial groups and a biological basis of race. In other words, the essentialist theory parallels beliefs associated with natural kind categories such as "tiger" and "gold" (cf. Rothbart & Taylor, 1992), and represents the notion that categories possess core, underlying properties that are independent of human perception (Tate & Audette, 2001). In contrast, the social constructionist theory of race parallels beliefs associated with human artifacts such as "chair" and "table," and posits that categories do not possess unalterable, inherent properties (e.g., an overturned crate can be considered a chair) but are created by human perceivers due to their motives to simplify and group items by function.

Holding an essentialist theory of race orients racial minority members to perceive a more rigid, impermeable interracial boundary than does holding a social constructionist theory of race. Under the essentialist theory framework, racial minority members feel that they can never become full-fledged members of the mainstream, host cultural group. This perception makes it difficult for minority group members to switch to the mainstream cultural frame and would eventually affect real-life outcomes, such as expatriates' adaptation to their adopted culture and cross-cultural management, in which bicultural managers adjust their management practices in different cultural contexts. I review evidence for this below.

IDENTIFICATION WITH MAINSTREAM CULTURE. As noted, one assumption for the lay theory approach is that people may hold multiple theories in a certain domain but one of those theories may be more chronically accessible to an individual because he or she has been using it more frequently than the other theory. If that is the case, then we should also be able to activate the accessibility of a certain theory by persuading participants that that theory is supported by stronger scientific evidence. In fact, we used this method to temporarily activate the accessibility of each of the lay theories. Specifically, in the study (No et al., 2008, Study 2), we randomly assigned Asian American participants into one of the two lay theories of race induction conditions. Participants in the essentialist theory induction condition read an essay, allegedly from *Time*, which advocated that "there is essence underlying racial groups. The concept of race has divided humankind into meaningful social groups based on differences in their innate qualities." By contrast, participants in the social constructivist theory induction condition read an essay, also allegedly from *Time*, which claimed that "the meaning of race is socially constructed. It is used to characterize different social groups." As a cover story for reading the essay, we told participants that they were going to participate in a reading comprehension task and that they would eventually be asked questions regarding the main theme of the article and how persuasive and convincing it was.

Readers of the two articles were similarly proficient in identifying the main theme and found the articles similarly persuasive and convincing. Unbeknownst to the participants, however, we were really interested in how they would identify with their ethnic culture and the mainstream American culture after reading the article. Our prediction was that the Asian American participants in the essentialist theory induction condition would find it harder to later identify with the mainstream American culture than would those participants in the social constructionist theory induction condition. Indeed, we found that participants who were in the essentialist theory condition identified significantly less with the mainstream American culture than did their counterparts in the social constructionist theory condition. Interestingly, these two groups were similar high in identifying with their Asian identity.[1] Therefore, it seems that as we predicted, the essentialist theory induction created somewhat

---

[1]Interestingly, this result differs from the typical results of permeability of intergroup boundaries in that previous research typically found that members of a low-status group identify with their ingroup less when the intergroup boundaries are perceived as permeable than impermeable (e.g., Ellemers, Van Knippenberg, de Vries, & Wilke, 1988; Ellemers, Van Knippenberg, & Wilke, 1990). Although the social constructionist theory of race may orient ethnic minority members to view the interethnic boundaries as fluid, it does not necessarily undermine their native ethnic identity.

of a cognitive barrier that blocked our racial minority participants from passing into the mainstream culture. (We were careful in debriefing the participants afterward, such that we did not jeopardize participants' identification with the American culture.)

SWITCHING BETWEEN CULTURAL FRAMES. In another study (Chao et al., 2007, Study 1), we examined whether lay theories of race were related to efficiency in switching between cultural frames. We first measured participants' endorsement of lay theories of race. In the main study, we presented participants with a cultural priming task that was similar to the one just described. However, this time we presented participants with cultural icons one at a time immediately followed by a target word (or nonword). The target words were either Chinese values (e.g., filial, collectivist), American values (freedom, individualist), or nonwords (strings of scrambled letters). As such, we used Chinese and American icons as primes to activate participants' corresponding knowledge systems and then examined their subsequent performance in recognizing Chinese and American cultural value words in a lexical decision task. We predicted that for people who endorse the essentialist theory of race, because they keep Chinese cultural knowledge separate from American cultural knowledge, it would be harder for them to switch rapidly between the Chinese and American cultural frames. Therefore, it should take these participants more time to identify the target words in the trials in which the primes and words were a cultural mismatch (i.e., Chinese primes with American value words, or American primes with Chinese value words). In fact, we found that Chinese American participants who strongly endorsed the essentialist theory of race took longer to identify target words in culturally mismatched trials than did those who endorsed the essentialist theory of race less strongly.

The findings revealed that in trials that required rapid switching between cultural frames (American-prime-Chinese-word trials and Chinese-prime-American-word trials), the stronger the participants believed in racial essentialism, the longer they took to identify the target words. This further suggested that bicultural individuals who endorse essentialism perceive rigid boundaries between the Chinese and American cultures and think of the two cultures as separate entities.

As the essentialist theory of race is associated with perceiving more rigid cultural group boundaries and more difficulty in switching between cultural frames than the social constructionist theory, this effect may also manifest itself in more effort and stress when bicultural individuals discuss their experiences with both cultures. To test this idea, we conducted the Cultural Attachment Interview (CAI; Hong et al., 2006) among 60 Chinese American biculturals (Chao et al., 2007, Study 2). The CAI examines the degree to which bicultural individuals have come to develop coherent narratives about their experiences in Chinese and American cultures. During the interviews, we acquired data on participants' changes in electrodermal activity (skin conductance level) as an indication of their preparation for action in response to anxiety, stress, and perceived threat. The study revealed that stronger endorsement of essentialist beliefs was associated with increased electrodermal response when the participants talked about their bicultural experiences. This suggested that discussing personal experiences within the two cultures may be highly stressful and threatening for bicultural individuals who endorse an essentialist belief about race, as they need to reconcile and integrate the seemingly rigid interracial boundaries and competing cultural attributes (e.g., cultural values).

ASSIMILATION VERSUS CONTRAST EFFECTS IN CULTURAL PRIMING. At the outset of this discussion, we mentioned the cultural priming procedures in which participants display responses that match the culture primes (an assimilation effect). However, this assimilation effect is not inevitable. For Asian Americans who believe in an essentialist theory, seeing the American primes may remind them of their Asian identity and that they might never become "true" Americans. Therefore, it is possible that they would not assimilate into the American primes and would even react against them and respond in typically "Asian" ways when primed with American icons (a contrast effect). To test this idea, we (No et al., 2008, Study 4) examined the pattern of emotional projection among Asian Americans. Prior work by Cohen and Gunz (2002) examined the projection of emotional experiences onto generalized others among European Canadians and foreign-born Asian Canadians. Consistent with previous cross-cultural research findings on independent and interdependent self-construals (e.g., Markus & Kitayama, 1991), European Canadians displayed a pattern of egocentric projection in which emotions felt by the self were projected onto others (e.g., feeling "anger" and projecting "anger" onto others), whereas Asian Canadians showed a pattern of relational projection and perceived others as experiencing the complementary emotion felt by the self (e.g., feeling "anger" and projecting "fear" onto others).

Accordingly, we predicted that overall Asian Americans would show more egocentric projection and less relational projection when primed with American cultural icons and more relational projection and less egocentric projection when primed with Asian cultural icons. However, we argued that this pattern would be moderated by participants' lay theories of race such that those who more strongly endorsed an essentialist theory of race would be less likely to display assimilation effects toward the American primes. This is because the American primes would elicit intergroup comparison processes, reminding the Asian Americans who endorse an essentialist theory of their essential, unalterable differences that set them apart from the White majority group. This study was conducted with Korean Americans, and the findings were consistent with our predictions. Specifically, whereas participants who endorsed the social constructionist theory assimilated toward the American cultural primes (i.e., responding with more egocentric projection and less relational projection), those who endorsed the essentialist theory did not show such assimilation. In contrast, essentialists showed the opposite pattern when primed with the American cultural icons such that they responded with less egocentric projection and more relational projection.

This lack of assimilation toward American cultural primes among people who endorse an essentialist theory of race raises the question of whether individuals are unwilling versus unable to switch between cultural frames. To the extent that the cultural icons were effective in activating the corresponding cultural knowledge, the lack of assimilation found in this study may be indicative of a motivational reluctance to frame switch among those who endorse essentialist race beliefs. In short, the findings suggest that the essentialist theory, in comparison to the social constructionist theory, is associated with a more discrete representation of cultures, thereby making it harder for minority group members to switch rapidly between cultural frames; it also dampens their tendency to assimilate toward the majority cultural frames.

EXPATRIATE ADAPTATION AND CROSS-CULTURAL MANAGEMENT. How might the lay theories of race predict real life outcomes? Adaptation of expatriates is a case in point. Not only do expatriates face the challenge of living and working in a new culture but many of them also change their status from a racial majority in their own country to a racial minority in the host country. Therefore, their lay theories of race should also affect their tendency to approach versus avoid the new host culture. To understand these processes, we (Hong & Zhang, 2006) conducted a survey in Beijing, China to examine the acculturative tendencies of Caucasian expatriates from Western countries (America, Europe, and Australia). Our research assistants recruited Western expatriates at bars in the Hou Hai (后 海) district in Beijing, an area that is known to be frequented by expatriates. The expatriates ($N = 88$) were asked to respond to our lay theories of race measure, together with a measure of Chinese language proficiency, length of stay in China, and their extent of engagement in Chinese cultural practices and activities in the past 6 months (e.g., "When I listened to music, _____% of the time I listened to Chinese music;" "During the past 6 months, _____% of the films I watched were in Chinese;" "When I ate at home, _____% of the time the food was prepared in Chinese style;" "Now, _____% of my friends are Chinese"). The results revealed that the stronger the expatriates held an essentialist theory of race, the less likely they were to engage in Chinese cultural practices and activities. This correlation remained significant even when proficiency in the Chinese language and length of residence in China were statistically controlled. These findings suggest that the essentialist theory of race also hinders Caucasian expatriates' acculturation into Chinese (the host) culture. More important, they hint that the effects of endorsing an essentialist theory of race not only apply to Asian Americans, who typically possess less sociopolitical power and status than White Americans, but also to White expatriates, a racial minority group that enjoys relatively high status in China. As such, the essentialist theory of race appears to set up an impermeable interracial boundary for groups regardless of their relative power.

In a recent study, my colleagues and I (Friedman et al., in press) investigated how the cultural frame switching tendency is related to the managerial decisions of a group of Taiwanese managers who have experiences studying or working in Western countries. Presumably, these Taiwanese managers are bicultural individuals (i.e., have acquired Chinese and Western cultural knowledge). Would we find that they display Western (Chinese) managerial practices when exposed to Western (Chinese) primes? In the study, we examined the bicultural identity integration (BII) of Taiwanese managers instead of the lay theories of race because the managerial situations in Taiwan usually did not involve interracial relations (hence, the measure of lay theories of race was no longer applicable). BII, proposed by Benet-Martinez and colleagues (Benet-Martinez & Haritatos, 2005; Haritatos & Benet-Martinez, 2002), refers to bicultural individuals' subjective perception that their two identities are overlapping, nonantagonistic, and integrated easily into everyday thought and behavior. Previous research (Benet-Martinez, Leu, Lee, & Morris, 2002) showed assimilation effects of cultural priming among biculturals who are high on BII but contrast effects among those who are low on BII.

In our study, we assessed the level of integration between the Chinese self and Western self for the Taiwanese managers, and how integration moderates the effect of cultural frame switching tendency on their pay allocation, a common managerial decision. Results showed that only those managers who had a highly integrated bicultural identity showed the cultural frame switching tendency, such that they made more equal pay allocations between the efficient and less efficient employees (a typical Chinese response) in the Chinese priming condition and more equitable pay allocations to the efficient employee (a typical Western response) in the Western priming condition. Managers who had a less integrated bicultural identity did not display much difference in their method of pay allocation across the two priming conditions. These findings parallel the effects found for lay theories of race. Only those who are at ease with their two cultural identities can switch smoothly between cultural frames.

RACIAL CATEGORIZATION AND PROCESSING. Recently, we extended our research to examine whether lay theories of race are associated with basic cognitive processing of race related information, including detection of subtle facial features of ethnic groups and categorization of target individuals into racial groups. In five studies (Chao, Hong, & Chiu, 2011), we have shown that believing in an essentialist theory of race is linked to an increased tendency to engage in race-based categorization (categorizing celebrities into Black vs. White racial groups, rather than categorizing them along other dimensions, such as actors vs. basketball players), higher efficiency in learning race-related categories (in an implicit learning task), greater sensitivity to discern phenotypic racial differences when performing racial categorization, and greater tendency to adhere to hypodescent principle in perceiving racial groups (i.e., excluding targets from the White category when they show any, even minimal, features of Blacks).

Furthermore, when making inferences about the psychological traits of a racial group, perceivers who endorse the essential theory of race weigh the behaviors of group members with salient phenotypic characteristics (e.g., skin color, facial features) more heavily than the behaviors of those with less salient phenotypic characteristics. The results have supported our contention that the essentialist theory of race serves as a background assumption within which people interpret race-related information and derive meaning out of it, a process we tried to demonstrated earlier using Figure 9.2.

Implications for Building a Multicultural Society

In this chapter, I have differentiated two intimately linked processes that result from multicultural exposure—the multicultural mind and multicultural self. The former is related to the process of acquiring and applying new cultural knowledge after extensive immersion in the new culture. The latter is related to the process of evaluating one's identity in relation to the new culture, which could facilitate or hinder the acquisition and application of the new cultural knowledge. When an identity is not at risk, such as when there is no identity threat or the interracial boundary is perceived to be permeable and nonrigid, individuals can freely navigate between cultures and use the multiple cultural knowledge systems as their resources; such a process is likely to occur when ethnic minority individuals hold a social constructionist theory of race or are high in bicultural identity integration, or in societies in which the interethnic boundaries are fluid. Conversely, when interracial boundaries are rigid, impermeable, and passing through them seems impossible, the cultural frame switching process can be jeopardized and individuals might even react against and retreat to their native culture when confronted with the mainstream culture; such a process is likely to occur when racial minority individuals hold an essentialist theory of race or are low in bicultural identity integration, or in societies in which interethnic boundaries are structured to be impermeable.

Because an essentialist theory of race has consistently been associated with detrimental consequences for ethnic minority and majority group members, it seems that debunking the myth of race would help all ethnic groups to resolve their rigid views about interethnic boundaries, thereby easing the acquisition and application of multicultural knowledge. However, despite the fact that we have shown some success in temporarily activating the accessibility of the lay theories of race experimentally (No et al., 2008, Study 2), changing people's lay theories of race could be more difficult than it may seem. For one, the *race* concept has long been entrenched in people's everyday discourse. (In writing this chapter, I felt great difficulty in restraining myself from using *race* or *racial groups*.) More important, it is hard because the essentialist theory often plays important functions for both groups. In ethnic majority groups, some members are motivated to endorse the essentialist theory, especially when the superiority of their groups is under threat because it would help to justify their dominance over minority groups (Morton, Postmes, Haslam, & Hornsey, 2009). This makes the essentialist theory of race a part of the legitimizing myth to justify the status quo (akin to the social dominance theory; Sidanius & Pratto, 1999) and is hard to dispute despite scientific evidence.

In ethnic minority groups, some individuals may also embrace the essentialist theory of race because it allows them to be differentiated from the ethnic majority group. This is useful when the minority group is lobbying for preferential treatment or seeking legitimacy in breaking away from a majority group. For example, Liu (2009) examined how stem cell research in Taiwan serves the purpose of finding unique "Taiwanese genetic characteristics" and thus a biological basis for a unique Taiwanese identity, which then can be used to claim independence from Mainland China.

In our view, however, it is not about stopping people from using racial categories (or making people "color-blinded"; see Plaut, Thomas, & Goren, 2009), which would not cure the root of the problem. Rather, a more thorough remedy would be to steer people away from making inferences from observable differences among ethnic groups to deep-seated, unalterable dispositions. Understanding the differences among ethnic groups (in norms, values, and sociohistorical circumstances of different groups) and at the same time appreciating the within-group variations as well as between-group overlaps are important. The key message is that there is not a monolithic, homogenous group and any differences between ethnic groups cannot be attributed to deep-seated dispositions.

As globalization is proceeding at an unprecedented speed, not only are immigrants or sojourners confronted with new cultures but many countries are also facing the rapid import of foreign ideas and practices. This means that whether one goes to a new country or not, managing multiculturalism is a pressing necessity rather than a luxury. Societies that are successful in managing multiculturalism would be more likely to enjoy intergroup harmony and peace and at the same time reap the benefits of having a more creative and innovative workforce (cf. Leung, Maddux, Galinsky, & Chiu, 2008). Through examining the intricate interplay between multicultural mind and multicultural self, our research has provided pointers toward successful management of multiculturalism.

References

Benet-Martinez, V., & Haritatos, J. (2005). Bicultural Identity Integration (BII): Components and psychosocial antecedents. *Journal of Personality*, *73*, 1015–1050. doi:10.1111/j.1467-6494.2005.00337.x

Benet-Martinez, V., Leu, J., Lee, F, & Morris, M. W. (2002). Negotiating biculturalism: Cultural frame switching in biculturals with oppositional versus compatible cultural identities. *Journal of Cross-Cultural Psychology*, *33*, 492–516. doi:10.1177/0022022102033005005

Bond, M. H. (Ed.). (2010). *Oxford handbook of Chinese psychology*. Oxford, England: Oxford University Press.

Bonham, V. L., Warshauer-Baker, E., & Collins, F. S. (2005). Race and ethnicity in the genome era: The complexity of the constructs. *American Psychologist*, *60*, 9–15. doi:10.1037/0003-066X.60.1.9

Celious, A., & Oyserman, D. (2001). Race from the inside: An emerging heterogenous race model. *Journal of Social Issues*, *57*, 149–165. doi:10.1111/0022-4537.00206

Chao, M. M., Chen, J., Roisman, G., & Hong, Y. (2007). Essentializing race: Implications for bicultural individuals' cognition and physiological reactivity. *Psychological Science*, *18*, 341–348. doi:10.1111/j.1467-9280.2007.01901.x

Chao, M. M., Hong, Y., & Chiu, C. (2011). *Essentializing race. Racial categorization and itsiImplications on racialized perceptions*. Manuscript submitted for publication.

Cheryan, S., & Monin, B. (2005). "Where are you really from?": Asian Americans and identity denial. *Journal of Personality and Social Psychology*, *89*, 717–730. doi:10.1037/0022-3514.89.5.717

Cohen, D., & Gunz, A. (2002). As seen by the other: Perspectives on the self in the memories and emotion perceptions of Easterners and Westerners. *Psychological Science*, *13*, 55–59. doi:10.1111/1467-9280.00409

Deaux, K. (2006). *To be an immigrant*. New York, NY: Russell Sage Foundation.

Devos, T., & Banaji, M. R. (2005). American = White? *Journal of Personality and Social Psychology*, *88*, 447–466. doi:10.1037/0022-3514.88.3.447

Dweck, C. S. (1999). *Self-theories: Their role in motivation, personality, and development*. Philadelphia, PA: The Psychology Press.

Dweck, C. S., Chiu, C., & Hong, Y. (1995). Implicit theories and their role in judgments and reactions: A world from two perspectives. *Psychological Inquiry*, *6*, 267–285. doi:10.1207/s15327965pli0604_1

Ellemers, N., Van Knippenberg, A., de Vries, N., & Wilke, H. (1988). Social identification and permeability of group boundaries. *European Journal of Social Psychology*, *18*, 497–513. doi:10.1002/ejsp.2420180604

Ellemers, N., Van Knippenberg, A., & Wilke, H. A. (1990). The influence of permeability of group boundaries and stability of group status on strategies of individual mobility and social change. *British Journal of Social Psychology*, *29*, 233–246. doi:10.1111/j.2044-8309.1990.tb00902.x

Fairchild, H. H., Yee, A. H., Wyatt, G. E., & Weizmann, F. M. (1995). Readdressing psychology's problems with race. *American Psychologist*, *50*, 46–47. doi:10.1037/0003-066X.50.1.46

Friedman, R., Liu, W., Chi, S. S.-C., Hong, Y., & Sung, L.-K. (in press). Cross-cultural management and bicultural identity integration: When does experience abroad lead to appropriate cultural switching? *International Journal of Intercultural Relations*.

Gelman, S. A., & Hirschfeld, L. A. (1999). How biological is essentialism? In D. L. Medin & S. Atran (Eds.), *Folkbiology* (pp. 403–446). Cambridge, MA: MIT Press.

Gil-White, F. (2001). Are ethnic groups biological species to the human brain? Essentialism in human cognition of some social groups. *Current Anthropology*, *42*, 515–553. doi:10.1086/321802

Gossett, T. F. (1997). *Race: The history of an idea in America* (Rev. ed.). New York, NY: Oxford University Press.

Haritatos, J., & Benet-Martinez, V. (2002). Bicultural identities: The interface of cultural, personality, and sociocognitive processes. *Journal of Research in Personality*, *36*, 598–606. doi:10.1016/S0092-6566(02)00510-X

Haslam, N., Rothschild, L., & Ernst, D. (2000). Essentialist belief about social categories. *British Journal of Social Psychology*, *39*, 113–127. doi:10.1348/014466600164363

Haslam, N., Rothschild, L., & Ernst, D. (2002). Are essentialist beliefs associated with prejudice? *British Journal of Social Psychology*, *41*, 87–100. doi:10.1348/014466602165072

Heider, F. (1958). *The psychology of interpersonal relations*. New York, NY: Wiley. doi:10.1037/10628-000

Higgins, E. T. (1996). Knowledge activation: Accessibility, applicability and salience. In E. T. Higgins & A. E. Kruglanski (Eds.), *Social psychology: Handbook of basic principles* (pp. 133–168). New York, NY: Guilford Press.

Hong, Y. Y., Benet-Martinez, V., Chiu, C., & Morris, M. W. (2003). Boundaries of cultural influence: Construct activation as a mechanism for cultural differences in social perception. *Journal of Cross-Cultural Psychology*, *34*, 453–464. doi:10.1177/0022022103034004005

Hong, Y. Y., Chao, M., & No, S. (2009). Dynamic interracial/intercultural processes: The role of lay theories of race. *Journal of Personality*, *77*, 1283–1310. doi:10.1111/j.1467-6494.2009.00582.x

Hong, Y. Y., Chiu, C., & Kung, T. M. (1997). Bringing culture out in front: Effects of cultural meaning system activation on social cognition. In K. Leung, U. Kim, S. Yamaguchi, & Y. Kashima (Eds.), *Progress in Asian social psychology* (pp. 135–146). Singapore: Wiley.

Hong, Y. Y., Coleman, J., Chan, G., Wong, R. Y. M., Chiu, C., Hansen, I. G., . . . Fu, H. (2004). Predicting intergroup bias: The interactive effects of implicit theory and social identity. *Personality and Social Psychology Bulletin*, *30*, 1035–1047. doi:10.1177/0146167204264791

Hong, Y. Y., Levy, S. R., & Chiu, C. (2001). The contribution of the lay theories approach to the study of groups. *Personality and Social Psychology Review*, *5*, 98–106. doi:10.1207/S15327957PSPR0502_1

Hong, Y. Y., Morris, M. W., Chiu, C., & Benet-Martinez, V. (2000). Multicultural minds: A dynamic constructivist approach to culture and cognition. *American Psychologist*, *55*, 709–720. doi:10.1037/0003-066X.55.7.709

Hong, Y. Y., Roisman, G. I., & Chen, J. (2006). A model of cultural attachment: A new approach for studying bicultural experience. In M. H. Bornstein & L. R. Cote (Eds.), *Acculturation and parent–child relationships: Measurement and development* (pp. 135–170). Mahwah, New Jersey: Lawrence Erlbaum.

Hong, Y. Y., Wan, C., No, S., & Chiu, C. (2007). Multicultural identities. In S. Kitayama & D. Cohen (Eds.), *Handbook of cultural psychology* (pp. 323–345). New York, NY: Guilford Press.

Hong, Y. Y., & Zhang, X. (2006). *Essentialist race belief predicts acculturation among a Caucasian expatriate sample in Beijing, China*. Unpublished raw data, Peking University, Beijing, China.

Keller, J. (2005). In genes we trust: The biological component of psychological essentialism and its relationship to mechanisms of motivated social cognition. *Journal of Personality and Social Psychology*, *88*, 686–702. doi:10.1037/0022-3514.88.4.686

Kelly, G. A. (1955). *The psychology of personal constructs*. New York, NY: Norton.

Kitayama, S., & Cohen, D. (2007). *Handbook of cultural psychology*. New York, NY: Guilford Press.

Kroeber, A. L., & Kluckhohn, C. (1963). *Culture: A critical review of concepts and definition*. New York, NY: Vintage Books.

Leung, A. K.-y., Maddux, W. W., Galinsky, A. D., & Chiu, C.-y. (2008). Multicultural experience enhances creativity: The when and how? *American Psychologist*, *63*, 169–181. doi:10.1037/0003-066X.63.3.169

LaFromboise, T., Coleman, H. L., & Gerton, J. (1993). Psychological impact of biculturalism: Evidence and theory. *Psychological Bulletin*, *114*, 395–412. doi:10.1037/0033-2909.114.3.395

Levy, S. R., Stroessner, S. J., & Dweck, C. S. (1998). Stereotype formation and endorsement: The role of implicit theories. *Journal of Personality and Social Psychology*, *74*, 1421–1436. doi:10.1037/0022-3514.74.6.1421

Lott, B. (in press). *Toward a multicultural psychology*. Boston, MA: Blackwell.

Liu, J. (2009). Taiwan modern: Stem cells, identity, and other hybrid things. *A talk at the Department of History*. University of Illinois at Urbana–Champaign.

Maalouf, A. (2000). In the name of identity: Violence and the need to belong. New York, NY: Arcade.

Markus, H. R., & Kitayama, S. (1991). Culture and the self: Implications for cognition, emotion, and motivation. *Psychological Review*, *98*, 224–253. doi:10.1037/0033-295X.98.2.224

Medin, D. L. (1989). Concepts and conceptual structure. *American Psychologist*, *44*, 1469–1481. doi:10.1037/0003-066X.44.12.1469

Medin, D. L., & Ortony, A. (1989). Psychological essentialism. In S. Vosniadou & A. Ortony (Eds.), *Similarity and analogical reasoning* (pp. 179–195). New York, NY: Cambridge University Press. doi:10.1017/CBO9780511529863.009

Medin, D. L., Unsworth, S. J., & Hirschfeld, L. (2007). Culture, categorization, and reasoning. In S. Kitayama & D. Cohen (Eds.), *Handbook of cultural psychology* (pp. 615–644). New York, NY: The Guilford Press.

Metcalfe, J., & Mischel, W. (1999). A hot/cool-system analysis of delay of gratification: Dynamics of willpower. *Psychological Review*, *106*, 3–19. doi:10.1037/0033-295X.106.1.3

Morton, T. A., Postmes, T., Haslam, S. A., & Hornsey, M. J. (2009). Theorizing gender in the face of social change: Is there anything essential about essentialism? *Journal of Personality and Social Psychology*, *96*, 653–664. doi:10.1037/a0012966

Murphy, G. L., & Medin, D. L. (1985). The role of theories in conceptual coherence. *Psychological Review*, *92*, 289–316. doi:10.1037/0033-295X.92.3.289

Ng, S., & Han, S. (2009). The bicultural self and the bicultural brain. In R. S. Wyer, Jr., C. Chiu, & Y. Hong, (Eds.), *Understanding culture: theory, research and application* (pp. 329–342). New York, NY: Psychology Press.

Ng, S. H., & Lai, J. C. L. (2009). Effects of cultural priming on the social connectedness of the bicultural self: A self-reference approach. *Journal of Cross-Cultural Psychology*, *40*, 170–186. doi:10.1177/0022022108328818

No, S., Hong, Y., Liao, H., Lee, K., Wood, D., & Chao, M. M. (2008). Race and psychological essentialism: Lay theory of race moderates Asian Americans' responses toward American culture. *Journal of Personality and Social Psychology*, *95*, 991–1004. doi:10.1037/a0012978

Norenzayan, A., Choi, I., & Peng, K. (2007). Perception and cognition. In S. Kitayama & D. Cohen (Eds.), *Handbook of cultural psychology* (pp. 569–594*)*. New York, NY: Guilford Press.

Ossorio, P., & Duster, T. (2005). Race and genetics: Controversies in biomedical, behavioral, and forensic sciences. *American Psychologist*, *60*, 115–128. doi:10.1037/0003-066X.60.1.115

Park, R. E. (1928). Human migration and the marginal man. *American Journal of Sociology*, *33*, 881–893. doi:10.1086/214592

Phinney, J. S. (1996). When we talk about American ethnic groups, what do we mean? *American Psychologist*, *51*, 918–927. doi:10.1037/0003-066X.51.9.918

Plaut, V. C., Thomas, K. M., & Goren, M. J. (2009). Is multiculturalism or colorblindness better for minorities? *Psychological Science*, *20*, 444–446. doi:10.1111/j.1467-9280.2009.02318.x

Prentice, D. A., & Miller, D. T. (2006). Essentializing differences between women and men. *Psychological Science*, *17*, 129–135. doi:10.1111/j.1467-9280.2006.01675.x

Ross, M., Xun, W. Q., & Wilson, A. E. (2002). The effect of language on the bicultural self. *Personality and Social Psychology Bulletin*, *28*, 1040–1050. doi:10.1177/01461672022811003

Rothbart, M., & Taylor, M. (1992). Category labels and social reality: Do we view social categories as natural kinds? In G. R. Semin & K. Kiedler (Eds.), *Language and social cognition* (pp. 11–36). London, England: Sage.

Sanchez-Burks, J., & Lee, J. (2007). Cultural psychology and workways. In S. Kitayama & D. Cohen (Eds.), *Handbook of cultural psychology* (pp. 346–369). New York, NY: Guilford Press.

Segall, M. (2002). *All of us are related, each of us is unique*. Retrieved from http://allrelated.syr.edu/

Sidanius, J., & Pratto, F. (1999). *Social dominance: An intergroup theory of social hierarchy and oppression*. New York, NY : Cambridge University Press.

Sui, J., Hong, Y., Liu, C. H., Humphreys, G. W., & Han, S. (2011). *Dynamic cultural modulation of neural responses to self-face recognition*. Manuscript submitted for publication.

Tadmor, C. T., Hong, Y., Chiu, C., & No, S. (2010). What I know in my mind and where my heart belongs: Multicultural identity negotiation and its cognitive consequences. In R. Crisp (Ed.), *The psychology of social and cultural diversity* (pp. 115–144). West Sussex, England: Wiley-Blackwell.

Tate, C., & Audette, D. (2001). Theory and research on "race" as a natural kind variable in psychology. *Theory & Psychology*, *11*, 495–520. doi:10.1177/0959354301114005

Tov, W., & Diener, E. (2007). Culture and subjective well-being. In S. Kitayama & D. Cohen (Eds.), *Handbook of cultural psychology* (pp. 691–713). New York, NY: Guilford Press.

Verkuyten, M., & Pouliasi, K. (2002). Biculturalism among older children: Cultural frame switching, attributions, self-identification and attitudes. *Journal of Cross-Cultural Psychology*, *33*, 596–609. doi:10.1177/0022022102238271

Verkuyten, M., & Yildiz, A. A. (2007). National (dis)identification and ethnic and religious identity: A study among Turkish Dutch Muslims. *Personality and Social Psychology Bulletin*, *33*, 1448–1462.

Ward, C., Bochner, S., & Furnham, A. (2001). *The psychology of culture shock* (2nd ed.). London, England: Routledge.

Wong, R. Y., & Hong, Y. (2005). Dynamic influences of culture on cooperation in the prisoner's dilemma. *Psychological Science*, *16*, 429–434.

Wyer, R. S., & Srull, T. K. (1986). Human cognition in its social context. *Psychological Review*, *93*, 322–359. doi:10.1037/0033-295X.93.3.322

Zhu, Y., Zhang, L., Fan, J., & Han, S. (2007). Neural basis of cultural influence on self-representation. *NeuroImage*, *34*, 1310–1316. doi:10.1016/j.neuroimage.2006.08.047

Zuckerman, M. (1990). Some dubious premises in research and theory on racial differences: Scientific, social, and ethical issues. *American Psychologist*, *45*, 1297–1303. doi:10.1037/0003-066X.45.12.1297

Part IV

Looking Back and Moving Forward

10

Building Solidarity Across Difference: Social Identity, Intersectionality, and Collective Action for Social Change

Shaun Wiley and Nida Bikmen

In this chapter, we address how people who occupy different social categories or locations can realize their common fate and act together on the basis of a common social identity. Patricia Hill Collins first raised this question in a 1993 article, arguing that the answer would require people to develop new ways of understanding race, class, and gender as well as "new categories of connection, new visions of what our relationships with one another can be," (p. 25). We use two traditions to the study of social categories in social psychology—intersectionality and social identity—to support and elaborate on Hill Collins' insight. We argue that to build equitable coalitions, people need to recognize the diversity in experiences with privilege and oppression across social categories and build new identities that encompass seemingly contrasting constituencies.

By *social category* we mean all of the distinct social groupings to which an individual belongs. By *social location*, in contrast, we mean one's position at the intersection of various social categories. For example, one may belong to the social categories of Black and working class and male, but one's social location is a Black, working-class man. The same individual can be seen as privileged or disadvantaged across multiple social categories. For example, a straight, Black, (non)disabled male occupies positions of power on the basis of being straight, (non)disabled, and male, but occupies a disadvantaged position on the basis of being Black. One of the key insights of the past 30 years in the social sciences is that the social locations are not isolated from one another. Rather, complex combinations of privileges and disadvantages emerge from individuals' multiple social locations (e.g., race/ethnicity, gender, social class, sexual orientation, able-bodiedness; Cole, 2009; Settles, 2006; Shields, 2008). This insight has been termed *intersectionality* and has implications for both psychological theorizing on social identity and organization of collective action for social change. To the extent that people become conscious of intersectionality, they can build alliances that move beyond single social categories such as race, gender, class, sexuality, or disability, to intersectional categories that reflect shared oppression (Cohen, 1997; Greenwood, 2008).

Recognizing shared oppression, however, is unlikely to unite people in action unless it results in the creation of a new, shared social identity. In fact, when different groups recognize that they face oppression from a common source, the differences within the groups may cause them to argue over "who is worse off" (Purdie-Vaughns & Eibach, 2008), a phenomenon that has been called *competitive victimhood* (Noor, Brown, & Prentice, 2008). For example, African American women and men, both disadvantaged in terms of their race in the United States, may be divided on how gender also contributes to their oppression and what to do about it. Adopting a shared social identity, we will argue, can ward off competitive victimhood and allow groups to act in spite of—and in the best cases in full acknowledgment of—power differences based on their social locations.

Building a shared social identity does not mean that group members have to ignore power differences within their group. Black men and women need not put aside gender differences to act in terms of a shared racial identity. Such an arrangement runs the risk of reproducing inequalities within social movements (Cole, 2008). By social identity, we mean "that part of an individual's self-concept which derives from his membership of a social group (or groups), together with the value and emotional significance attached to this" (Tajfel, 1978, p. 63). Social identities can be based on people's social locations. For example, gay men are more likely to take to the streets to the extent they identify as a gay activist (Stürmer & Simon, 2004). Social identities can also be formed around opinion-based groups (McGarty, Bliuc, Thomas, & Bongiorno, 2009) or shared values and beliefs (Subašić, Reynolds, & Turner, 2008). For example, activists occupying many different social locations may take to the streets because they identify themselves as "antiracist." These latter social identities, in turn, have the power to build solidarity across difference and remake the social world (Reicher & Hopkins, 2001a, 2001b).

In sum, we argue that intersectionality and social identity approaches are complementary for our understanding of how to build solidarity across differences without reproducing hierarchies within social movements. Recognizing commonalities across differences allows groups to build alliances that may not be obvious and may encourage social action. Several psychological processes facilitate this recognition, including intersectional consciousness and social identity complexity. Without a shared social identity, however, awareness of common oppression can devolve into competitive victimhood. At the same time, shared social identities can paper over real power differences among group members. We examine the way that leaders can define group identities to acknowledge power and use it to unite it in shared action.

We begin by reviewing some of the insights from research and theory on intersectionality, which has highlighted how the diversity within social locations and their relations to systems of power leads to similar experiences of privilege and disadvantage among people occupying vastly different social locations. Next, we review research on collective action as most commonly studied within the frames of social identity (Tajfel & Turner, 1986) and self-categorization (Turner, Hogg, Oakes, Reicher, & Wetherell, 1987) theories, and discuss recent research in social identity theory that highlights the power of social identities to recreate the social world. Finally, we call for additional research that would highlight leaders' roles in mobilizing solidarity across difference.

Intersectionality: Historical and Current Approaches

The origins of intersectional thinking can be found in the work of Black American scholars and leaders of the 19th century (see Lerner, 1973, cited in King, 1988). However, Black feminist activists and scholars (e.g., Collins, 1990; Combahee River Collective Statement, 1977/1995, cited in Cole, 2009), and critical race theorists (e.g., Crenshaw, 1995) are credited for articulating the concept. Intersectionality has been claimed to be the major contribution of feminist theory to social sciences (e.g., Cole, 2009; McCall, 2005; Shields, 2008), and it has become the dominant paradigm in women's studies (Davis, 2008). Psychology embraced the concept relatively late, even though feminist psychologists were writing about problems associated with disentangling gender, race, and other categories in research around the same time as other social scientists (e.g., Hurtado, 1989; Smith & Stewart, 1983). In the past 2 decades, intersectional theorizing and research became more visible in U.S. psychology. Several reviews of this work are now available (Cole, 2009; Shields, 2008).

In the political realm, intersectional thinking emerged from the conflicts Black women experienced in the feminist and racial justice movements in the United States. These movements, with their agendas articulated by White, middle-class women or Black men, respectively, failed to benefit Black women; instead, they were further marginalized in these groups (King, 1988). Hurtado (1989) suggested that although both White women and women of color are oppressed, because of White women's greater connection to the most powerful group in U.S. society, White men, each group's oppression is maintained through different mechanisms. White women are offered a share in power, however little, as the mothers, sisters, and partners of White men. Such power sharing is not a possibility for women of color, except in rare cases of tokenism. Instead, they become partners of men of color who are similarly oppressed by White men. Differences in their relationship to power makes the experiences of White women and women of color drastically different. When the variability in the experiences of a social category is not taken into account, the policies and services designed for that social group end up ignoring the needs of an important segment of the group. In her work on violence against women, Crenshaw (1995) discussed how interventions that were designed with White, middle-class women's experience with violence in mind fell short of addressing the needs of women of color who were more likely to lack adequate housing, social networks they could rely on, or access to information about resources from which they could benefit.

One way of conceptualizing the way different social categories influence one another is through an additive model, by which each subordinate social category increases one's disadvantage and each advantaged group membership increases one's privileges (e.g., Almquist, 1975). The way social categories interact, however, is often more complex, affording people both opportunities and disadvantages (Shields, 2008). For example, King (1988) showed that although White women have a higher income than Black women at lower levels of education, Black women benefit much more from a higher education degree compared with White women. (The same interaction effect was not found for White and Black men.) King (1988) and Hurtado (1989) suggested that the marginalized status of Black women also allowed them opportunities to develop survival skills and greater labor force participation that were not afforded to White women. Black female science students in Settles's (2006) research mentioned their greater likelihood to benefit from affirmative action policies compared with Black men or White women because these policies target both their subordinate category memberships as women and Blacks. Thus, intersections of multiple subordinate identities do not necessarily mean accumulated disadvantages; they can also provide distinct advantages.

Purdie-Vaughns and Eibach (2008) offered a theoretical treatment of this last point. In their model of *intersectional invisibility*, they suggested that people perceive groups in terms of their prototypical members. Ideologies of androcentrism, ethnocentrism, and heterocentrism define the normative person as male, White, and straight, respectively, so that when people think of a subordinate social group, they think of its most typical members. A few examples illustrate this point: Gay White men are the prototype of the category "gay," rather than gay Black men or lesbians of any color; Black men are the prototype of the category "Black," rather than Black women; straight White women are more prototypical of the category "women," than women of color or gay women. Accordingly, individuals who belong to multiple subordinate categories are not typical members of any category they belong to, which makes them socially invisible.

Invisibility carries both advantages and disadvantages. At the interpersonal level, it spares the individual the sting of face-to-face discrimination, as these forms of prejudice are directed at the more prototypical members of the subordinate social categories (e.g., gay men are more disliked than gay women; see Kite & Whitley, 1996). But invisibility also makes it harder for people with multiple social category memberships to be heard, recognized, represented, or to achieve positions of power within or outside either group. Black women's voices, for example, are less likely to be heard in social movements based on their gender *or* their race.

One reason that intersectional approaches have taken a longer time to appear in U.S. psychology than in other social sciences may be the emphasis on experimentation in much of the research on social categorization. Although other methods are employed, experiments make up an overwhelming majority of articles in social psychology's most impactful journals. As mentioned above, intersections of multiple group memberships are associated with various opportunities and disadvantages that are qualitatively different than the sum of the privileges and disadvantages of each group membership; they do not easily fit the factorial designs of psychology experiments or moderation analyses. Although some psychologists argue that quantitative measures with their linear assumptions fall short of examining the intersections of social group memberships (Bowleg, 2008), others have suggested that they can be reconceptualized to capture the complexities of these intersections (Cole, 2008, 2009; Settles, 2006; Warner, 2008).

The question about what kind of methodology is best suited to intersectional approaches may be answered by considering Cole's (2008) discussion of what Crenshaw (1995) called *structural (categorical) intersectionality*. Most psychological work on intersectionality has adopted the structural framework, which is suitable to a factorial design. Structural, or categorical, intersectionality examines how the experience of one group membership changes depending on membership in another social category. This framework is especially useful when the goal is to investigate outcome disparities between social categories. For example, in a comparison of U.S. cities with different economic systems, McCall (2005) found that gender disparity in wages was more pronounced for noncollege-educated women but not for college-educated women in Detroit, an industrial city. The pattern was reversed in Dallas, a postindustrial city.

However, Cole (2009) indicated that this framework, with its accompanying methodology, might not provide an adequate analysis of how categories are socially constructed through institutions, policies, and historical and current social hierarchies. Rather, it may place the source of the disparity (e.g., racial, gender) *within* the category itself. For example, Shih, Pittinsky, and Ambady (1999) examined susceptibility to stereotype threat on a math test among Asian women. Being categorized as Asian carries with it positive stereotypes about math performance, whereas being categorized as a woman carries negative stereotypes. The researchers found that it was not the category itself (Asian woman) that impacted group membership—it was the stereotypes associated with each category (Asian and woman). When the Asian category membership was made salient, participants did better on the math test; when the female category membership was made salient, they did worse. In other words, it was not belonging to the categories Asian and woman that made participants more or less susceptible to stereotypes; rather, it was the social meanings attached to those categories in a particular social context.

Cole (2009) argued that one key question for intersectional research in psychology is, "Who is included?" Much research in psychology suggests that social categories are not homogeneous and that within-group variability affects both the experiences of group members and how they are perceived by others. For example, in research on the development of same-sex attraction, Savin-Williams and Diamond (2000) found that sexual categories included so many different experiences—particularly among women—that their use failed to account for the full range of men and women's sexual behavior. In terms of others' perceptions, Kite and Whitley (1996) showed that attitudes toward gay men are more negative than attitudes toward lesbians.

Differences within social categories are about power as much as diversity. A second key aspect of intersectionality is how inequality shapes the experience of category memberships (Cole, 2009). Owing to their origins in activist work, intersectional approaches have always been about power. Paying attention to power and inequality enables researchers to identify the ways in which social categories are constructed by past and current societal hierarchies and unequal access to resources (Cole, 2008). For example, both Mahalingam and Leu (2005) and Cole and Zucker (2007) have shown that endorsement of traditional gender roles or femininity among Asian and Black American communities, respectively, was a form of resistance to social marginalization. Instead of locating the source of these values within the communities, these researchers attempted to understand the social forces that produced and maintained them.

Attending to the diversity of social locations within social categories and their relationships to power also implies that there are similarities across social categories, either because category memberships are cross-cutting or that groups may share a similar form of oppression. The second contribution of intersectionality to building solidarity across differences is that it allows people to see potential connections where they might otherwise be hidden.

The work of Cohen (1997) on gay activism illustrates this point. In her review, Cohen demonstrated that prevailing norms and state policies privilege White middle-class heterosexuality. Both historically and currently, anything outside of this normative sexuality, whether heterosexual or homosexual, has been marginalized through state policies and discourse. The ban on interracial marriage in the past and on gay marriage currently or the portrayals of poor women on welfare and young Black men as unable to control their sexual activity are examples of this point. Thus, instead of conceptualizing the dividing line as between gays and heterosexuals, Cohen suggests that an analysis of how both gays and nonnormative heterosexuals (e.g., single teen mothers, women on welfare, HIV-positive people of any sexual orientation) are targeted by similar policies and social norms would provide more avenues for coalition building. She gave the example of a movement that brought together heterosexual people of color, White and privileged lesbians and gay men, and formerly incarcerated people to protest the poor quality of health care for prisoners with AIDS. These various groups of people all suffered from government policies that denied them health care; thus, they shared grievances. By articulating how power (in policies or in the norms of communities) marginalizes people who belong to different social categories but who do not conform to normative sexuality, it was possible to form alliances that crossed the boundaries of established social categories.

This focus on commonalities helps to develop an understanding of how particular social, institutional, and political arrangements produce shared characteristics, as well as differences, among social categories. But perhaps more importantly, Cole (2008) suggested, commonalities can serve as a common ground from which social movements can be articulated. Accordingly, different social groups targeted or marginalized by similar policies or institutions can join forces on the basis of shared relationships to power, rather than shared identity, as identity groups are too heterogeneous to have all similar experiences. This perspective suggests an important path for social movements organizing that takes into account political intersectionality.

Everyday Understandings of Intersectionality and Solidarity Across Difference

How does intersectionality relate to establishing solidarity across difference in social movements without reproducing hierarchies? To answer this question, researchers need to examine how people conceive of intersectionality in their everyday lives. First, recognizing intersectionality makes people aware of the diversity of social locations represented within any given category. This means that members in the same category may have very different experiences, priorities, and values, but they may also differ in their social power—both within and outside a social movement. Not only do Black women have different experiences regarding racism and sexism than do White women (Hurtado, 1989), for example, but they are also less likely to been seen as leaders within the women's movement (Purdie-Vaughns & Eibach, 2008). Without attending to power differentials *within* social categories, social movements run the risk of reproducing some of the very hierarchies they mean to dismantle (Cole, 2008). Second, intersectionality draws people's attention to the similarities across seemingly different social categories in terms of their relationship to social power. Japanese and Muslims in the United States, for example, can unite on the basis of their shared exclusion by the U.S. government (Naber, 2004, cited in Cole, 2008). For the Japanese, this may be based on their forced internment during World War II. For Muslims, this may be based on profiling at airports and the experience of wiretapping following September 11, 2001.

One of the key insights that U.S. social psychology brings to this discussion is that people differ in their subjective construal of social relations. For some, intersectionality is readily apparent, whereas for others it is not. It is these perceptions of social relations, rather than the relations themselves, that drive behavior. Research on intersectional consciousness (Greenwood, 2008) and social identity complexity (Roccas & Brewer, 2002) has examined the extent to which individual group members appreciate the diversity in their group categorizations.

Intersectional political consciousness is

> a set of political beliefs and action orientations rooted in recognition of the need to account for multiple grounds of identity when considering how the social world is constructed, when deciding what corrective goals to pursue, and when selecting the appropriate means for pursuing these goals. (Greenwood, 2008, p. 38)

It is contrasted with a *singular consciousness*, which is the perception that group advantage and disadvantage can be defined along a single axis such as race, gender, social class, or (dis)ability. In a study of women activists, Greenwood (2008) found that members differed in the degree to which they saw gender as the primary category shaping women's experience or believed that gender was inextricably tied to other categories, such as race and class. Intersectional group consciousness moderated how women responded to diversity within an organization. Only when gender was seen as the single axis of women's oppression was diversity linked to lower solidarity. For women with an intersectional consciousness, diversity did not have a negative impact.

Although group members may differ in the endorsement of intersectionality, this does not mean that it has not shaped their experience. In fact, the rejection of intersectionality is likely to be greater among group members whose privilege allows them to feel entitled to speak for the group as a whole. Greenwood's (2008) study demonstrates that it is important to study participants' lay understandings of intersectionality. Intersectionality should be treated not only as a matrix of privilege and oppression that affects people's lives but also as a way of looking at the world that shapes the very structure of activist movements. An awareness of intersectionality, not just on the part of psychological researchers but also on the part of activists, can allow for groups to recognize, rather than ignore, their differences and keep them from seeing diversity as a threat.

Research on *social identity complexity* has also examined lay perceptions of cross-cutting social group memberships. Social identity complexity is the extent to which people see their ingroup memberships as neatly overlapping ("All people who belong to my respective ingroups are quite similar to each other") *versus* cross-cutting and diverse ("Some of my ingroup members may be very different from other ingroup members"; Roccas & Brewer, 2002). Whereas intersectional consciousness captures the multiply determined nature of disadvantage and privilege, social identity complexity is the degree to which people cognitively represent the actual diversity among their many ingroups (Miller, Brewer, & Arbuckle, 2009; Schmid, Hewstone, Tausch, Cairns, & Hughes, 2009). People who are high in social identity complexity generally have more positive attitudes toward diversity and toward outgroups. The construct represents an awareness of both the diversity within one's ingroups and by implication, the similarities across seemingly dissimilar groups. As such, social identity complexity should make representing ingroup diversity an important priority and building cross-group coalitions an obvious possibility.

Intersectional consciousness and social identity complexity should both facilitate the acceptance of diversity within categories and the formation of solidarity across them. For the former, this is because axes of oppression are interlocking and for the latter it is because social categories are cross-cutting. However, the recognition of shared oppression and category memberships does not always result in shared action. Instead, it can sow division. Minority group members exhibit *horizontal hostility*, or negative attitudes to a more mainstream minority group, when they think about the majority. Specifically, vegans' attitudes toward nonvegan vegetarians become much more negative when both are contrasted with "meat eaters" (White, Schmitt, & Langer, 2006). In a somewhat different vein, emphasizing similarities among social groups can increase group members' desire to emphasize differences between them, at least among people who are highly committed to the "different" groups in the first place (Jetten, Spears, & Postmes, 2004). Through these channels, social identity is required to transform the awareness of common grievances or crosscutting categorizations into collective action.

Social Identity and Self-Categorization: A Brief History

Early research on intergroup discrimination and collective action in psychology developed out of realistic conflict theory, based on the idea that competition between groups was likely to result from a dispute of resources; in particular, scarce resources. Groups were more likely to engage in collective action the more they were deprived of such resources (Sherif, 1966). Several problems with this approach revealed themselves fairly early on, however. First, it was clear that people who could be described as "objectively" deprived did not always experience their disadvantage that way. Rather, groups were more likely to engage in collective action when they perceived themselves to be relatively deprived compared with some outgroup that they saw as having what they should have (Gurr, 1970; Runciman, 1966). It also quickly became clear that people were more likely to engage in collective action when they felt deprived as group members, called *fraternal deprivation*, as opposed to being deprived as individuals (Runciman, 1966). These insights brought to the fore an emphasis on group identities in explaining collective action: It became evident that social action could be explained not only by social location but also by attachment to a particular group and one's perception of social relations.

Around the same time, research based on social identity theory was demonstrating that realistic conflict was not necessary to create social antagonism between groups (Tajfel & Turner, 1986). Participants in minimal group paradigm studies were randomly assigned to one-dimensional categories of people they did not know, with whom they shared no goals, and with whom they would never interact. They were then asked to assign resources to an ingroup member and an outgroup member. In the absence of any objective conflict, participants favored their ingroup over the outgroup. The studies demonstrated that realistic conflict was not necessary to create intergroup discrimination but that it could form simply by knowing the group to which one did (and did not) belong (Tajfel, Billig, Bundy, & Flament, 1971).

Social identity was the psychological mechanism put forward to explain the results. Groups could become subjectively meaningful, a part of the self. When they did, people strived to see their group as positive and unique, enlisting comparisons with other groups to do so. The actions that groups take given intergroup comparisons—assimilating, redefining their group, or active conflict—depended on shared beliefs about the social context; that is, how strict are the boundaries between the groups and how stable and fair the social system is seen to be (Reynolds & Turner, 2001; Tajfel & Turner, 1986).

Looking back at the minimal group paradigm, much of the empirical research assumed social categorization as a preexisting condition, defined by the experimenters as an independent variable. This led some to refer to it as the "maximal group experiment" because much of what is contested in real life—which are the most relevant categories, what is at stake, which are the most relevant outgroups, what it means to be an ingroup member—is defined by the researcher a priori (Reicher, 2004). Furthermore, categories tended to be studied one at a time without much emphasis on the diversity within them or how they relied on each other for meaning (see Chapter 6, this volume). Both tendencies contradict the arguments by theorists of intersectionality that we should conceptualize social categories as social processes rather than independent variables, and that we should focus on the way category memberships rely on one another for meaning (Cole, 2009; Helms, Jernigan, & Mascher, 2005). However, social identity theory offers a starting point for understanding when and why people who belong to marginalized groups will engage in social change by attending to the way they construct subjectively meaningful categories in relation to systems of social power.

While the social identity approach addressed the question of when and why psychological groups would fight for social change, it left questions about when and why a particular group would come to be psychologically important unanswered. *Self-categorization theory* aimed to fill in this gap (Reynolds &

Turner, 2001). In short, the theory argued that people would come to identify in terms of a certain categorical relationship when it fits with their existing knowledge, motives, and beliefs, but also when the category meaningfully explains differences among groups of people in a given situation (Turner et al., 1987). Two important tenets of self-categorization theory are that identities are hierarchically organized and that they depend on one another—and on the context of comparison—for meaning. In other words, being Black means something different if it describes what kind of woman one is than if it describes what kind of American one is. What's more, being Black has a different meaning when making a comparison with White Americans than when making a comparison with Caribbean immigrants. Self-categorization theory moved toward acknowledging two important aspects of intersectionality: We all belong to multiple, cross-cutting groups and these groups depend on each other and on their relationship to power for meaning (Cole, 2009).

In summary, early research in psychology acknowledged the importance of social identity in addition to shared disadvantage as important drivers for collective action. Furthermore, social identities were not defined in essentialist terms. Self-categorization theory assumed that individuals had multiple, hierarchically-organized identities. Social identity theory assumed identities took their meaning from the relations of power within a society. In this way, both theories balanced materialist notions about the structure of identity—that they relate to people's actual experience in the social structure—with idealist notions—that beliefs about the social structure imbue them with meaning. In practice, however, identities tended to be studied one at a time, with the emphasis placed on the effects of social categories, rather than how they came to be constructed and redefined in the first place.

Social Identity and Collective Action

How does social identity relate to establishing solidarity across difference in social movements without reproducing hierarchies? Shared social identities are the psychological basis for collective action. People who strongly identify with a group are more likely to engage in collective action on its behalf (Deaux, Reid, Martin, & Bikmen, 2006; de Weerd & Klandermans, 1999; Lalonde & Cameron, 1993; Simon et al., 1998; van Zomeren, Postmes, & Spears, 2008; Veenstra & Haslam, 2000). Furthermore, shared social identity is necessary to transform common fate (Campbell, 1958) into common action. In a study of Canadians' support of sweatshop workers, Subašić et al. (2010) found that a strong belief in common fate only increased majority group members' support for a disadvantaged group in the context of a shared identity. Without a shared identity, shared maltreatment by an authority can lead to competitive victimhood, in which different maltreated groups fight over who has it worst. When both Canadian consumers and sweatshop workers were united by a common identity, the perception of shared unjust treatment by the same corporation increased the likelihood of collective action. In contrast, in the absence of a shared identity, common fate actually made collective action *less* likely (although it is not entirely clear why this is so). Social identities allow common oppression to be interpreted as a shared grievance and thus are central to establishing solidarity across difference (Subašić et al., 2008).

Within social psychology, most of the research on collective action takes singular demographic groups as their starting point and examines the extent to which these groups become psychologically meaningful and mobilize people for action. Collective action may be mobilized differently for members of a category occupying different social locations. For example, Deaux et al. (2006) showed that the kind of social beliefs that drive willingness to engage in collective action on behalf of the ingroup depend on one's immigration status (U.S.-born vs. foreign-born) and ethnicity. For U.S.-born Whites, willingness to engage in collective action was predicted by acceptance of social inequality, whereas for native-born Blacks and Latinos, it was predicted by rejection of social inequality. For foreign-born participants, both White and of color, collective action orientation was predicted by greater endorsement of social diversity.

Emphasizing a shared social identity can come at a cost if it privileges some members of a group over others. The first author's recent research with men and women in Latino immigrant organizations provides an example (Wiley, 2009). For men, identifying with ethnic organizations is a source of respect and power in a society that devalues them. For women, in contrast, identifying with the organizations does not afford respect. Rather, women manage their marginalization by reaffirming traditional values such as family and religion, as has been observed in other contexts (e.g., Cole & Zucker, 2007; Mahalingham & Leu, 2005). The same values that allow women to resist marginalization outside the group reinforce male privilege within it. This creates a situation in which, in the context of a shared identity, the position of men and women are quite different. In his ethnographic work, Smith (2006) noted a similar phenomenon:

> Men tend to participate more in transnational public life than women do, while women tend to do more of the everyday settlement work in New York, especially things like enrolling children in school, and private transnational life, such as caregiving for the third generation. Settlement activities can increase women's power and autonomy in the United States, while public, transnational activities tend to create institutions that reproduce or create arenas over which men have power. (p. 122)

Thus, women increase their status outside the group by attending to the needs of others in their family and their community, performing idealized cultural identities. This leaves them little time or influence within ethnic organizations. Within the group men's interests dominate and less attention is paid to the interests of immigrant women. In sum, shared social identities can transform common disadvantage into shared grievances and keep groups from fracturing over "who has it worse." At the same time, they may recreate power differences within groups that threaten their potential for social change.

Articulating a Common Identity Out of Shared Oppression

We argue that building solidarity across differences requires an integration of intersectional and social identity perspectives. On the one hand, intersectionality attends to important differences in power within groups and allows alliances to expand into unexpected directions. On the other hand, those alliances are unlikely to hold together without the creation of a shared identity that respects subgroup difference and addresses power differentials among those subgroups. Such identities are not easily built. Understanding how they are created requires attending to the dynamics of leadership.

Cole (2008) gave an excellent example of how activists can create new identities that do not gloss over important differences between groups within a movement but make it possible for them to act together. Activist Loretta Ross was approached by a feminist organization to mobilize women of color for a demonstration focusing primarily on abortion rights. Ross saw how this focus left out the concerns of women of color, whose rights to parent were often targeted by schools, law enforcement, and foster care systems. She negotiated to redefine the demonstration in terms of the broader term *reproductive rights*, which allowed both White women and women of color to represent the way that they are disadvantaged by existing policies under a shared umbrella. Rather than abortion rights versus the right to parent, a shared identity allowed both White women and women of color to be aggrieved at each other's respective disadvantages without papering over either. The presence of a shared, superordinate identity can help ensure that groups that are oppressed within a single system (albeit in different ways) do not descend into competitive victimhood.

Recent work in the social identity tradition has argued for the world-making power of social identities (Reicher, Haslam, & Hopkins, 2005; Reicher & Hopkins, 2001a, 2001b). Our social identities not only reflect the social structure—although they are in many ways limited by social realities—but they also have the power to *remake* it by getting people to think of themselves in different ways and form different alliances as a result. Leaders who can successfully define the boundaries of group membership (i.e., who is included), the norms and values that membership entails, and the interest of the group will be able to mobilize members to action. Thus, the power of leaders depends on their ability to create a social identity or redefine the meaning of belonging to an existing social category. In that sense, leaders are "entrepreneurs of identity" (Reicher et al., 2005, p. 557).

Social category definition as articulated by leaders has great power to determine members' behaviors. For example, Reicher, Cassidy, Wolpert, Hopkins, and Levine (2006) examined how Bulgarian leaders argued for the protection of Jews in the Second World War. (Bulgaria, they noted, was the only country to end the war with a larger Jewish population than it started with.) First, leaders defined Jews as part of Bulgaria's ingroup, effectively creating a form of intersectional consciousness (Greenwood, 2008). Second, they promulgated group norms that solidarity for the most threatened members of the group was a core component of the identity, and that the group would be diminished if it let anything happen to its Jewish members. This analysis shows how solidarity in diverse social movement organizations can be built on the foundation of shared identity with the scaffolding of norms that attend to differences in power. It demonstrates how leaders can create new identities that encourage group members to think of the inclusive reality of intersectionality.

Conclusion

The groups around which political activists organize not only hold the seeds of division but also the opportunity for coalition. It would seem a requirement of any successful political group would be that its leadership is skilled at strengthening its seams and expanding its edges. Incorporating lessons from research on political intersectionality seems important for action that leads to social change.

We suggest that an intersectionality approach to collective action must focus on coalition building among many different groups on the basis of common suffering or fate, as Cole (2008, 2009) did. In addition, we stress the importance of articulating a common identity for the coalition. Part of the reason that common fate builds solidarity is because recognizing shared maltreatment at the hands of some powerful group or institution makes people more likely to identify with one another (Campbell, 1958; Haslam & Turner, 1992). In other words, if people see their shared interests they can work together. Thus, the processes of intersectional consciousness and social identity complexity may be effective ways of building solidarity across differences because they forge new identities, not because they leave social identities aside.

The challenge of political solidarity is how to deal with power differences within organizations. As Cole (2008) asked, "How can coalitions among members of social groups with unequal political and economic power avoid reproducing existing inequality in practice?" (p. 448). Recent work on intergroup contact underscores the problem. Positive interactions between high- and low-status groups can lead the low-status group members to falsely expect that the high-status group members will join their cause (Saguy, Tausch, Dovidio, & Pratto, 2009). It is only when shared identity and differential relations to social power are addressed simultaneously can a more equitable solidarity be built.

References

Almquist, E. (1975). Untangling the effects of race and sex: The disadvantaged status of Black women. *Social Science Quarterly*, *56*, 129–142.

Bowleg, L. (2008). When Black + lesbian + woman ≠ Black lesbian woman: The methodological challenges of qualitative and quantitative intersectionality research. *Sex Roles*, *59*(5–6), 312–325. doi:10.1007/s11199-008-9400-z

Campbell, D. (1958). Common fate, similarity, and other indices of the status of aggregates of persons as social entities. *Behavioral Science*, *3*(1), 14–25. doi:10.1002/bs.3830030103

Cohen, C. J. (1997). Punks, bulldaggers, and welfare queens: The radical potential of queer politics? *GLQ: A Journal of Lesbian and Gay Studies, 3*, 437–465.

Cole, E. R. (2008). Coalition as a model for intersectionality: From practice to theory. *Sex Roles*, *59*, 443–453. doi:10.1007/s11199-008-9419-1

Cole, E. R. (2009). Intersectionality and research in psychology. *American Psychologist*, *64*, 170–180. doi:10.1037/a0014564 s

Cole, E. R., & Zucker, A. N. (2007). Black and White women's perspectives on femininity. *Cultural Diversity and Ethnic Minority Psychology*, *13*(1), 1–9. doi:10.1037/1099-9809.13.1.1

Collins, P. H. (1990). *Black feminist thought: Knowledge, consciousness, and the politics of empowerment*. New York, NY: Routledge.

Collins, P. H. (1993). Toward a new vision: Race, class and gender as categories of analysis and connection. *Race, Sex and Class: An Interdisciplinary Journal*, *1*(1), 25–46.

Combahee River Collective (1977/1995). Combahee River Collective statement. In B. Guy-Sheftall (Ed.), *Words of fire: An anthology of African American feminist thought* (pp. 232–240). New York, NY: New Press.

Crenshaw, K. (1995). Mapping the margins: Intersectionality, identity politics, and violence against women of color. In K. Crenshaw, N. Gotanda, G. Peller, & K. Thomas (Eds.), *Critical race theory: The key writings that formed the movement* (pp. 357–383). New York, NY: New Press.

Davis, K. (2008). Intersectionality as buzzword: A sociology of science perspective on what makes a feminist theory successful. *Feminist Theory, 9*(1), 67–85. doi:10.1177/1464700108086364

Deaux, K., Reid, A., Martin, D., & Bikmen, N. (2006). Ideologies of diversity and inequality: Predicting collective action in groups varying in ethnicity and immigrant status. *Political Psychology, 27*, 123–146. doi:10.1111/j.1467-9221.2006.00452.x

de Weerd, M., & Klandermans, B. (1999). Group identification and political protest: Farmers' protest in the Netherlands. *European Journal of Social Psychology, 29*, 1073–1095. doi:10.1002/(SICI)1099-0992(199912)29:8<1073::AID-EJSP986>3.0.CO;2-K

Diamond, L. & Savin-Williams, R. (2000). Explaining diversity in the development of same-sex sexuality among young women. *Journal of Social Issues, 56*, 297–313. doi:10.1111/0022-4537.00167

Greenwood, R. (2008). Intersectional political consciousness: Appreciation for intragroup differences and solidarity in diverse groups. *Psychology of Women Quarterly, 32*(1), 36–47. doi:10.1111/j.1471-6402.2007.00405.x

Gurr, T. (1970). *Why men rebel*. Princeton, NJ: Princeton University Press.

Haslam, S. A., & Turner, J. C. (1992). Context-dependent variation in social stereotyping 2: The relationship between frame of references, self-categorization, and accentuation. *European Journal of Social Psychology, 22*, 251–277. doi:10.1002/ejsp.2420220305

Helms, J. E., Jernigan, M., & Mascher, J. (2005). The meaning of race in psychology and how to change it: A methodological perspective. *American Psychologist, 60*, 27–36. doi:10.1037/0003-066X.60.1.27

Hurtado, A. (1989). Relating to privilege: Seduction and rejection in the subordination of White women and women of color. *Signs: Journal of Women in Culture and Society, 14*, 833–855. doi:10.1086/494546

Jetten, J., Spears, R., & Postmes, T. (2004). Intergroup distinctiveness and differentiation: A meta-analytic integration. *Journal of Personality and Social Psychology, 86*, 862–879. doi:10.1037/0022-3514.86.6.862

King, D. H. (1988). Multiple jeopardy, multiple consciousness: The context of a Black feminist ideology. *Signs: Journal of Women in Culture and Society, 14*, 42–72. doi:10.1086/494491

Kite, M. E., & Whitley, B. R. (1996). Sex differences in attitudes toward homosexual persons, behaviors, and civil rights: A meta-analysis. *Personality and Social Psychology Bulletin, 22*, 336–353. doi:10.1177/0146167296224002

Lalonde, R. N., & Cameron, J. E. (1993). An intergroup perspective on immigrant acculturation with a focus on collective strategies. *International Journal of Psychology, 28*(1), 57–74. doi:10.1080/00207599308246918

Lerner, G. (1973). *Black women in white America: A documentary history*. New York, NY: Vintage.

Mahalingam, R., & Leu, J. (2005). Culture, essentialism, immigration, and representations of gender. *Theory & Psychology, 15*, 839–860. doi:10.1177/0959354305059335

McCall, L. (2005). The complexity of intersectionality. *Signs: Journal of Women in Culture and Society, 30*, 1771–1800. doi:10.1086/426800

McGarty, C., Bliuc, A., Thomas, E., & Bongiorno, R. (2009). Collective action as the material expression of opinion-based group membership. *Journal of Social Issues, 65*, 839–857. doi:10.1111/j.1540-4560.2009.01627.x

Miller, K., Brewer, M., & Arbuckle, N. (2009). Social identity complexity: Its correlates and antecedents. *Group Processes & Intergroup Relations, 12*(1), 79–94. doi:10.1177/1368430208098778

Naber, N. C. (Interviewer) & Abdulhadi, R. (Interviewee). (2004). *Rabab Abdulhadi* [Interview transcript]. Retrieved from Global Feminisms: Comparative Case Studies of Women's Activism and Scholarship, Interview Transcripts: United States. Website: http://www.umich.edu/~glblfem/us.html

Noor, M., Brown, J. R., & Prentice, G. (2008). Prospects for intergroup reconciliation: Social psychological predictors of intergroup forgiveness and reparation in Northern Ireland and Chile. In A. Nadler, T. Malloy, & J. D. Fisher (Eds.), *Social psychology of intergroup reconciliation: From violent conflict to peaceful coexistence* (pp. 97–114). Oxford: Oxford University Press.

Purdie-Vaughns, V., & Eibach, R. P. (2008). Intersectional invisibility: The distinctive advantages and disadvantages of multiple subordinate-group identities. *Sex Roles*, *59*, 377–391. doi:10.1007/s11199-008-9424-4

Reicher, S. (2004). The context of social identity: Domination, resistance, and change. *Political Psychology, 25*, 921–945.

Reicher, S., Cassidy, C., Wolpert, I., Hopkins, N., & Levine, M. (2006). Saving Bulgaria's Jews: An analysis of social identity and the mobilization of social solidarity. *European Journal of Social Psychology*, *36*(1), 49–72. doi:10.1002/ejsp.291

Reicher, S., Haslam, S. A., & Hopkins, N. (2005). Social identity and the dynamics of leadership: Leaders and followers as collaborative agents in the transformation of social reality. *The Leadership Quarterly*, *16*, 547–568. doi:10.1016/j.leaqua.2005.06.007

Reicher, S., & Hopkins, N. (2001a). *Self and nation*. London, England: Sage.

Reicher, S., & Hopkins, N. (2001b). Psychology and the end of history: A critique and a proposal for the psychology of social categorization. *Political Psychology, 22*, 383–407. doi:10.1111/0162-895X.00246

Reynolds, K. J., & Turner, J. C. (2001). Understanding prejudice, discrimination, and social conflict: A social identity perspective. In M. Augoustinos & K. J. Reynolds (Eds.), *Us and them: Understanding the psychology of prejudice and racism* (pp. 160–178). London, England: Sage.

Roccas, S., & Brewer, M. (2002). Social identity complexity. *Personality and Social Psychology Review*, *6*, 88–106. doi:10.1207/S15327957PSPR0602_01

Runciman, W. G. (1966). *Relative deprivation and social justice: A study of attitudes to social inequality in twentieth century England*. Berkeley, CA: University of California Press.

Saguy, T., Tausch, N., Dovidio, J., & Pratto, F. (2009). The irony of harmony: Intergroup contact can produce false expectations for equality. *Psychological Science*, *20*, 114–121. doi:10.1111/j.1467-9280.2008.02261.x

Schmid, K., Hewstone, M., Tausch, N., Cairns, E., & Hughes, J. (2009). Antecedents and consequences of social identity complexity: Intergroup contact, distinctiveness threat, and outgroup attitudes. *Personality and Social Psychology Bulletin*, *35*, 1085–1098. doi:10.1177/0146167209337037

Settles, I. H. (2006). Use of an intersectional framework to understand Black women's racial and gender identities. *Sex Roles*, *54*, 589–601. doi:10.1007/s11199-006-9029-8

Sherif, M. (1966). *The psychology of social norms*. Oxford, England: Harper.

Shields, S. (2008). Gender: An intersectionality perspective. *Sex Roles*, *59*, 301–311. doi:10.1007/s11199-008-9501-8

Shih, M., Pittinsky, T., & Ambady, N. (1999). Stereotype susceptibility: Identity salience and shifts in quantitative performance. *Psychological Science*, *10*, 80–83. doi:10.1111/1467-9280.00111

Simon, B., Loewy, M., Stürmer, S., Weber, U., Freytag, P., Habig, C., . . . Spahlinger, P. (1998). Collective identification and social movement participation. *Journal of Personality and Social Psychology*, *74*, 646–658. doi:10.1037/0022-3514.74.3.646

Smith, R. (2006). *Mexican New York: The transnational lives of new immigrants*. Berkeley: University of California Press.

Smith, A., & Stewart, A. J. (1983). Approaches to studying racism and sexism in Black women's lives. *Journal of Social Issues*, *39*(3), 1–15. doi:10.1111/j.1540-4560.1983.tb00151.x

Stürmer, S., & Simon, B. (2004). The role of collective identification in social movement participations: A panel study in the context of the German gay movement. *Personality and Social Psychology Bulletin*, *30*, 263–277. doi:10.1177/0146167203256690

Subašić, E., Reynolds, K. J., & Turner, J. C. (2008). The political solidarity model of social change: Dynamics of self-categorization in intergroup power relations. *Personality and Social Psychology Review*, *12*(4), 330–352. doi:10.1177/1088868308323223

Subašić, E., Schmitt, M. T., & Reynolds, K. J. (2010). *We are all in this together: Common fate, shared identity meaning, and collective action in solidarity with the disadvantaged*. Manuscript submitted for publication.

Tajfel, H. (1978). *Differentiation between social groups*. London, England: Academic Press.

Tajfel, H., Billig, M., Bundy, R., & Flament, C. (1971). Social categorization and intergroup behaviour. *European Journal of Social Psychology*, *1*, 149–178. doi:10.1002/ejsp.2420010202

Tajfel, H., & Turner, J. C. (1986). The social identity theory of intergroup behavior. In S. Worchel & W. G. Austin (Eds.), *The psychology of intergroup relations* (pp. 7–24). Chicago, IL: Nelson-Hall.

Turner, J., Hogg, M., Oakes, P., Reicher, S., & Wetherell, M. (1987). *Rediscovering the social group: A self-categorization theory*. Cambridge, MA: Basil Blackwell.

van Zomeren, M., Postmes, T., & Spears, R. (2008). Toward an integrative social identity model of collective action: A quantitative research synthesis of three sociopsychological perspectives. *Psychological Bulletin*, *134*, 504–535. doi:10.1037/0033-2909.134.4.504

Veenstra, K., & Haslam, S. A. (2000). Willingness to engage in industrial protest: Exploring social identification in context. *British Journal of Social Psychology*, *39*, 153–172. doi:10.1348/014466600164390

Warner, L. R. (2008). A best practices guide to intersectional approaches in psychological research. *Sex Roles*, *59*, 454–463. doi:10.1007/s11199-008-9504-5

White, J., Schmitt, M., & Langer, E. (2006). Horizontal hostility: Multiple minority groups and differentiation from the mainstream. *Group Processes & Intergroup Relations*, *9*, 339–358. doi:10.1177/1368430206064638

Wiley, S. (2009). *"There's a place for us:" Ethnically-relevant organizations as a resource for immigrants to manage collective identities* (Doctoral dissertation). Retrieved from ProQuest Dissertations and Theses database. (UMI No. 3378661)

11

Categories We Live By

Kay Deaux

Social categories have a long and deep history within social psychology, as numerous writers in this volume have discussed. Used both when we attempt to understand the world around us and when we position ourselves within that social world, categories are basic to our everyday experience. As Philogène (see Chapter 2, this volume) notes, discussions of social categories—conceived as both structure and process—emerge in numerous theories across disciplines, continents, and eras. In my own work over the years, social categories have played a key role, underlying questions related to gender, ethnicity, and immigration.

Because what appears to be the same social category is often used by observer and actor alike, both reflecting some broader societal consensus as to the ways in which the social world is organized and interpreted, it is easy to assume that the same processes and understandings are involved. Indeed, it seems most parsimonious to make this assumption—even if, as Bodenhausen (2010) noted, investigators often restrict themselves to one perspective or the other. An alternative viewpoint, however, argues that significant differences in categorical usage exist, a possibility raised by several authors in this volume. In fact, Wiley and Bikmen (Chapter 10, this volume), although suggesting that the terms *social category* and *social location* can be used interchangeably, indirectly raise some of the distinctions that I believe exist. On the assumption that isomorphism between observer and actor category usage is problematic, this chapter explores some differences in the way that observers and targets use social categories. I focus on three specific issues: (a) the functional purposes of social categories, (b) assumptions of stability and flexibility, and (c) categorical content and meaning. In addition, I consider the circumstances of convergence and divergence in the use of categories by observer and by actor, and I also speak briefly to the consequences of categories in social and political life. Before elaborating on these points, however, let me briefly sketch out the ways in which categories are used by observers and by actors.

A Brief Chronicle of Category Usage

"The human mind must think with the aid of categories," asserted Gordon Allport more than 50 years ago (Allport, 1954/1958, p. 19 in abridged version). Since then, fueled by the tremendous growth in social cognition research, categorization has become fundamental to our understanding of social perception. From the voluminous literature that now exists, let me draw a few key points that are relevant to the argument I make here. A fundamental goal of observers is to make sense of their social world, accomplishing this in part by abstracting key elements and simplifying the categories that they use. Complexity is in some respects the enemy—necessary to engage if simple categories fail, but rarely the first option. As Allport (1958) observed, "We like to solve problems easily" (p. 20).

At a very basic level of perceiving others, we use fundamental categories such as gender, ethnicity, and age to organize our encounters. Because these categories are so broad, subcategories necessarily develop, as research on gender subtyping has shown (Deaux, Winton, Crowley, & Lewis, 1985; Vonk & Ashmore, 2003). In other cases, one or two discrepant individuals may simply be dismissed as exceptions, requiring no change or elaboration of the basic category. But in the end most observers like to keep things simple. Fewer categories are easier to handle, requiring fewer decisions as to what a person might be like. Similarly, assuming that all members of the category share numerous traits and characteristics allows greater clarity and predictability (even if that certainty is often misplaced). A need to reduce uncertainty, posited by Hogg and Abrams (1993; Hogg, 2007) to underlie the adoption of social identities, may in fact be operating more strongly for observers than it is for actors.

The question of how actors use categories inevitably invokes the work of Henri Tajfel as a starting point. Social identity theory (Tajfel, 1978) is premised on the idea that people claim membership in social categories (ingroups) and define themselves in reference to those who are members of other groups or categories (outgroups). In identifying themselves as one of a group of people who share some key features individuals are able to position themselves in their social world. With further developments of this perspective, most notably in the shape of self-categorization theory (Turner, Hogg, Oakes, Reicher, & Wetherell, 1987; Turner, Oakes, Haslam, & McGarty, 1994), the cognitive processes involved in self-definition have been much more thoroughly examined and the influence of context on category usage by actors has been more fully articulated. For the most part a parallelism between observer and actor is assumed. As Bodenhausen (2010) noted, although self-categorization is "framed in terms of how the categorization of the self changes across situations, the theory assumes corresponding patterns in the categorization of others" (p. 2).

Both perspectives, that of the observer and that of the actor, are reflected in the chapters in this volume, sometimes as separate concerns and sometimes combined in the analysis. The chapters by Esses and her colleagues (Chapter 7), by Eagly (Chapter 4), and by Fiske and Lee (Chapter 8), for example, consider how categories are used by observers to make judgments about other people in their environment. For Esses and her colleagues the question is how refugees are represented in the media, and how these categorical representations affect the attitudes and perceptions of Canadian citizens toward members of these groups. Eagly focuses specifically on the category of leaders and explores how women do or do not fit the template, as it has been defined in the past in terms of its primarily male occupants. Fiske and Lee used the stereotype content model (Fiske, Cuddy, Glick, & Xu, 2002) to position the attitudes of people toward various social groups, showing how two basic dimensions—warmth and competence—are fundamental to all categorical judgments. Although positions of groups vary along these two dimensions, the underlying simplicity of a two-dimensional model reinforces the argument that observers are quite economical in their judgments of others. Indeed, Fiske and her colleagues have argued for the universality of these two dimensions of judgment, showing impressive consistency in the judgments of people in a wide array of countries throughout the world.

Other chapters in this volume put the spotlight on the categories that actors themselves use to characterize their own identities. Curtin and Stewart (Chapter 5) use a case study approach to examine the identity dynamics of two feminist activists, one an African American woman from Texas and the other an Indian woman who is a product of the still-influential caste system. Major (Chapter 1) looks at gender and ethnicity as key identity categories as well, with a particular emphasis on the strategies people use as they deal with the devaluation of their identity category by others. Hong (Chapter 9) addresses the concept of multicultural identities, considering the ways in which people who are exposed to and participate in two different cultures adjust their thoughts and behaviors across different contexts. Greenwood (Chapter 6) pushes the combinatorial idea further in her analysis of intersectionality, in particular as it is evidenced in the political consciousness of women. Wiley and Bikmen (Chapter 10) also look at actors and the ways in which they position themselves within multiple groups as they develop collective approaches to social action.

A number of these chapters speak to the interplay (or the confrontation) between identities applied by others and those claimed by the actors themselves, an issue to which I return later. First, however, let me describe some of the critical ways I believe the use of categories differs between observers and actors.

What Functions Do Categories Serve?

For observers, a principal function of social categories is to simplify the social world by providing a limited vocabulary with which to more easily operate. Rather than having to process all aspects of every person encountered, social categories allow the observer to make some quick assessments, placing new people into familiar old boxes. As Tajfel (1969) said early on in his thinking about the role of categorization, "In each relevant situation we shall achieve as much stereotyped simplification as we can without doing unnecessary violence to the facts" (p. 82). Even when people have more than one category at their disposal to use when encountering another person, evidence suggests that "stereotypes tend to be activated and applied in an 'either/or' manner" (Bodenhausen, 2010, p. 7). Purdie-Vaughns and Eibach (2008) moved from simplification to elimination in their analysis of the ways in which observers deal with people who are members of multiple subordinate groups, suggesting that these nonprototypical people are subject to "intersectional invisibility." In other words, categories are a means of reduction, compressing and simplifying the operating rules. The stereotype content model that Fiske and Lee describe in this volume (Chapter 8) also supports the notion of simplicity of categorization, wherein just two dimensions are used to respond to a wide variety of social groups.

Whereas category usage by observers has a primarily reductionist function, I would argue that the categories used by actors serve a more extensive agenda.[1] Social identity categories can expand the meaning of the self (Aron et al., 2004), provide a basis for self-esteem and buffer the self from negative input from others (Tajfel, 1978; Major, Chapter 1, this volume), or position a person for interaction with others (Philogène, Chapter 2, this volume; Wiley & Bikmen, Chapter 10, this volume). In Deaux, Reid, Mizrahi, and Cotting (1999), we provided evidence for seven distinct functions of social identification, including self-insight and understanding, intergroup comparison and competition, and ingroup cooperation and cohesion. As we demonstrated in that paper, identity groups vary in which functions they are most likely to serve for the individual, and individuals can satisfy their various needs by identifying with a variety of social categories.

Aron et al. (2004) contended that expansion of the self is a central human motivation, and, I would argue, social identities are one way to satisfy this motivation. In linking oneself to others, one typically expands some aspects of the self, adding material, knowledge, and social assets that one did not possess before. Thus, in contrast to the reductionist tendency in evidence when observers use categories, the actor can find added meaning in the adoption of a social category and the linkages with others who belong to that category.

Social identities open up a sense of possibilities for the actor and within the language of self-categorization theory take "into account people's context-specific, relational characteristics" (Oakes, 1996, p. 105). In so doing they can make explicit the power relationships between members of different groups and suggest strategies for interaction. In Chapter 1, this volume, Major focuses specifically on members of categories that are devalued by some segments of society as she describes the ways in which members of stigmatized groups use their group membership to buffer them from negative evaluations and thus protect their self-esteem. Within this extensive and impressive program of research, Major and her colleagues have also shown the importance of strength of identification as a moderator of various psychological processes, emphasizing the variability that can be found within most identity categories. They found, for example, that highly identified Latino American students felt more depressed and threatened after reading an article that described prejudice against Latinos than did Latino students with weaker ethnic identification. The demonstrated importance of identity strength as a moderator of a broad

---

[1]Initial identification with a category can have the goal of simplification as well, as Hogg's (2007) uncertainty-identity theory posits. The central premise of this theory is that "social categorization reduces or protects [people] from uncertainty because it depersonalizes perception" (Hogg, 2007, p. 112). Although manipulating uncertainty may indeed motivate people to identify more strongly with a category, that evidence does not rule out the possibility that identities (particularly those identities that are significant in one's daily life) serve a great many other functions for their occupants, including the satisfaction of goals and motivations that go beyond simple strength of identification.

range of outcomes is further support for the argument that what appears to be the same category can be used in different ways by different actors.

Establishing one's social position in a broader cultural system also sets the stage for action within that system, as the chapters by Philogène (Chapter 2) and by Wiley and Bikmen (Chapter 10) discuss. In their analyses, social identities give individuals greater agency (Philogène, Chapter 2) and provide a basis for collective action by group members, transforming a sense of common fate into common action (Wiley & Bikmen, Chapter 10). This engagement in projects beyond the self is one of the most dramatic functions of social categories, extending the boundaries of self in behavioral as well as cognitive and affective ways.

In sum, available evidence suggests a far greater range of functions served by social categories for the actor than for the observer. For the observer, categories are a primarily cognitive way to simplify the world, reducing possibilities and limiting alternatives for subsequent engagement. For the actor, in contrast, identifying with social categories expands self-definitions and enlarges the potential agenda for action.

Stability and Flexibility

Both observers and actors have some flexibility in the categories they use, in theory recognizing that there are multiple possibilities. From the observer's perspective, this element of choice has been considered primarily in terms of the cognitive availability of cues and the consequent salience of one category over another. Certain categories are more available to the observer because they are more often used by that individual, leading the person to apply those categories more readily in both familiar and new situations. Cues in the environment are another source of category salience, which facilitates the use of certain categories for observers in particular contexts, at least partially independent of any prior history of use. Certainly observers have some flexibility in their use of categories: They can use or even create subcategories when a more global category is not sufficient, and they can use multiple categories in a combined fashion (Bodenhausen, 2010; Crisp & Hewstone, 2007). For the most part, however, flexibility in category usage as studied by social psychologists has been demonstrated in terms of systematic situational influences rather than in more permanent changes in the category repertoire.

Flexibility on the part of the actor is implicit in the assumption that people have multiple identities and ample data and theory are available to support this assumption. From the perspective of self-categorization theory, for example, variability in the salience of identities is primarily a cognitive calculation, assessing the fit between one's own characteristics and the salient features of the situation (Turner et al., 1987). Often actions taken consistent with one versus another identity are relatively automatic. Consider, for example, the different stereotype threat patterns that Shih, Pittinsky, and Ambady (1999) observed in Asian women when either their Asian or their gender identity was primed. Similarly, the work of Hong and her colleagues on cultural frame-switching shown by Chinese American bicultural individuals nicely illustrates the ways in which situations can influence the identity display of actors (see Hong, Chapter 9, this volume). When their participants were presented with Chinese cultural icons such as the Great Wall of China, they reacted in more typically Chinese ways; when American primes were presented, their participants acted in a more American fashion. In a further illustration of the importance of fit, Wong and Hong (2005) found that priming either American or Chinese icons causes differences in the display of cooperation only when bicultural participants are interacting with friends, in which the context is an appropriate fit, and not with strangers.

Flexible use of identity categories can also be under more deliberate conscious control. A revision of the original self-categorization position, with its stress on cognitive matching of salient cues, considers these more strategic aspects of identity performance (Klein, Spears, & Reicher, 2007; Wiley & Deaux, 2011). From this perspective, choices among identities are consciously motivated, chosen in order to enact a desired identity in the face of a particular audience. West Indian immigrants, for example, may emphasize their accent when replying to a White interrogator in order to clearly distinguish themselves from native-born African Americans. Indeed, people may seek out particular audiences for the express purpose of presenting a desired identity to that group, taking the lead rather than playing only a reactive role to the categorical assumptions of others. Hong's proposal for a dynamic constructivist approach to understanding bicultural behavior is consistent with this position, in that she posits that people "flexibly shift their responses and use culture as a cognitive resource for grappling with their experiences" (Chapter 9, this volume, p. 171).

Curtin and Stewart (Chapter 5, this volume) remind us that the identity categories claimed by actors can also change over time, exemplified by an African American woman whose feminist identity was consciously articulated many years after her ethnic identity was well established. Consideration of changes in all elements of identity over time (Ashmore, Deaux, & McLaughlin-Volpe, 2004) can add a valuable developmental perspective to the immediate situational perspective most often adopted by social psychologists.

To conclude, I suggest that stability and flexibility operate somewhat differently in actors and observers. For the observer, the first choice is typically one of stability, using those categories that have worked most often in the past. Circumstances can prompt the use of alternative categories or a combination of available categories, as Crisp and Hewstone (2007) discussed in detail and as social psychological experimentation can readily demonstrate. For the actor, however, flexibility seems more fundamental to the use of categories, in large part because multiple identities are almost always operating in the person and choices are being made about what situations to enter and engage in as well as how to respond to the categorical assumptions of others.

Categorical Content

A critical question in the comparison of observer and actor usage is whether the meanings associated with a social category by the observer map onto the meanings associated with an identity bearing the same name. The quick assumption once again is that they do, allowing members of a culture to have a common basis of communication. Within any society, a variety of social representations are formed, communicated, and shared, allowing common understandings of frequently-encountered persons and events (Deaux & Philogène, 2001; Philogène, Chapter 2, this volume). The needs of communication should thus press for common meanings associated with commonly-used categories—particularly when, as Cherry (Chapter 3, this volume) notes, the assumptions underlying common categories can change from one historical period to another.

The study of stereotypes, as originally defined in terms of consensus, is one instantiation of a social representation. Thus, observers generally agree that women and men, or the old and the young, or Mexicans and Chinese and Italians, typically possess certain characteristics. (A caution: When stereotypic traits are assessed in terms of percentages of people endorsing a characteristic, agreement is typically below, sometimes well below, 100%.) The work of Fiske and her colleagues provides impressive evidence of the universality of warmth and competence as the key dimensions used in the judgment of others (Fiske, Cuddy, & Glick, 2007; Fiske & Lee, Chapter 8, this volume).

A number of chapters in this volume illustrate the ways in which widely shared meanings are associated with a particular category and serve as a way of determining who should and should not be part of the category. Research on leadership is a good example. Consensually defined images of successful leaders—a long-standing "gentlemen's agreement" among those who have dominated political and business leadership—show a high level of correspondence with cultural definitions of men, masculinity, and agency (Eagly, Chapter 4, this volume), allowing men entrance into the category and excluding women from it. As Hong (Chapter 9, this volume) discusses, meanings associated with some social categories such as race can be characterized in essentialist terms, conveying the notion that underlying properties "are independent of human perception" (Hong, Chapter 9, this volume, p. 176). Essentialist beliefs thus give added stability to the meaning system and allow little room for divergence between actor and observer.

A more constructivist interpretation of categories allows for greater variability on the part of observers. Within social representation theory, for example, the concept of positioning is based on the assumption that segments of a society have different experiences and access to different information, hence the meanings that they associate with the same category may differ (Clémence, 2001). Differences in the meanings associated with race and color of skin in different societies throughout the world also attest to the variable meaning system that can be associated with a similar category (Hong, Chapter 9, this volume; Telles, 2004).

Consistent with the earlier discussion of flexibility, the shared meanings of a category can change over time. Stereotypes of Chinese immigrants, for example, have shifted dramatically over the past century in the United States (Deaux, 2006). In the early part of the 20th century Chinese were typically viewed as superstitious and sly, consistent with government policies that banned Chinese immigration. At the beginning of the 21st century these images had dramatically changed, as Chinese became a favored immigrant group, a "model minority" that is viewed as smart, hard-working, and polite. Social and political events continue to exert an influence on ethnic stereotypes in particular, evidenced most recently by the increasingly negative images held of Muslims in many parts of the world (e.g., Verkuyten, 2010).

The stereotypic content of a category can change over time, but observers continue to strive for simplicity and consensus in their categories; actors, in contrast, are both more expansive and more variable. Actors can essentially choose to define a category for themselves, taking on some of the consensually agreed-upon elements but also adding and subtracting characteristics as they see fit (Deaux, 1992). Further, individuals or small groups of category members can challenge the meaning of a shared category, providing a new sense of what it means to be a member of the group. When Helen Reddy sang *I am Woman (Hear me Roar)* in the early 1970s, she gave new content to the category, describing women as strong and invincible (and winning a Grammy award in the process). As a consequence, many women may have found it satisfying to incorporate traits of strength into their identity definition without needing to claim a more politically charged feminist identity.

Curtin and Stewart's (Chapter 5, this volume) intensive analysis of the life narratives of two activist women offers a vivid illustration of the ways in which the meanings of a shared category may differ. On all of the elements specified by Ashmore et al. (2004), Curtin and Stewart point to ways in which their two selected women differed in their identity descriptions, evidencing, for example, different affective tone and social linkages for their feminist activist identities. These two women—one African American, one Indian—had dramatically different life experiences set in widely divergent social and political contexts. And yet they shared a common identity, together with the dozens of other women interviewed by Stewart and her colleagues as part of the Global Feminism Project.

Greenwood (Chapter 6, this volume) also speaks to the variations in meaning within an identity category, using work on intersectionality and political consciousness to problematize *woman* as an identity category. As she discusses, Black and White women may have quite different ideas about what it means to be a woman; similarly, lower paid working-class women see their gender in ways different from the middle-class professional woman. For women in some positions within the society, economic and racial themes may be inextricably linked to the sense of being a woman; for others, these concerns may seem quite distinct and apart from a sense of gender identity.

These differences in meanings within and between categories form the wellspring for intersectional analyses, which I discuss in greater detail in the next section. For now, I just point to these variations to support the claim that actor identities are characterized by much more diversity and heterogeneity than observer categories typically show.

When Categories Converge—or Not

The dance of social life involves encounters between actors and observers; many of these encounters involve assumptions about social categories, as perceived and as adopted. In tune with these realities, many models of social interaction try to take into account the existence and salience of both observer and actor categories. The Deaux and Major (1987) model, as one example, specifically points to the beliefs about gender categories that observers bring to an encounter and the gender-related schema of the actors in that situation. In another example, Major (Chapter 1, this volume) focuses on people who are members of a stigmatized group. How do these actors interpret the views of others—are they based on categorical assumptions or individual assessments—and then how does the individual cope with potential threats to identity? Much of Major's work considers people's involuntary stress reactions to negative evaluations as they relate to category membership, and how they voluntarily develop the means to deal with these threats.

The actors in Major's model develop ways to react to the evaluations and actions of others that are based on a category to which they belong and that as a result of that category membership have negative consequences for the self (and the more strongly they identify with the group, the more severe are the consequences). In Eagly's (Chapter 4, this volume) analysis of leadership, the actor (in this case a woman) can be seen trying to develop ways to become a member of a category to which others may not consider her a member. As she notes, "Given the double bind of cross-pressures from leadership roles and the female gender role, it is not surprising that female leaders report that achieving an appropriate and effective leadership style is one of their greatest challenges" (p. 71). Thus, in the face of assumptions by others as to what the category of leader requires, women who see themselves as potential leaders must define a strategy whereby both they and their audience agree that the actor is a legitimate member of the category. As her analysis of the literature shows, these strategies are context-dependent as the style that women adopt depends on who the audience is; for example, are the leadership roles typically more or less dominated by men? In the domain of interest to Eagly, the "observer" is often institutionally based and supported, such that the shared consensus of the organization renders considerable force to the categorical assumptions that the individual encounters.

Contemporary research on intersectionality raises fundamental questions about the potential fault lines between the categories of observers and of actors. This line of work can, in fact, be seen as arising from the perspective of actors who are resisting and rebelling against the categorical assignment of others— others, in this case, the pervasive representations of a society. From an observer's viewpoint, parsimony is an advantage, and the quick application of some very fundamental categories, such as gender or ethnicity, can seem an appropriate way to deal with initial encounters. Homogenizing the membership of a category, using what is perceived to be the common denominator or the most salient exemplar, lets the observer make quick assumptions and be on his or her way (Purdie-Vaughns & Eibach, 2008). Thus the dominant exemplar of Blackness becomes Black men and the dominant image of feminists is White women, as Greenwood (Chapter 6, this volume) discusses in more detail. Greenwood also echoes the voices of others in describing how researchers themselves become the observers in this intersectional analysis. "Researchers should be wary," she warns, "of imposing their definitions of identity onto others" (Chapter 6, this volume, p. 122).

Actors challenge both the simplicity of the categories and the inflexibility of their application. From the perspective of the actor who claims membership in multiple identity categories, who imbues each of these categories with personal meaning, and who has the option to present these categories flexibly across time and situation, single-category assignment is very likely to be resisted. When the category is a broad one, as in the case of gender, accepting a globally-based set of assumed characteristics and interactive possibilities is clearly too restrictive and unacceptable. Even with somewhat more limited categories, such as feminist activist, Curtin and Stewart (Chapter 5, this volume) show us how diverse the meaning and connections can be for women who are part of those general groups.

Actors who are joining with other actors in pursuit of common objectives can play the role of observer and actor simultaneously. Their views of the other group and their definitions of their own group then become the site for negotiation and redefinition, as both Greenwood (Chapter 6, this volume) and Wiley and Bikmen (Chapter 10, this volume) describe. Wiley and Bikmen point out that in "recognizing commonalities across differences," groups may be able to build alliances that allow them more effectively to reach mutually desired goals. For Greenwood, the concept of intersectional consciousness is a critical moderator of the ability of subgroup members to arrive at a position of superordinate solidarity. Wiley and Bikmen also point to the potential for leaders as "entrepreneurs of identity" (Reicher, Haslam, & Hopkins, 2005) to frame the situation in such a way as to encourage common understandings and goals.

Recognition of disjunction between categories of observer and actor can lead to a number of corrective processes. Observers can, for example, complicate their categories, not only forming subtypes for a more particularized vision of others but also by recognizing heterogeneity in whatever level of category they use. Actors can alter the meanings generally associated with a category, choosing attributes that fit and ignoring those that are not consistent with their own meaning system. Actors also have considerable flexibility to choose their form of identity presentation and to choose their audiences as well (Wiley & Deaux, 2011). They can live between and outside of rigid category boundaries, often doing so with minimal stress (Benet-Martínez, in press; Hong, Chapter 9, this volume). Thus, the issue is not whether there can be compatibility between the categories used by actors and observers; rather, the question is when and how the two perspectives can mesh in ways that facilitate the communication and interaction of both parties.

Categories and Their Consequences

Ultimately, the study of social categories is important because categories have consequences. The labels that people use affect the actions that they take toward members of those labeled categories; the identities that people claim affect the choices they make for personal and collective activity.

Work described by Esses and her colleagues (Chapter 7, this volume) illustrates the potential consequences of category usage in the broad domain of immigration policy and the treatment of refugee groups. Using a real editorial that appeared in Canadian papers along with an experimenter-created parallel that defined the characteristics of refugees more favorably, Esses and her colleagues show how the meanings associated with categorical membership can affect attitudes not only toward refugees themselves (who in the "real" editorial condition were seen as less admirable and more contemptible) but also toward broad-scale immigration and refugee policy. The dehumanization associated with images of refugees in the Esses work (Chapter 7, this volume) resonates with the work of Fiske and her collaborators (2002) on the stereotype content model (SCM). In the SCM, groups that are both disliked and considered low in competence—a position occupied by first-generation immigrants in general and especially those who are undocumented or have Latin American or African origins—are the ones most likely to be the recipient of active attacks as well as passive neglect. Media statements that place immigrants in this unfavorable position are likely to promote these kinds of negative behavior; more optimistically, messages that would move a group's position up the dimension of warmth would be predicted by SCM to facilitate more positive, helping actions toward members of immigrant groups.

Eagly's work on leadership (Chapter 4, this volume) provides another strong example of the consequences of categorical beliefs. The labyrinth that Eagly describes as the path of women seeking leadership positions is built on the basis of assumptions about the (mis)fit between the categories of gender and leader. As Eagly cites, ample evidence shows that women are targets of employment discrimination, receiving lower performance ratings, for example, than men in male-dominated jobs. Similarly, audit studies show that women fare less well than men when applying for jobs. These differential judgments, when shown in experimental studies, can be attributed only to the assumptions made about gender as a relevant category. In some cases, more finely tuned gender subcategories only compound the problem. Research on the "maternal wall" (Biernat, Crosby, & Williams, 2004), for example, shows that the more specified category of "working mother" brings with it negative consequences that are not associated with working women who do not have children. (For men, in contrast, being a father can result in more favorable evaluations.)

In the actions of actors, identifications with categories clearly have consequences as well. In a striking demonstration of the effects of categorical identification, Hong (Chapter 9, this volume) and her colleagues show how Taiwanese managers who defined themselves in terms of a highly integrated bicultural identity made differential decisions about pay allocations depending on the prime they received—a behavioral manifestation of cultural frame switching. If primed by Chinese images, they made more equal pay allocations to efficient and inefficient employees; if primed by Western images, they showed a preference for equity over equality in their pay recommendations.

The analysis by Wiley and Bikmen (Chapter 10, this volume) of the conditions under which people are likely to form coalitions to effect collective action provides yet another illustration of the consequences of categorization. Theirs is an analysis that goes beyond the individual encounter to a consideration of forces that can make changes in the conditions and power relationships among groups in a society, picking up on the work of Reicher (1996) and others that links social identity to social change.

Conclusion

In framing this chapter in terms of differences that I see between the ways in which observers and actors employ categories, I do not mean to suggest that there are no commonalities of usage. Certainly there are occasions when the two players share meanings and satisfy similar functions, and many of those have been described or assumed in much that has been written before. But because the assumptions often lead us to ignore distinctions that can exist between the two cases, I focus my discussion on what I see as some of the critical differences between the two. These, probably more than the similarities, need to be explored in order to increase possibilities for effective social interaction.

I, along with all the authors in this volume, believe in the ubiquity and the power of social categories in our everyday lives. Whether accepted easily or challenged regularly, social categories shape our perception and channel our actions. These categories are, in many respects, social constructions, but they are anything but ephemeral; rather, these categories are formed and used because they reflect important features of our environment, and as such they are deeply imbedded in our practices. Further, although their usage is heavily influenced by immediate context both in the application by observers and in the presentations of actors, social categories are carried with us wherever we go, ready to be employed with or without conscious intent in our everyday experience.

References

Allport, G. W. (1954/1958). *The nature of prejudice* (Abridged). Garden City, NY: Doubleday Anchor.

Aron, A., McLaughlin-Volpe, T., Mashek, D., Lewandowski, G., Wright, S. C., & Aron, E. N. (2004). Including others in the self. *European Review of Social Psychology, 15,* 101–132. doi:10.1080/10463280440000008

Ashmore, R. D., Deaux, K., & McLaughlin-Volpe, T. (2004). An organizing framework for collective identity: Articulation and significance of multidimensionality. *Psychological Bulletin, 130,* 80–114. doi:10.1037/0033-2909.130.1.80

Benet-Martínez, V. (in press). Multiculturalism: Cultural, social, and personality processes. In K. Deaux & M. Snyder (Eds.), *The handbook of personality and social psychology.* New York, NY: Oxford University Press.

Biernat, M., Crosby, F. J., & Williams, J. C. (Eds.). (2004). The maternal wall: Research and policy perspectives on discrimination against mothers. *Journal of Social Issues, 60*(4).

Bodenhausen, G. V. (2010). Diversity in the person, diversity in the group: Challenges of identity complexity for social perception and social interaction. *European Journal of Social Psychology, 40,* 1–16.

Clémence, A. (2001). Social positioning and social representations. In K. Deaux & G. Philogène (Eds.), *Representations of the social* (pp. 83–95). Oxford, England: Blackwell.

Crisp, R. J., & Hewstone, M. (2007). Multiple social categorization. *Advances in Experimental Social Psychology, 39,* 163–254. doi:10.1016/S0065-2601(06)39004-1

Deaux, K. (1992). Personalizing identity and socializing self. In G. Breakwell (Ed.), *Social psychology of identity and the self-concept* (pp. 9–33). London, England: Academic Press.

Deaux, K. (2006). *To be an immigrant.* New York, NY: Russell Sage Foundation.

Deaux, K., & Major, B. (1987). Putting gender into context: An interactive model of gender-related behavior. *Psychological Review, 94,* 369–389. doi:10.1037/0033-295X.94.3.369

Deaux, K., & Philogène, G. (Eds.). (2001). *Representations of the social*. Oxford, England: Blackwell.

Deaux, K., Reid, A., Mizrahi, K., & Cotting, D. (1999). Connecting the person to the social: The functions of social identity. In T. Tyler, R. M. Kramer, & O. P. John (Eds.), *The psychology of the social self* (pp. 91–113). Mahwah, NJ: Erlbaum.

Deaux, K., Winton, W., Crowley, M., & Lewis, L. L. (1985). Level of categorization and content of gender stereotypes. *Social Cognition, 3*, 145–167. doi:10.1521/soco.1985.3.2.145

Fiske, S. T., Cuddy, A. J., & Glick, P. (2007). Universal dimensions of social perception: Warmth and competence. *Trends in Cognitive Sciences, 11*, 77–83. doi:10.1016/j.tics.2006.11.005

Fiske, S. T., Cuddy, A. J., Glick, P., & Xu, J. (2002). A model of (often mixed) stereotype content: Competence and warmth respectively follow from perceived status and competition. *Journal of Personality and Social Psychology, 82*, 878–902. doi:10.1037/0022-3514.82.6.878

Hogg, M. A. (2007). Uncertainty-identity theory. *Advances in Experimental Social Psychology, 39*, 69–126. doi:10.1016/S0065-2601(06)39002-8

Hogg, M., & Abrams, D. (1993). Towards a single-process uncertainty-reduction model of social motivation in groups. In M. A. Hogg & D. Abrams (Eds.), *Group motivation: Social psychological perspectives* (pp. 173–190). New York, NY: Harvester Wheatsheaf.

Klein, O., Spears, R., & Reicher, S. (2007). Social identity performance: Extending the strategic side of SIDE. *Personality and Social Psychology Review, 11*, 28–45. doi:10.1177/1088868306294588

Oakes, P. (1996). The categorization process: Cognition and the group in the social psychology of stereotyping. In W. P. Robinson (Ed.), *Social groups and identities* (pp. 95–119). Oxford, England: Butterworth Heinemann.

Purdie-Vaughns, V., & Eibach, R. P. (2008). Intersectional invisibility: The distinctive advantages and disadvantages of multiple subordinate-group identities. *Sex Roles, 59*, 377–391. doi:10.1007/s11199-008-9424-4

Reicher, S. (1996). Social identity and social change: Rethinking the context of social psychology. In W. P. Robinson (Ed.), *Social groups and identities* (pp. 317–336). Oxford, England: Butterworth Heinemann.

Reicher, S., Haslam, A. S., & Hopkins, N. (2005). Social identity and the dynamics of leadership: Leaders and followers as collaborative agents in the transformation of social reality. *The Leadership Quarterly, 16*, 547–568. doi:10.1016/j.leaqua.2005.06.007

Shih, M., Pittinsky, T. L., & Ambady, N. (1999). Stereotype susceptibility: Identity salience in quantitative performance. *Psychological Science, 10*, 80–83. doi:10.1111/1467-9280.00111

Tajfel, H. (1969). Cognitive aspects of prejudice. *Journal of Social Issues, 25*, 79–97. doi:10.1111/j.1540-4560.1969.tb00620.x

Tajfel, H. (Ed.). (1978). *Differentiation between social groups: Studies in the social psychology of intergroup relations*. London, England: Academic Press.

Telles, E. E. (2004). *Race in another America: The significance of skin color in Brazil*. Princeton, NJ: Princeton University Press.

Turner, J. C., Hogg, M. A., Oakes, P. J., Reicher, S. D., & Wetherell, M. S. (1987). *Rediscovering the social group*. Oxford, England: Blackwell.

Turner, J. C., Oakes, P. J., Haslam, S. A., & McGarty, C. (1994). Self and collective: Cognition and social context. *Personality and Social Psychology Bulletin, 20*, 454–463. doi:10.1177/0146167294205002

Verkuyten, M. (2010). *Justifying discrimination of Muslim immigrants: A discursive analysis of the extreme right*. Unpublished manuscript.

Vonk, R., & Ashmore, R. D. (2003). Thinking about gender types: Cognitive organization of female and male types. *British Journal of Social Psychology, 42*, 257–280. doi:10.1348/014466603322127247

Wiley, S., & Deaux, K. (2011). The bicultural identity performance of immigrants. In A. Azzi, X. Chryssochoou, B. Klandermans, & B. Simon (Eds.), *Identity and participation in culturally diverse societies: A multidisciplinary perspective* (p. 49–68). West Sussex, England: Wiley-Blackwell.

Wong, R. Y., & Hong, Y. (2005). Dynamic influences of culture on cooperation in the prisoner's dilemma. *Psychological Science, 16*, 429–434.

Index

About the Editors

Shaun Wiley, PhD, is an assistant professor of psychology at The College of New Jersey. His research focuses on collective identity and intergroup relations among marginalized and immigrant groups. Specifically, it examines how members of disadvantaged groups deal with discrimination and low status and the factors that influence the relationship among people's multiple social identities.

Gina Philogène, PhD, is an associate professor of psychology at Sarah Lawrence College, where she has been on the faculty since 1998. Her PhD is from the École des Hautes Études en Sciences Sociales, Paris. Her interests are in social and cultural psychology, history of psychology, race and social identity, as well as social representations. She is the author or editor of three books: *From Black to African American: A New Representation* (Greenwood-Praeger, 1999), *The Representations of the Social: Bridging Theoretical Traditions* (with Kay Deaux; Blackwell, 2001), and *Racial Identity in Context: The Legacy of Kenneth B. Clark* (American Psychological Association, 2004). She is the recipient of several grants from the National Science Foundation as well as the American Psychological Association. She is currently working on a book analyzing the role of group denominations in civil societies.

Tracey A. Revenson, PhD, is professor of psychology at the Graduate Center of the City University of New York. Her research centers on stress and coping processes among individuals, couples, and families facing chronic physical illnesses; the influence of interpersonal relationships on adaptation; and the influence of gender on health. She was the founding editor-in-chief of the journal *Women's Health: Research on Gender, Behavior, and Policy,* serves as associate editor of the *Annals of Behavioral Medicine,* and is on the editorial board of *Health Psychology.* Dr. Revenson served as president of the Division of Health Psychology of the American Psychological Association in 2005. She is the author or editor of six volumes, including *Couples Coping With Stress, The Handbook of Health Psychology*, and *Ecological Research to Promote Social Change.*